8/95

 St. Louis Community College

Forest Park
Florissant Valley
Meramec

Instructional Resources
St. Louis, Missouri

GAYLORD

CASEBOOKS ON MODERN DRAMATISTS
VOL. 15

AUGUST WILSON

GARLAND REFERENCE LIBRARY
OF THE HUMANITIES
VOL. 1626

CASEBOOKS ON MODERN DRAMATISTS

KIMBALL KING
General Editor

SAM SHEPARD
A Casebook
edited by Kimball King

CARYL CHURCHILL
A Casebook
edited by Phyllis R. Randall

CHRISTOPHER HAMPTON
A Casebook
edited by Robert Gross

HAROLD PINTER
A Casebook
edited by Lois Gordon

DAVID RABE
A Casebook
edited by Toby Silverman Zinman

LANFORD WILSON
A Casebook
edited by Jackson R. Bryer

HOWARD BRENTON
A Casebook
edited by Ann Wilson

DAVID STOREY
A Casebook
edited by William Hutchings

PETER SHAFFER
A Casebook
edited by C.J. Gianakaras

ALAN AYCKBOURN
A Casebook
edited by Bernard F. Dukore

DAVID MAMET
A Casebook
edited by Leslie Kane

SIMON GRAY
A Casebook
edited by Katherine H. Burkman

DAVID HARE
A Casebook
edited by Hersh Zeifman

JOHN ARDEN AND MARGARETTA D'ARCY
A Casebook
edited by Jonathan Wike

AUGUST WILSON
A Casebook
edited by Marilyn Elkins

AUGUST WILSON

A Casebook

edited by

Marilyn Elkins

GARLAND PUBLISHING, Inc.
New York & London / 1994

Library of Congress Cataloging-in-Publication Data

August Wilson : a casebook / edited by Marilyn Elkins.
      p.   cm. — (Garland reference library of the
humanities ; vol. 1626. Casebooks on modern dramatists ; vol. 15)
    ISBN 0–8153–0922–8
    1. Wilson, August—Criticism and interpretation.
2. Afro-Americans in literature.   I. Elkins, Marilyn
Roberson.   II. Series: Garland reference library of the
humanities ; vol. 1626.   III. Series: Garland reference
library of the humanities. Casebooks on modern dramatists ; vol. 15.
PS3573.I45677Z56   1994
812'.54—dc20   94–27256
                                          CIP

Printed on acid-free, 250-year-life paper
Manufactured in the United States of America

Contents

General Editor's Note

Like O'Neill, Kaufman, Sherwood, Wilder, Williams and Albee, August Wilson is one of seven American playwrights who has won two Pulitzer prizes. His mastery of vernacular speech combined with a poet's instinct for creating striking images and sounds have made him the modern world's most visible African-American playwright. Committed to writing a cycle of ten plays that will recreate each decade of the twentieth century in terms of black experience, Wilson has planned an epic project that will help to redefine contemporary American culture and history. Leading scholars in African-American studies have contributed a wide range of essays to this volume including an interview with the playwright himself that reveals his idealistic purposes and imaginative approach to the theater and staging.

The editor of *August Wilson: A Casebook* is Marilyn Elkins, assistant professor of English at California State University in Los Angeles. Ideally suited to collect and appraise essays on Wilson, Elkins served as an African-American studies Fulbright lecturer in France during the 1993–1994 academic year. She has published articles in the *Journal of American Culture* and *American Literary Realism* and is presently writing an article on Toni Morrison for the *Oxford Companion to American Literature*. Elkins's central study of an important American novelist was also recently published under the title, *Kay Boyle: Metamorphizing the Novel. Kay Boyle's Narrative Innovations*.

Kimball King

Acknowledgments

I am grateful for a 1986 National Endowment for the Humanities Grant which allowed me to attend a summer seminar in contemporary drama at Columbia University. Under the direction of Howard Stein, the seminar provided participants with numerous opportunities to converse with directors and playwrights. I appreciate Howard's generosity in giving me these opportunities and his willingness to share his theatrical contacts and acumen so freely. I am especially grateful for his arranging our visit to the O'Neill Center where we met Lloyd Richards. Having seen the 1984 Broadway production of *Ma Rainey's Black Bottom*, I already suspected that August Wilson was destined to become one of America's outstanding playwrights and used this occasion to ask Lloyd Richards a rather foolish question about Wilson's potential. I cannot recall Richards's exact response, but the quality and intensity of his remarks convinced me that the powerful play I had seen was only the beginning of a remarkable career. Meeting Richards and seeing *Joe Turner's Come and Gone* several times that summer deepened my interest in Wilson's work. The long hours I spent discussing the poetic speech of Wilson's characters with Wilbur Johnson, a fellow NEH participant, further convinced me that Wilson offers a unique contribution to contemporary drama.

Therefore, I was particularly grateful when Kimball King asked me to edit this volume of Wilson criticism. The perfect editor, Kimball offered me excellent advice when asked, but he never intruded. I would be remiss if I failed to mention my gratitude to Harriet, as well. An academic couple who possess a wonderful blend of intelligence and generosity, the Kings have aided me tremendously in pursuing my academic goals.

In addition, the following people were especially encouraging and helpful with the preparation of this volume: Elizabeth Spencer, Lee Greene, Ann Trapasso, Marty Fehsenfeld, Trudier Harris, Linda Wagner-Martin, Helena Woodard, Laurence Avery, Mary Kemp Davis, Martha Cook, Lavinia Jennings, Carl Selkin, Phyllis Korper, and Adrienne Makowski.

Finally, I must express my gratitude to California State University, Los Angeles for awarding me an Affirmative Action Grant which allowed me to complete the volume on schedule and to my contributors for completing their perspicacious essays in a timely manner.

Introduction

When August Wilson received his second Pulitzer Prize for *The Piano Lesson* in 1990, he joined the elevated company of seven other playwrights who have won this award at least twice: Eugene O'Neill, George S. Kaufman, Robert E. Sherwood, Thornton Wilder, Tennessee Williams, and Edward Albee. The winner of Bush, McKnight, Rockefeller, and Guggenheim Foundation Fellowships in playwriting, Wilson also had the distinction in 1988 of having two plays running simultaneously on Broadway: *Joe Turner's Come and Gone* and *Fences.* Clearly, he is one of America's most prominent playwrights.

Beginning his writing career as a poet, Wilson switched to drama in the '60s, cofounding the Black Horizon Theatre, a company that featured activist drama. At the outset, he envisioned theatre as a means to raise the collective community's consciousness about black life in twentieth-century America. He has committed himself to writing a cycle of ten plays which will rewrite the American history of each decade of this century so that black life, as it was and is lived, becomes a more fully acknowledged part of America's theatrical history.

What he writes, however, is not *agitprop.* Wilson draws his multidimensional characters fully and avoids the pat answers of such theatre. He effects, instead, a powerful theatrical experience and trusts his audience to reach political conclusions which develop as a logical extension of his plays' narrative situations. He accomplishes this difficult task partly through his focus on the poetry of everyday language. Perhaps he no longer considers himself a poet, but his fine ear for vernacular speech and his ability to infuse the language of ordinary people with the stuff of poetry are an essential, distinguishing factor of his plays. His poetic gift, therefore, remains highly evident in his efforts as a dramatist who often seems to speak for black America.

Throughout his theatrical career, in addition to being considered as a spokesperson for the black experience, Wilson has also been considered a playwright of startling imagination and depth. But because he eschews more traditional, Western approaches to dramatization, his work has been slow to receive the kind of in-depth, critical analysis it clearly deserves. Consequently, as the editor of this collection, I was faced with the task of locating Wilson-scholars-in-the-making to supplement the fine work which I had already been promised by existing Wilson scholars. This task, while initially frustrating, proved extremely rewarding and has allowed me to include essays by outstanding, younger scholars who are just beginning their major work on Wilson. Their essays provide fresh, new insight into Wilson's work—perceptions which often stem from the use of critical and cultural theory. They add to the volume's firm grounding in African American criticism that contextualizes Wilson's work within that tradition and in analyses which evaluate his work within the more general tradition of Western drama as a whole.

As editor of a volume which undertakes to deal with Wilson's dramatic accomplishment, I was also faced with the challenge of assembling this perceptive, comprehensive commentary in a cohesive manner. I wanted the essays, as a whole, to adumbrate the multiple perspectives that can be brought to bear upon August Wilson's work and to attest to its multilayeredness. Towards realizing that effect, my chronology provides a brief sketch of his remarkable career, and the volume's twelve original essays are organized around five distinct aspects of Wilson's work: the impact of his acknowleged influences, his use of traditional aspects of African American culture, the use of contemporary cultural theory as a means to understanding and evaluating his work, an investigation of his creative and collaborative method, and recent interviews with both Wilson and his director-of-choice, Lloyd Richards. Because Sandra G. Shannon has recently published a comprehensive annotated bibliography of primary and secondary Wilson materials in *May All Your Fences Have Gates: Essays on the Drama of August Wilson,* edited by Alan Nadel (1993), I have decided not to replicate her efforts here. The Works Cited section at the end of each individual essay provides the necessary information for any material which is not covered by Shannon's article.

The essays begin with explorations of the relationship between Wilson's work and that of his consciously acknowledged influences. Mark William Rocha looks at the influence of Romare Bearden, Imamu Amiri Baraka, Jorge Luis Borges, and the blues upon Wilson's work: what Wilson, himself, refers to as his four B's. Tracing connections between each of these entities and the body of Wilson's work, Rocha provides concrete examples of the ways in which their influence is exemplified in Wilson's plays. Moving toward a more theoretical approach, Rocha argues that Wilson uses these sources to develop his own sign system. This system provides his plays with an interdisciplinary perspective that requires an understanding of African American cultural icons for a thorough and rewarding decoding. For Rocha, Wilson creates a highly specialized lexicon of the black experience. Entering that experience requires mastery of its special vocabulary; Rocha argues that would-be interpreters and teachers of Wilson must steep themselves in the richness of these Wilson influences.

Looking at another acknowledged influence, Joanne Gordon follows a slightly different route than that of Rocha. She compares *Fences* and *"Master Harold" . . . and the Boys* as a method of illustrating and illuminating Wilson's unique political vision. As someone who has successfully directed Athol Fugard's work, Gordon brings theatrically based experience to bear on her understanding of Fugard which, in turn, fuels her analysis of the ways in which the two playwrights use the theatre as a vehicle for politics. Gordon's analysis illuminates the political agendas of both authors. Although Fugard and Wilson write to effect social change, their goals emerge as quite different. Gordon concludes that while Fugard dreams of a world without distinctions based on race, Wilson asks African Americans to reject the predominant culture and discover their own uniqueness. Wilson's goal moves toward empowering African Americans to acknowledge and celebrate their difference.

These opening essays help provide an understanding of some of the major influences upon Wilson's work and the way in which he has incorporated and modified those influences. Yet there are other, less articulated but perhaps more instrumental components of Wilson's writing. Eileen Crawford, Trudier Harris, Patricia M. Gantt, and Pamela Jean Monaco look at these more pervasive elements in Wilson's work.

Eileen Crawford's essay can be read as an illustration of the way in which a thorough knowledge of the blues—its performers and its cultural importance within the African American community—can provide a richer, more resounding interpretation of a single Wilson play. She provides a close reading of *Ma Rainey's Black Bottom* that demonstrates her in-depth knowledge of Wilson's lexicon of the blues, exemplifying the kind of Wilson scholarship that Rocha calls for in the conclusion of his essay. Crawford traces the ways in which Wilson infuses his knowledge of both Ma Rainey and her music into the dramatic unity of the play, making that knowledge pivotal for an informed analysis of both characterization and action. She concludes that the audience must know the history of the blues to realize the sheer inevitability of the play's final resolution and to appreciate its cultural and political resonance.

Continuing the exploration of Wilson's use of the African American cultural tradition, Trudier Harris brings her considerable acumen in the fields of folklore and African American literature to bear upon Wilson's use of African American folklore. While she focuses on *Joe Turner's Come and Gone*, she includes examples from his other plays for further elucidation. She also carefully places Wilson's use of folklore within a broader and more comprehensive context. She argues that Wilson uses African American folk belief or secular mythology, as she comes to name it, as a source of religious conversion that overwrites Christianity. She analyzes the way in which Wilson merges the secular and the sacred and interprets his approach as an innovative use of African American spirituality and folklore that gives its practitioners a private source of internal strength. For Harris, Wilson has reclaimed the folklore tradition and restored it to its original spiritual meaning within African American culture.

As a scholar of Southern literature and folklore, Patricia Gantt analyzes Wilson's Broadway canon to interpret the ways in which Southern icons and remembrances undergird the plays' action and characterization. Noting that Wilson's characters usually refer to the South as "down there," she posits that Wilson looks into the Southern past and incorporates its pain and conflict as a means of reaffirming his characters' sense of who they are. The Southern language—terms such as "fixing to," "ain't studying," and "hungrier than a mule"—and food—such as biscuits, greens, and grits—give visual and verbal concession of the Southern inheritance of Wilson's characters. Despite their universal acknowledgement of the South's destructive effect upon their lives and psyches, they are still strongly influenced by that past and treat it ambivalently. Converting that site of shared suffering into a source of strength and empowerment becomes the primary challenge for Wilson's characters. Gantt concludes that the plays suggest a great part of African American humanity comes directly from its Southern heritage and that reclaiming that heritage is integral to black identity.

Pamela Jean Monaco contextualizes August Wilson's work within the larger body of twentieth-century African American theatre. She traces his movement away from the more didactic drama of the '60s towards what she terms "ritualistic drama," arguing that Wilson relies upon cultural rituals which reaffirm his audience's values. By recreating these rituals on stage, Wilson confirms the possibilities that exist when one can recontact one's ancestors and reach a deeper understanding of one's present strength. Monaco contends that Wilson presents the African heritage as a repository of spiritual values and survival skills and offers his audience access to their mythical ancestors as the true possessors of the sacred.

While these approaches to Wilson's work offer a solid background for understanding his dramatic project, applying cultural analysis in its less literal sense to his work broadens and extends (our understanding of) its contemporary social relevance. Looking at the works as they reflect issues of postmodernism and gender politics is particularly rewarding.

Towards that end, Gunilla Theander Kester presents a theoretical approach to the metaphoric relationship between

African American history and the black body as they are presented in *Fences* and *Joe Turner's Come and Gone*. She argues that Wilson's recoding of the poetics of memory shifts from a spatialized, and therefore static, metaphorics of the past toward a dynamic metaphorics of the black body, making the writing of the body a central locus of change and difference. Consequently, she sees Wilson as offering a progressive revision of Africa and the Diaspora, one which shows the futility of being entrapped in nostalgia for an unapproachable past. She concludes that while his stylistic shifts between the mimetic and the metaphoric disturb the pervasive realistic impression of the plays, this juxtaposition constitutes the major postmodern quality of Wilson's work, making it both visionary and revisionary.

Kim Marra argues, however, that Wilson's work to date fails to provide women with an important role in his revisionary process. Marra analyzes the gender ideology endemic in the construction of each of Wilson's published plays. As a feminist theatre critic, she carefully establishes a theoretical paradigm derived from leading exponents of black feminist thought and then applies this paradigm in a critical analysis of the female characters in the Wilson canon. She sees Wilson's treatment of women as reflecting the dominant culture's anxieties surrounding powerful women. She posits that white supremacism has degraded black matriarchy and that Wilson's male characters, having internalized the phallocentric ethos of the dominant culture, feel that they must overthrow women to become men. She suggests, also, that Wilson's commercial success may partly rest upon this reinforcement of dominant gender ideology because it shifts blame for racial ills from white capitalist patriarchy onto black women, a subtext that is acceptable to the white-male-dominated critical establishment and middle-class theatre audiences.

Moving from the broader issues of culture to the more specialized arena of creative method, Joan Fishman looks at Wilson's work as a craftsman, reviser, and collaborator. As part of her dissertation on August Wilson, Fishman analyzed the various manuscript changes of the five drafts of *Fences*. She looks at the way in which these changes allow Wilson to reinforce his theme without sacrificing the unity of the play. As *Fences* was developed, Wilson refined the level of responsibility in each of the characters and, thereby, elucidated the double bind of the pursuit of personal goals and the commitment to family. Her analysis affords a deeper understanding of this theme as it is manifest in the play. Her essay also creates a thumbnail sketch of Wilson at work: an ecclectic and highly dedicated artist who labors over each change, even when those changes occur collaboratively.

Sandra G. Shannon also provides us with a portrait of Wilson at work, but her essay reflects more upon the personal ramifications of his collaboration with Lloyd Richards. Chronicling the history of Wilson's relationship with Richards, Shannon draws a finely detailed portrait of both their method and friendship. Detailing the unprecedented extent of the Wilson-Richards collaboration, Shannon explores its underlying reasons. She traces similarities in the mens' background as a partial explanation for their closeness and concludes that, regardless of its impetus, the relationship has evolved into that of a father-and-son team. She concludes that Wilson has elected Richards as his surrogate father and that Richards welcomes a "son" who will continue to use his "father's" artistic vision and business savvy.

As a fitting conclusion to the volume, Richard Pettengill, the dramaturg at the Goodman Theatre who had the good fortune to work with both Lloyd Richards and August Wilson on productions of *Piano Lesson* and *Two Trains Running*, permits the author and his director/mentor to speak the final words of the volume. Pettengill's interview with Richards articulates some of the ways in which Richards has facilitated solutions to dramatic problems in Wilson's plays. With his comments on *Two Trains Running*, Richards also helps us understand Wilson's characterization in this play and increases our awareness of Wilson's reliance upon setting and geographical location for their dramatic impact.

Pettengill's interview with August Wilson is noteworthy in many respects. Wilson makes extensive comments about his conceptualization and analysis of *Two Trains*; he offers his most lengthy public exploration of the underlying economic basis for the African American's status in contemporary American society; he takes a retrospective look at the importance and accomplishment of each of his plays; and he discusses *Seven Guitars,* his play which is currently being revised for its Broadway production. Wilson argues that economic empowerment is essential for black America to recover its sense of identity and self-worth and suggests methods for accomplishing this task. The interview offers an important personal assessment by Wilson, one that will prove invaluable for future scholars. It serves, therefore, as an appropriate finale to this collection which honors an outstanding American playwright.

Marilyn Elkins

Chronology

1945 August Wilson is born Frederick Kittel on "The Hill," a racially mixed area of Pittsburgh, Pennsylvania, to Frederick Kittel, a German baker, and Daisy Wilson Kittel, a cleaning woman, on April 27. His maternal grandmother migrated to Pittsburgh, by foot, from North Carolina. The fourth of six children, he grows up in a two-room apartment behind a grocery store on Bedford Avenue.

1959 Wilson's stepfather, David Bedford, relocates the family to a white suburb where Wilson encounters increased racism.

1961 After being falsely accused of plagiarism, Wilson drops out of Gladstone High School.

1963 Wilson enters the army and wrangles a discharge after one year's service.

1965 On April 1, Wilson buys his first typewriter, determined to become a writer. In the fall, he moves into a rooming house and begins earning his keep through what will become a long and varied assortment of menial jobs. He hears Bessie Smith for the first time and discovers the blues. He helps form the Centre Avenue Poets Theatre Workshop.

1968 Along with Rob Penny, Wilson founds Black Horizons Theatre Company on the Hill.

1969 Wilson's stepfather, David Bedford, dies. Wilson marries Brenda Burton, a Muslim.

1970 Birth of daughter, Sakina Ansari.

1972 Dissolution of Wilson's marriage. He intensifies his efforts as a poet.

1973 Wilson writes "Morning Statement," a poem that he, borrowing a term from Robert Duncan, often cites as evidence of his achieving "surety."

1976 Wilson sees Athol Fugard's *Sizwe Bansi Is Dead*, which encourages him about his own ability to write drama.

1978 Wilson moves to St. Paul to write plays for Claude Purdy. He begins working as a scriptwriter for the Science Museum of Minnesota.

1980 Wilson becomes associate playwright with Playwrights Center, Minneapolis, and receives a Jerome fellowship. At the suggestion of Rob Penny, Wilson begins submitting his work to the Eugene O'Neill Theatre Center National Playwrights Conference. *Jitney, Black Bart and the Sacred Hills,* and *Fullerton Street* will all be rejected before his work is accepted.

1981 Wilson marries Judy Oliver, a social worker. *Black Bart,* a musical satire, is produced in St. Paul.

1982 *Jitney* (two-act play) is produced at the Allegheny Repertory Theatre in Pittsburgh, and *Ma Rainey's Black Bottom* is accepted for workshop production at the O'Neill. Wilson receives a Bush fellowship and meets Lloyd Richards for the first time in New York City.

1983 Death of Daisy Wilson in March from lung cancer. Wilson joins New Dramatists, New York. *Fences* is produced at the O'Neill.

1984 *Ma Rainey* opens at the Yale Repertory Theatre on April 6 and at the Cort Theatre on Broadway on October 11. Wilson attends opening night in a borrowed tuxedo. *Joe Turner's Come and Gone* is accepted at the O'Neill. Wilson receives a Rockefeller fellowship.

1985 *Ma Rainey's Black Bottom* wins New York Drama Critics' Circle Award and a Tony nomination. *Fences* opens at the Yale Repertory on April 30. Wilson receives a McKnight fellowship.

1986 *Joe Turner's Come and Gone* opens on April 29 at Yale Rep. Wilson receives a Whiting Foundation Award for *Ma Rainey* and a Guggenheim fellowship.

1987 *Fences* opens at 46th Street Theatre in New York on March 26. It wins the New York Drama Critics Circle Award, the Drama Desk Award, the Tony, and the Pulitzer. *The Chicago Tribune* selects Wilson as Artist of the Year, and he receives the John Gassner Outer Critics' Circle award for best American playwright. *The Piano Lesson* opens on Nov. 26 at the Yale Rep.

1988 *Joe Turner's Come and Gone* opens on March 26 at the Ethel Barrymore Theatre on Broadway. It is nominated for a Tony and wins the New York Drama Critics' Award. Wilson is added to the list of Literary Lions by the New York Public Library.

1990 *The Piano Lesson* opens on April 16 at the Walter Kerr Theatre on Broadway. It wins the Drama Desk award, the New York Drama Critics' Circle award, a Tony nomination, the Outstanding Play Award from American Theatre Critics, and the Pulitzer Prize. *Two Trains Running* opens on March 27 at the Yale Rep. Wilson moves to Seattle and begins the official dissolution of his second marriage.

1991 Wilson is elected to the American Academy of Arts and Sciences.

1992 *Two Trains Running* opens on April 13 at the Walter Kerr Theatre on Broadway. It receives a Tony nomination and the American Theatre Critics' Association Award.

1993 Wilson wins the Bush Artists fellowship.

August Wilson

August Wilson and the Four B's
Influences

Mark William Rocha

> In terms of influence on my work, I have what I call my
> four B's: Romare Bearden; Imamu Amiri Baraka, the
> writer; Jorge Luis Borges, the Argentine short-story writer;
> and the biggest B of all: the blues.
>
> > *August Wilson, "How to Write a Play"*

Few American playwrights have been as explicit in naming
influences as August Wilson. In the dozens of interviews Wilson
has granted in the eight years since *Ma Rainey's Black Bottom*
appeared on Broadway in 1984, Wilson has been unusually
forthcoming not only in citing his influences but in explaining
specifically how the four B's can be found in his plays. And
indeed when I interviewed Wilson on January 24, 1992, I found
him to be so eager to discuss the four B's that at one point he
enthusiastically took up a book of Romare Bearden's works,
turned to the work entitled *Mill Hand's Lunch Bucket*, and
reviewed in animated detail how it served as the source for *Joe
Turner's Come and Gone*.

  To be sure, a good deal of Wilson's citation of the four B's
may be ascribed to a generous and magnanimous soul who is
sincerely grateful to those who have nourished his art. There is
also behind Wilson's acknowledgment of indebtedness a sense of
homage and respect that characterizes an African sensibility, for
as Wilson notes, "In Africa a man is judged not by what he has
but by what is owed to him" (Rocha 29). But I also want to argue

here that Wilson's consistent invocation of his four B's goes beyond the expression of gratitude and respect, and is part of a conscious, deliberate, programmatic effort to turn every interview he gives, and certainly the one he gave me, into a scene of instruction. Wilson doesn't just talk about his four B's, he *teaches* them, not merely as discrete influences, but as constituent elements of an African American cosmology. In offering his four B's—Bearden, Baraka, Borges, and the Blues—Wilson not only inscribes a theory of African American literature but also names the creators of the sign system he inhabits. To read or see a Wilson play without learning about the four B's is, in the vernacular, "not to see where he's coming from."

But before we see where Wilson is coming from, it is worth a moment to clarify where Wilson is *not* coming from, because Wilson has also been unusually explicit in stating who has *not* influenced him, which I take as further evidence of Wilson's instructional agenda with regard to the four B's. Despite the fact that in 1987 he told the *Los Angeles Times* that he is "sitting in the same chair as Shakespeare, confronting the same problems as Arthur Miller and Eugene O'Neill" (Arkatov 35), Wilson has insisted many times that he has never read any of the canonical Western playwrights. In 1988 he commented, "I haven't read Ibsen, Shaw, Shakespeare. . . . I'm not familiar with *Death of a Salesman*. I haven't read Tennessee Williams. I very purposefully didn't read them" (Savran 292). And when I spoke with Wilson and referred to Aristotle and the Western theory of tragedy, Wilson made a point of saying he had never read the *Poetics* even though in 1990 he told *The Boston Globe*, "As far as playwriting goes, it's Aristotle" (Kelly).

I do not raise this to reveal a discrepancy in Wilson's testimony. Rather I wish to call attention to *why* Wilson goes so far out of his way to disconnect himself from the Western tradition of drama, even though his plays reside comfortably within that tradition. I do of course hold it as improbable that Wilson, a playwright who has collaborated for eight years with Lloyd Richards and the Yale Repertory Theater, has never read O'Neill or Miller. Consider, for one example, that it is nearly impossible to avoid one reading of *Fences* as a deliberate point-to-point signifyin(g) parody of *Death of a Salesman*. It is thus all the more significant that Wilson argues so vociferously for himself as liberated from Western influence. I therefore interpret Wilson to be "facing" the Western tradition, to use a vernacular term from the vocabulary of Signifyin(g) compiled by Henry Louis Gates. Gates explains, ". . . 'In your face' is a standard Signifyin(g) retort, meaning that by which you intended to confine (or define) me I shall return to you squarely in your face" (66). Gates offers Signifyin(g) as the basis for an intertextual theory of literary history in which an African American writer like Wilson would both repeat and revise the work of literary antecedents, which in Wilson's case means "getting in the face" of the American triumvirate of O'Neill, Miller, and Williams. While Wilson's facing, especially of O'Neill, may also be usefully read under the paradigm of Harold Bloom's psycho-drama of the strong poet displacing his ancestor, Wilson's response to the anxiety of influence extends beyond the text of his plays to include his aggressive public act—an act of black signifyin(g)—of "calling O'Neill out" by publicly refusing his influence. When informed he had won his second Pulitzer Prize in 1990 for *The Piano Lesson,* Wilson's first comment was, "Well, O'Neill won four, so I guess I better get going" (Fitzgerald 33).

Wilson's obvious desire to "get over on" the Western tradition is first and foremost what bonds him so strongly to his brother-poet Baraka, who in his quest for a post-white, post-American, post-Western form is the discoverer of the African American literary landscape in which Wilson has found a place. Baraka has spent his entire career "facing" the Western tradition, no clearer instance of which comes from his autobiographical novel, *The System of Dante's Hell* (1965), when the Prodigal asks, "Who is T. S. Eliot? So what?" (134). Without Baraka posing this question, August Wilson would not be possible.

Baraka is Wilson's brother-poet for several reasons. First, the two are closer together in age than one might think, Baraka born in 1934 and Wilson in 1945. But more importantly, both poets experienced an almost ritual exorcism of Western poetic influence that was enacted in the year 1965—the year that Malcolm X was killed. Kimberly Benston has called 1965 Baraka's "year of crossroads," during which he divorced his wife and moved uptown to Harlem, whereupon he set himself to realizing the dead prophet Malcolm X's dream of a black nation (Benston, *Baraka* 43). Wilson, in characteristically mythic fashion, designates April 1, 1965, only a few weeks after Malcolm X's death, as the birth of his life as a poet:

> That was the day I made a commitment to being a writer. I spent $20 for a typewriter ... I didn't even have enough left over to take the bus home, so I carried it up the street, plopped it down on the kitchen table in my basement apartment, sat down and plunked out my name. I didn't know how to type. I just wanted to see what AUGUST WILSON looked like. I saw it there, standin' up on the paper, and said, "That's alright, man, all right." (Kelly)

This is an unmistakable answer to Baraka's call in "Poem for Black Hearts," to "quit stuttering and shuffling, look up" in the name of the "Great Malcolm" *(Selected Poetry* 104). Moreover, the central image of the black poet alone with his typewriter in his underground cell, in addition to recalling of course Ellison's *Invisible Man*, recalls precisely the same image in Baraka's play, *A Recent Killing*, the story of a black soldier who is jailed for aiding a rebellion and who graduates to a new resolution for action symbolized by the tableau of a gun leaning against the typewriter by his bed. It is crucial to see that Wilson met Baraka through Malcolm X. Wilson wrote one of his early plays on Malcolm X (the play is yet unpublished but has been performed in Minnesota and elsewhere by Minneapolis's Playwright's Center). More recently, *Two Trains Running* refers explicitly to Malcolm X and his problematic relationship within the black community (I.2.40–41). Wilson must therefore be identified, as he so forthrightly identifies himself, as a Black Nationalist. The overtly political agenda of Black Nationalism is every bit as much at the heart of Wilson's plays as Baraka's, and when we grant Baraka as one of Wilson's four B's, we put the claws back on the tiger, something that is quite necessary in light of the surprisingly benign, almost cuddly August Wilson we are given in the press. If by comparison to Baraka's, Wilson's plays seem less political, it is because our sense of the term political is too much caught up with confrontation, with the "facing of the Man" which so concerns Baraka. Yet a closer look within

Wilson's plays will show that he continues and deepens the motif of facing the white man which Baraka developed so fully.

Benston has recently proposed the scenario of "facing" as an organizing metaphor for African American literary history. Benston's "facing tradition" perfectly comprehends the intertextual relationship of Wilson and Baraka, especially with respect to "the face-to-face encounter that constitutes a primal scene in African American literature: confrontation with the face of mastery" *(PMLA* 100). It is no exaggeration to say that Baraka's plays are about little else but this black-white confrontation: Clay's confrontation with Lula in *Dutchman* and Walker's confrontation with Easley in *The Slave* are two of the best-known of such scenes, but the examples in Baraka's plays are legion and achieve an apotheosis in *Slave Ship*, Baraka's "historical pageant" which predicts a final triumphant confrontation over the white man. One might then say that Baraka taught Wilson how to *do* the facing of the white man, a lesson Wilson applies to every one of his five major plays that currently constitute his historical cycle: in *Ma Rainey* we have Levee's confrontation with the record producer Sturdyvant, in *Joe Turner* it's Herald Loomis's facing of the prison warden Joe Turner, in *Fences* it's Troy Maxson's facing of his boss Mr. Rand, in *The Piano Lesson* it's Boy Willie's facing of his family's slavemaster Sutter, and in *Two Trains Running* it's Hambone's facing of the grocery store owner Lutz. Like Baraka's, Wilson's plays are organized around these facings with the signal difference that in Wilson's plays the confrontation occurs off-stage so that emphasis is placed not so much on the confrontation itself but upon how the black community invests itself in that face-to-face encounter.

Wilson has noted that the Baraka plays that he liked most were the ones published in the volume *Four Black Revolutionary Plays* (1969), which served as the main fare of the Black Horizons Theater of Pittsburgh, which Wilson founded with Rob Penny in 1968 and operated until 1972. Wilson thus not only subscribed to but lived the well-known Barakan manifesto, "The Revolutionary Theater," directing many of Baraka's plays. The experience had a profound effect, for Wilson transported three quintessentially Barakan elements to his own plays: the motion of history as the emergence of the African "Geist" out of the bones of the Middle Passage, the enactment of the ritual dance in which personal experience and racial history converge, and, most importantly, the quest for one's song that is ultimately realized in the blues.

Clay's epiphanic speech in *Dutchman* aptly expresses the significance of the blues in Baraka and serves as a stepping-off point for considering Wilson's biggest B of all. Clay has finally been stirred to speak the truth of his experience to Lula which his appearance belies. He rages at whites who misinterpret black culture and experience:

> They [the ofays] say, "I love Bessie Smith." And don't even understand that Bessie Smith is saying, "Kiss my ass, kiss my black unruly ass." Before love, suffering, desire, anything you can explain, she's saying, and very plainly, "Kiss my black ass." And if you don't know that, it's you that's doing the kissing. (Jones sc. 2, 34–35)

"Kiss my black ass" would be a suitable subtitle for Wilson's *Ma Rainey's Black Bottom*, the first of his "blues plays." The twenty-year gestation period of *Ma Rainey* dates back to the day in 1965 when August Wilson was transfixed and transformed by his discovery of Bessie Smith and came to an understanding of her coded message, which Baraka revealed not only through Clay but through such books as *Blues People* (1963). Wilson has often recounted how he bought a record player and a pile of old 78's for a few dollars and then found Bessie Smith's "Nobody in Town Can Bake a Jelly Roll Like Mine." He played the record twenty-two times in a row:

> I was stunned . . . It was one of the most beautiful songs I'd ever heard. I thought, "This person is talking to me. This is mine."
>
> I began to look at people in the rooming house [where I lived] differently. I had seen them as beaten. I was twenty, and these were old people. I didn't see the value to their lives. You could never have told me there was a richness and fullness to their lives. I began to see it. (Brown 122)

If Baraka is Wilson's brother, then Bessie Smith may well be figured as Wilson's mother, for she gave birth to Wilson as what Houston Baker would call a "blues detective" who is able to decipher black forms by looking to "the limitless freedom of myth and fictive discourse" (122). It took Wilson nearly twenty years to decipher fully in *Ma Rainey's Black Bottom* (1984) what Bessie Smith first brought into Wilson's view. In this first play of the current cycle, Ma Rainey becomes the embodiment of an African American cultural history which she pronounces with full authority:

> White folks don't understand about the blues. They hear it come out, but they don't know how it got there. They don't understand that's life's way of talking. You don't sing to feel better. You sing cause that's a way of understanding life. (II.67)

Wilson best elaborates the monumental importance of the blues to his plays:

> I think that what's contained in the blues is the African American's response to the world. We are not a people with a long history of writing things out; it's been an oral tradition . . .
>
> The thing with the blues is that there's an entire philosophical system at work. And I've found that whatever you want to know about the black experience in America is contained in the blues . . .
>
> So it [the blues] is the Book. It is our sacred book. Every other people has a sacred book, so I claim it as that. Anything I want to know, I go there and find it out. (Livingston 32)

Wilson's plays are replete with knowledge from his sacred book of the blues. The title of *Joe Turner* comes from a W.C. Handy song, *Ma Rainey* is of course about the real-life "Mother of the Blues," and *Fences*, *The Piano Lesson*, and *Two Trains Running* each contain numerous epigrams, allusions, and lyrics drawn from specific blues songs. In Wilson's plays, the blues are what Baker identifies as "the expressive site where American experience is named" (64), and constitute an ontology that is the very idea of America itself: that the sign "America" signifies the broken promise of presence. All blues songs begin from the ontological awareness of the American condition as the sign of

an absence, a broken promise—usually the specific premise is
"my lover's gone"—and the blues is the form blacks invented to
mediate this absence. So when August Wilson discovered the
blues, he in effect discovered America.

In Wilson, the blues is *the* American language for telling
and confronting the tragic reality of an America that is always
already absent. Any American history is as much about our
future as about our past, and Wilson's American history in the
current cycle asserts that the sign of "America" itself can only be
read into the future as a tragedy, as an experiment that *must* fail
because it was committed to the impossible from the beginning.
As James Baldwin first pointed out thirty years ago, Americans
do not wish to face the reality expressed in the blues that life is
tragic and the only fact we have is the final absence of death.
Wilson's "blues plays" may be taken together as an enactment of
Baldwin's prescription that, "one ought to rejoice in the *fact* of
death—ought to decide, indeed, to *earn* one's death by
confronting with passion the conundrum of life" (124).

One black way of confronting the conundrum of life with
passion is through ritual, and it is on this ground that Wilson
met Romare Bearden (1912–1988), the African American artist
best known for his collages of black life created during the 1960s
and 1970s. Wilson holds Bearden in reverential esteem, for
Bearden has not only served as the explicit inspiration for at least
two of Wilson's plays—*Joe Turner* and *The Piano Lesson*—Bearden
also serves Wilson as a kind of father-figure (both grew up in
Pittsburgh), a personification of the ideal for a black artist.
Indeed, Wilson has adopted Bearden's credo as his own: "I try to
explore, in terms of the life I know best, those things which are
common to all cultures" (Wilson "How to Write a Play").

The life Bearden knew best was characterized by *The
Prevalence of Ritual*, the title of a series of collages that were
collected in a volume in 1971, a volume which had a catalyzing
effect on Wilson. Wilson describes the moment as a young
struggling poet when he first encountered Bearden:

> [*The Prevalence of Ritual*] lay open on the table . . . I looked.
> What for me had been so difficult, Bearden made seem so
> simple, so easy. What I saw was black life presented on its
> own terms, on a grand and epic scale, with all its richness

and fullness, in a language that was vibrant and which,
made attendant to everyday life, ennobled it, affirmed its
value, and exalted its presence . . . I was looking at myself
in ways I hadn't thought of before and have never ceased
to think of since. (Payne)

Bearden offered Wilson a new visual language that created
a world populated by conjure women, trains, guitar players,
birds, masked figures, and the rituals of baptisms, funerals,
dinners, parades. Wilson was of course impressed by the black
experience Bearden represented, but he was equally interested in
his mode of representation. Wilson volunteers the creation story
of this new black form.

One day [in 1963] Bearden and some of his colleagues had
arranged to work together on a collaborative work—it was
supposed to be a collage of black life at that time—but
when it came time to actually do it, Bearden was the only
one who showed up. So he went ahead and just started
doing it on his own. (Rocha 31–32)

Bearden "riffed" on the quintessentially twentieth-century
language of collage, first introduced by Picasso in his Cubist
experiments, to create a form capable of expressing what Ralph
Ellison has called the "sharp breaks, leaps in consciousness,
distortions, paradoxes, reversals, telescoping of time and Surreal
blending of styles, values, hopes and dreams which characterize
much of Negro American history" (qtd. in Bearden 9). Wilson
describes the structure of his own plays as having this collagist
form:

In Bearden you've got all these pieces. There's an eye here,
a head over there, a huge oversized hand on a small body.
It's like that with me. I've got all these images, and the
point is how *I* put them together. The pieces are always
there; it's how I put them together, the relationships
between them that counts. (Rocha 32)

The first Bearden work to compel a Wilson play was *Mill
Hand's Lunch Bucket* (1978), part of Bearden's series called
"Pittsburgh Memories." When I showed Wilson a detail from it
in *Memory and Metaphor*, a retrospective volume on Bearden, he
welcomed the chance to explain how it gave birth to *Joe Turner's*

Come and Gone, pointing to each element of its tableau as he went along:

> It's Pittsburgh, so you can see the steel mill through the window there. Seth is coming down the steps on the left and Bertha is standing at the center. Between them you can see the figure of a man seated, and he's hunched over, looking down. I wanted to know more about that man. What burden was he shouldering? So I started writing down his story and he became Herald Loomis. (Rocha 32)

Even the character names in *Joe Turner* were supplied by another Bearden painting in the same series, *Miss Bertha and Mr. Seth*. Wilson has called *Joe Turner* his favorite play, which may have something to do with its being the most Beardenesque of his five plays. *Joe Turner* was the third play Wilson wrote in the current cycle. The very next play he wrote, *The Piano Lesson*, was also inspired by a Bearden painting of the same title, so years hence critics may be speaking of the two plays as comprising Wilson's "Bearden period." But it would be a mistake to limit Bearden's influence on Wilson to these two plays because the Bearden sensibility suffuses each of the plays to some degree. In the playbill of the Yale Rep production of *Two Trains*, for example, Wilson includes a detail from Bearden's 1968 collage, *Family Dinner*, which could serve as a subtitle for this play that takes place entirely in Memphis' restaurant. And Wilson's affinity for Bearden has its common source in the blues. Bearden himself was explicit, saying: "I paint out of the tradition of the blues, of call and recall. You start a theme and you call and recall" (64). Wilson writes plays out of the same tradition; his is a drama of call and recall. Bearden helped to give Wilson a field of reference for the blues that made of the blues idiom a historical language. So Bearden is as indispensable to Wilson as Baraka and the blues. Extending the familial metaphor, with Baraka as his brother, Bessie and Bearden may be taken as Wilson's artistic mother and father.

Where does Jorge Luis Borges (1899–1986) fit into Wilson's family? Possibly as a learned Latin cousin from whom Wilson has taken lessons in aesthetics. Wilson's debt to the Argentinian fabulist has been the least explored of the four B's, but he was no less emphatic about the influence of Borges:

> It's the *way* Borges tells a story. In Borges, it's not what
> happens, but *how*. A lot of times, he'll tell you what's
> going to happen up front, as in ["The Dead Man"] in
> which we're told at the beginning that a nobody from the
> slums will be shot in the head as a leader of his people. All
> of the interest is in how the story is going to be told.
> (Rocha 31)

Reading Borges has also taught Wilson the ethics of
listening which are so important in the black communities in his
plays:

> With Borges you've got all these wires carrying electrical
> impulses, but they don't all connect up. When you
> encounter one of those little breaks, I think he wants you
> to stop and say, "Now wait a second, how does *that*
> connect?" That's why so many of his stories are about
> writing stories, like ["Pierre Menard, Author of the
> *Quixote* "]. (Rocha 31)

Wilson's interest in storytelling is the basis of his strongest bond
with Borges. Mary Lusky Friedman has recently identified a
"Borgesean Paradigm" that may be usefully applied to Wilson:

> Reduced to its most schematic outline, the fantasy that
> informs each one of Borges' tales tells the following story:
> A mishap sets in motion a protagonist, who responds to
> the calamity by setting out on a journey. In the course of
> this journey Borges' hero travels through surroundings
> that are progressively more impoverished and irreal until
> at last he arrives at a structure that walls him in. Immured
> there, he is privy to a marvelous but blighting experience,
> an experience that blasts his selfhood and annihilates him.
> (6)

This also serves as an apt description of Wilson's
protagonists, each of whom conducts a Borgesean quest to locate
or lose a text. So Loomis in *Joe Turner* ultimately finds his "song
of self-sufficiency" rooted in the blues; Levy in *Ma Rainey*
unsuccessfully tries to transcend his father's revenge tragedy by
selling Sturdyvant his own songs, which are not rooted in the
blues; Berniece in *The Piano Lesson* exorcises the ghost of Sutter
by locating herself in the song of her ancestors; Troy Maxson in
Fences invests his legacy for his son in the song of Old Blue;

Hambone in *Two Trains Running* demands a ham instead of a chicken, a quest which is inscribed in his last words, "Black is beautiful." As with Borges's protagonist-narrators, Wilson's characters experience an annihilation which paradoxically creates a narrated self. Like Borges, Wilson presents meta-drama after meta-drama in which the primary self-reflexive topic of the plays is the very creation of text itself.

In the Wilsonian quest, as in the Borgesean journey, "the very act of narrating may be seen as a verbal journey . . . [Borges's] fictional speakers advertise their narrations alternately as ways of retrieving a valued memory from oblivion or of exorcising an experience so unsettling that it undermines the narrator's mental integrity" (Friedman 6). Seen in this light, Wilson's obsession with the past is less that of a historian than of a Borgesean trickster who both delights and despairs in the knowledge that the past is a life-long process of (re)invention.

Many other lines can be drawn from Borges to Wilson: the primacy of myth, the principle of irreality in which magic is viewed in anthropological terms as a complete system, the humor that equips one to face absurdity, and the postmodern stance that all significant human experience is textual. Friedman's Borgesean Paradigm, which views Borges's stories as repeated "attempts to resolve conflicts arising from his ambivalence for his father" (vii), further suggests a possible visceral identification by Wilson for Borges. Wilson's father, Frederick August Kittel, was white and abandoned his family when Wilson was a child. As an adult, Wilson legally adopted his mother's family name. These facts have heretofore gone unexamined. But a future biography of Wilson will benefit from a detailed assessment of the way Wilson's plays, like Borges's stories, enact an exorcism of the father and then a quest for a refigured father.

But perhaps most importantly, Borges may be viewed as the master signifier upon the Western literary tradition so fully represented by his father's library. Borges thus grants Wilson access to the Western tradition without the need for Wilson's deference to it. Through the mediation of Borges, Wilson is able to find a usable past in the Western tradition and identify himself as a writer not of America but of the intercultural Americas.

This adumbration of August Wilson's four B's is intended only to suggest the outline of these influences. It bears reiterating that the four B's are much more than discrete influences whose traces are to be sifted out of Wilson's plays, but together form the sign system from which Wilson's plays are written. Approached in this way, the four B's provide the growing numbers who read Wilson with an extraordinary opportunity to attain a truly interdisciplinary perspective. Reading Wilson requires that we learn about the blues and American music, about Bearden and modern art, about Baraka and Black Nationalism, and about Borges and the postmodern. Now that Wilson's plays are routinely anthologized, he has replaced Lorraine Hansberry as everyone's "obligatory" black playwright. This time let us be sensitive readers and learn that difference is *different* and take August Wilson with his four B's as he clearly asks us to do.

WORKS CITED

Arkatov, Janice. "August Wilson: His Way." *Los Angeles Times* 7 June 1987, Calendar: 35

Baker, Houston. *Blues, Ideology, and Afro-American Literature.* Chicago: University of Chicago Press, 1984.

Baldwin, James. *The Fire Next Time.* New York: Dell, 1962.

Baraka, Amiri. *Selected Poetry of Amiri Baraka/Leroi Jones.* New York: William Morrow, 1969.

———. *The System of Dante's Hell.* New York: Grove Press, 1965.

Bearden, Romare. *Memory and Metaphor: The Art of Romare Bearden 1940–1987.* Oxford University Press: 1991.

Benston, Kimberly. *Baraka: The Renegade and the Mask.* New Haven: Yale University Press, 1976.

———. "Facing Tradition: Revisionary Scenes in African American Literature." *PMLA* 105 (Jan 1990): 98–109.

Brown, Chip. "Light in August." *Esquire* April 1989: 116+.

Fitzgerald, Maureen. "The Heat of August." *Philadelphia Inquirer Magazine* 15 July 1990: 33+.

Friedman, Mary Lusky. *The Emperor's Kites: A Morphology of Borges' Tales.* Durham: Duke University Press, 1987.

Gates, Henry Louis, Jr. *The Signifying Monkey.* Oxford: Oxford University Press, 1988.

Jones, Leroi. *Dutchman. Two Plays by Leroi Jones.* New York: William Morrow, 1964: 1–38.

Kelly, Kevin. "August Wilson's True Stories." *The Boston Globe* 29 April 1990: B29.

Livingston, Dinah. "Cool August." *Minnesota Monthly* October 1987: 25–32.

Payne, Les. "Jazz Came Alive on His Canvas." *Newsday* 9 Dec 1990, Currents: 6.

Rocha, Mark William. "A Conversation with August Wilson." *Diversity: A Journal of Multicultural Issues* 1 (Fall 1992): 24–42.

Savran, David. *In Their Own Words.* New York: Theater Communication Group, 1988: 288–305.

Wilson, August. *Fences. Three Plays.* Pittsburgh: University of Pittsburgh Press, 1991: 94–192.

———. "How to Write a Play Like August Wilson." *The New York Times* 10 Mar 1991, sec. 2: 5.

———. *Joe Turner's Come and Gone. Three Plays.* Pittsburgh: University of Pittsburgh Press, 1991: 193–289.

———. *Ma Rainey's Black Bottom. Three Plays.* Pittsburgh: University of Pittsburgh Press, 1991: 1–93.

———. *The Piano Lesson.* New York: Plume, 1990.

———. *Two Trains Running.* New York: Plume, 1993.

Wilson and Fugard
Politics and Art

Joanne Gordon

There are two distinct approaches one can take in assessing the significance of *Fences*. One can emphasize the universal qualities of the play, hailing Wilson as a new Arthur Miller and drawing parallels between *Fences* and *Death of a Salesman,* or one can focus on Wilson's distinct voice and concentrate on the political significance of the piece. Although these two approaches are not necessarily mutually exclusive, an emphasis on either the universal or particular does affect how one regards the work.

One can undoubtedly find parallels between Wilson's work and that of Miller, but this kind of approach tends to minimize the unique quality of the playwright's voice and message. Wilson sees himself as a kind of chronicler, taking the oral tradition of Africa and setting it down in a uniquely African American form. He insists that African Americans must rediscover their own history if they are to come to terms with their present. The relationship of a race to its past is crucial, Wilson argues, and until recently African Americans relied almost exclusively on a white interpretation of their history. The playwright is determined to redress this omission and fill the void. He contends:

> Writing our own history has been a very valuable tool, because if we're going to be pointed toward a future, we must know our past. This is so basic and simple yet it's a thing that Africans in America disregard. . . . One of the things I'm trying to say in my writing is that we can never

really begin to make a contribution to the society except as
Africans. (quoted by Savron 295–6)

Wilson wants his audience to share in his own pride in
what it means to be an African in America. He insists that his
characters respond in a way true to their own identities and
milieu and never try to suppress their own culture and natural
inclinations. Wilson's characters are primarily African
Americans rather than Americans who happen to be black. His
intention is to contain within his plays the whole complex
totality of black culture in America. Each detail is included to
enrich the audience's appreciation of and understanding for the
complex cultural reality of the African American heritage. One
should not ignore or deemphasise this philosophic commitment.
Wilson is a political artist. He has an agenda and a specific aim
in creating his plays. He insists:

> As African-Americans, we should demand to participate
> in society as Africans. That's the way out of the vicious
> cycle of poverty and neglect that exists in 1987 in America,
> where you have a huge percentage of blacks living in the
> equivalent of South African townships, in housing
> projects. (Savron 299)

Wilson eschews the melting pot metaphors of liberal white
America and rejects assimilationist rhetoric, " I think that the
process of assimilation to white America was a big mistake. We
don't want to be like you" (Savron 304).

Although the playwright is obviously not oblivious to the
general suffering of mankind, his focus is far more specific. He
feels compelled to make concrete the oral traditions of Africa as
expressed and experienced by the African American community.
His resonance may be vast, but the scope of his vision is specific.
Wilson is clear and unambiguous about the political intentions of
his work:

> All art is political. It serves a purpose. All of my plays are
> political but I try not to make them didactic or polemical.
> Theatre doesn't have to be agitprop. I hope that my art
> serves the masses of blacks in America who are in
> desperate need of a solid sure identity. I hope that my
> plays make people understand that these are African
> people, that is why they do what they do. If blacks

> recognize the value in that, then we will be on our way to
> claiming our identity and participating in society as
> Africans. (Savron 304)

It is this overt political philosophy that connects Wilson's work
to that of another artist: Athol Fugard.

Fugard is white, but he is acutely aware of the pain and
inequity that the political system of his native South Africa has
wrought on the lives of his black countrymen. Consequently, he
has dedicated his life and art to defining the reality of
oppression. He has stated that the "true meaning" of his "life's
work" is "just to witness" as "truthfully" as he can " the
nameless and the destitute" of his "one little corner of the world"
(quoted by Walder, 2). He feels compelled to bear witness to the
perversion of justice and the impact that an obscene set of laws
can have on the lives of individuals. As Dennis Walder explains:

> Fugard's theatre is radical, even extreme; but it is in
> response to an extreme situation. He lives in a society
> familiar the world over for its unique system of racial
> oppression. Brutality and degradation are, of course, to be
> found elsewhere than in South Africa. But there is a level
> and quality of humiliation, suffering and despair in the
> lives of millions of ordinary South Africans—mostly, but
> not exclusively black—which demands recognition.
> Fugard's plays help obtain that recognition. (2)

Fugard does not deal exclusively with the lives of black
South Africans. He has chronicled in his plays the distortion of
all relationships under the rule of apartheid. Like Wilson, the
subjects and objects of his work are distinct and unique. One can
extrapolate certain universal statements about the general
condition of humanity from his work, but it is not in these
generalizations that his power lies. Fugard has provided the
world with a very distinct and individual insight into the
particular problems of a particular society, and it is in this
revelation of contemporary South Africa that his strength as a
playwright is to be found. He asserts:

> as a South African I want to talk to other South Africans
> about what is happening here and now. Now, being a
> South African means that I have got to acknowledge the
> fact that my whole style of living, everything, comes down

to. . . . how many decisions have I got that are not related to my white skin? (quoted by Walder 17)

Just as Fugard wants his fellow South Africans to acknowledge how their entire lives are being distorted by an obscene set of archaic laws, Wilson needs his fellow African Americans to recognize and embrace their African selves. Like Wilson, Fugard gives the voiceless masses of South Africa a mouth and in the delineation of the special nature of their pain, he provides the powerless disenfranchised of South Africa with a sense of self and pride. Consequently, it is both interesting and instructive to examine the similarities and differences between the work of these two men. By comparing *Fences* to one of Fugard's finest works, *"Master Harold" . . . and the Boys*, one can learn more about the work of both playwrights and, perhaps more significantly, see that Wilson's true contribution to dramatic art lies in his unique political vision.

Wilson has acknowledged his indebtedness to Fugard:

> . . . something happened when I saw *Sizwe Bansi Is Dead* at the Pittsburgh Public Theater in 1976. I thought, "This is great. I wonder if I could write something like this?" Most of the plays that I have seen are Fugard plays, so he's probably had an influence without my knowing it. Among the fourteen or so plays I've seen have been *Blood Knot*, *Sizwe Bansi*, *"Master Harold". . . . and the Boys* and *Boesman and Lena*. (quoted by Savron 292)

Wilson has never consciously mimicked Fugard, but the connection between the artists is strong. Not only do both playwrights have a clearly articulated mission in writing their plays, but the need to define what it means to be black in a repressive society is central to the work of both men.

Fences and *"Master Harold". . . . and the Boys* share many interesting similarities. Both plays are set in the 1950s, a time of *de facto* segregation in America, just prior to the upheavals of the civil rights movement, and in South Africa where the rigid laws of the Nationalist government were beginning to be clearly articulated. These different but closely related societies, both rife with prejudice and suspicion, are vividly evoked in the densely realized fabric of the dramas. The two plays deal with the pivotal relationship between a young boy and his father (or, in Fugard's work, paternal surrogate). In Wilson's play, Troy, a big lusty man, tries to prevent his son from experiencing the pain and frustration he has suffered all his life as a black man in American. His attempts to guide, shelter and protect the boy lead to the gradual disintegration of the relationship between father and son. In Fugard's work, Hally, a young white South African, is taught by Sam, a black man employed by his mother. The path that these two relationships follow serves as the spine of the works. On one level one can see the evolving relationships as universal human dramas, archetypal father/son conflicts. But in both the world of Wilson and Fugard, it is clear that the fundamental relationships are defined primarily by the sociological contexts of the characters' lives. Neither pair could have evolved, nor could their problems have arisen, in any situation other than the particular political context created by the playwrights.

"Master Harold". . . . and the Boys is Fugard's most clearly autobiographical work. It is based on a personal encounter that the playwright had tried to suppress. Ultimately, his guilt forced him to confront his demons and exorcise them in a work of art. As a young teenager Fugard had befriended a black employee, Sam Samela, who worked in his mother's tearoom. Their relationship had been extremely close until one fateful afternoon when the trust and love was shattered. Fugard recalls his traumatic confrontation with Sam:

> Can't remember now what precipitated it, but one day there was a rare quarrel between Sam and myself. In a truculent silence we closed the cafe, Sam set off home to New Brighton on foot and I followed a few minutes later on my bike. I saw him walking ahead of me and, coming out of a spasm of acute loneliness, as I rode up behind him I called his name, he turned in mid-stride to look back and, as I cycled past, I spat in his face. Don't suppose I will ever deal with the shame that overwhelmed me the second after I had done that. (quoted by Benson 26)

It is this relationship and incident that provide the basis for the play. Young Hally (Fugard's alter-ego) returns to the tearoom after school on a wet afternoon. He is alone with the two servants, Sam and Willie. Willie is a gentle, simple man who serves as an audience for the more volatile Hally and Sam. It is clear that the relationship between the boy and Sam is extremely close. It is loving and strong. At the same time it is carefully constrained by the unstated rules of apartheid. Sam, although clearly an intelligent, mature man, defers to the boy, and Hally makes a number of clearly unself-conscious racist comments. The two have a series of jovial sparring battles revolving around the youngster's homework and Hally's distorted sense of superiority is clear.

Although there is a sense of class distinction, the perverse effects of South Africa's racial politics are not immediately overt. In fact, the relationship between boy and man is clearly that of parent and child. Hally has to write an essay for school, and he and Sam become enraptured by Sam's description of the ballroom championships in which he and Willie are about to compete. Ballroom dancing becomes a focal image of the kind of harmony that could be possible in a world without racial or political conflict. As Sam poetically explains to his young charge:

> There are no collisions out there, Hally. Nobody trips or stumbles or bumps into anybody else. That's what that moment is all about. To be one of those finalists on that dance floor is like. . . . like being in a dream about a world in which accidents don't happen. (Fugard 45)

But the harmony of the afternoon is shattered when Hally's mother calls from the hospital to inform them that the boy's father is returning home. It is immediately clear that Hally despises his own father, who is a cripple and an alcoholic. The story of how he and Sam once had to carry the drunken man home provides one of the most painful moments of the play. Sam understands the boy's confusion and pain and has tried to shield him from the humiliation and inevitable anger. But Sam cannot forever protect the boy, and the youngster's shame for his father and sense of self-loathing boil up until Hally vents his fury on the gentle Sam:

> Hally: Don't turn your back on me! I haven't finished talking.
> (He grabs Sam by the arm and tries to make him turn around,
> Sam reacts with a flash of anger)

Sam: Don't do that, Hally! All right, I'm listening. Well? What do you want to say to me?

Hally: To begin with, why don't you start calling me Master Harold, like Willie.

Sam: Do you mean that?

Hally: Why the hell do you think I said it?

Sam: And if I don't?

Hally: You might just lose your job. (54)

It is at this moment that personal and political world fuse in a brilliant theatrical *tour de force*. Fugard shows that the angry impotent boy is able to take out his frustration and pain on the older man because of the system in which he lives. He has grown up being taught that as a white he is inherently superior to any black person. Although he loves and respects Sam, he does not know how to vent his frustration, and ultimately the play climaxes as Hally spits in Sam's face. All the ugliness of apartheid is encapsulated in this traumatic gesture.

What does this play tell us about *Fences*? In precisely the same way as Fugard subtly reveals the pernicious effects of a perverse system on the individual without ever being overtly didactic, so Wilson shows how the relationships between his characters are defined, not by their simple humanity , but by their sociological context.

Troy's relationship with his son deteriorates, not because the two are essentially incompatible, but because Troy fears that Cory will suffer the same disappointments and indignities that he suffered as an African American man trying to compete in a white world. There are elements of jealousy and unreasonableness in Troy's attempts to thwart Cory's ambition to get a football scholarship, but the driving force that determines his actions is his perception of his place in a racist society. He attempts to explain this to his son:

If they got a white fellow sitting on the bench. . . . you can bet your last dollar he can't play! The colored guy got to be twice as good before he get on the team. That's why I don't want you to get all tied up in them sports. Man on the team and what it get him? They got colored on the

> team and don't use them. Same as not having them. All
> them teams the same. (Wilson 36)

Just as Sam attempts to define his relationship both to
Hally and the world in terms of the extended metaphor of
ballroom dancing, so Troy attempts to explain his relationship to
the world and his son in terms of baseball. As the two angry and
hurt men confront each other Troy threatens:

> I'm going to tell you what your mistake was. See. . . . you
> swung at the ball and didn't hit it. That's strike one. See,
> you in the batter's box now. You swung and you missed.
> That's strike one. Don't strike out! (Wilson 56)

He knows that he has made many mistakes and acknowledges
his fallibility in a poignant confession to his wife. Sports are not
only the subject matter of his disputes, but baseball imagery
structures his world:

> . . . Maybe I come into the world backwards, I don't know.
> But . . . you born with two strikes on you before you come
> to the plate. You got to guard it closely . . . always looking
> for the curved ball on the inside corner. You can't afford to
> let none get past you. You can't afford a call strike. If you
> go down, you . . . you go down swinging. (Wilson 66)

Both playwrights choose metaphors that are organic to the
character's lives to explain their emotional entanglements.
Fugard's play opens with Sam teaching Willie how to dance, and
it is clear as the play progresses that it is Sam's ability to dance
over the tortuous terrain of South Africa's political system that
gives him his dignity and insight, just as Troy once felt his own
sense of strength and manhood in his ability to play ball. But
gradually the reality of being a black man in the early 1960s in
America has stripped him of his power and his pride. He feels
his sense of self diminish and asserts his remaining power in his
apparently cruel dictatorial behavior over his son.

Only Rose, Troy's wife, who has suffered so much because
of her husband's cruelty, infidelity and thoughtlessness,
understands the true nature of the relationship between father
and son. Like her creator, Rose recognizes the necessity of
acknowledging the pain of the past in order to embrace the
future. Troy has been determined to cut himself off from the boy

in order to prevent the boy's making the same mistakes as he did. He insists to Rose, "I don't want him to be like me! I want him to move as far away from my life as he can get" (Wilson 46). But, in the final moments of the play Rose explains to her son, "Your daddy wanted you to be everything he wasn't. . . . and at the same time he tried to make you everything he was" (96).

Neither Wilson nor Fugard needs to stand on a soapbox. Their message is dramatized in the living context of their dramas. The titles alone serve as a key to the political intentions of the playwrights. In *Fences* Wilson creates a man desperately trying to fence in his dignity, his pride and his family and fence out the humiliation of white America. Fugard's title encapsulates a system that elevates a callow youth to the position of "Master" (the term is used frequently in the play with increasing irony) and reduces a grown man to the position of "boy."

The similarity between the two plays can be extended beyond their narrative structure. There is a unity of style that is interesting. Both playwrights work essentially within the tradition of the well-made play; a gradually evolving conflict is ultimately resolved in the final moments of the drama. Yet neither is confined by the form. They both use musical metaphors to describe their style: Wilson acknowledges his conscious use of the blues, and Fugard claims to be influenced by the purity of form in the Bach sonatas. In both dramatists' work the colloquial interchanges of the vernacular are balanced by long arias in which the characters elaborate around the central theme. It is in these long monologues that much of the playwrights' power can be found. When Troy tries to explain his impotence and anger at a world in which his needs and ambitions have been frustrated and curtailed, he uses the apparently simple terms of his own language and the structuring metaphor is that of the archetypal American pastime—baseball—yet the dialogue sings with a poetic intensity:

> When I found you and Cory and a halfway decent job . . . I was safe. Couldn't nothing touch me. I wasn't going to strike out no more . . . I was safe. I had me a family. A job. I wasn't gonna get that last strike. I was on first looking for them boys to knock me in. To get me home. (66–7)

Wilson understands and captures the music of Troy's soul in his language. He does not resort to overtly poetic or sophisticated thought or language structures, but captures the essence of the man's frustration in the distinct speech patterns of the character's essential self.

Fugard's technique is similar. As the tension between Sam and Hally mounts the boy makes a cruel racist joke about a "niggers arse" not being "fair." His cruelty pushes Sam to shatter the calm exterior he has developed over the years of repression. He pulls down his pants and reveals his backside for Hally to inspect and vents his hurt in a poignant threnody:

> Ja, well, you've done it . . . Master Harold. Yes, I'll start calling you that from now on. It won't be difficult anymore. You've hurt yourself, Master Harold. I saw it coming. I warned you, but you wouldn't listen. You've just hurt yourself *bad*. And you're a coward, Master Harold. The face you should be spitting in is your father's . . . but you used mine, because you think you're safe inside your fair skin . . . and this time I don't mean just or decent. (56–7)

In both these examples it is clear that the playwrights create from inside the world of the characters. The impetus is the character's pain. It is not imposed. The language is the voice of the characters. But through these monologues, the playwrights are able to convey the results of political systems that repress and wound and destroy. The personal is transcended and the political is made concrete.

Yet the political message is not confined to the large climactic moments and huge arias. The reality of oppression is woven into all the minutiae of the plays and is constantly reemphasized. Troy's concern about his job after he has demanded that he be given the right to drive the garbage truck like the white workers is an example of how a system has attempted to restrict the man. His false confidence and unrepressed pride shine through his exchanges with his friend Bono. The pernicious effects of inverse prejudice and fear are equally clear when he describes the treatment of African Americans even in a restaurant owned by a fellow black man:

Man bought him that restaurant down there . . . fixed it up real nice . . . and then didn't want nobody to come in it! A Negro go in there and can't get no kind of service. I seen a white man go in there and order a bowl of stew. Pope picked all the meat out of the pot for him. Man ain't had nothing but a bowl of meat. Negro come behind him and ain't got nothing but the potatoes and carrots. (26)

Fugard is equally subtle but insistent. When Hally describes a caning he received at school, Sam compares it to the treatment of black prisoners:

Sam: That's the way they do it in jail.

Hally: Really?

Sam: Ja. When the magistrate sentences you to " strokes with a light cane."

Hally: Go on.

Sam: They make you lie down on a bench. One policeman pulls down your trousers and holds your ankles, another pulls your shirt over your head and holds your arms . . .

Hally: Thank you! That's enough.

Sam: . . . and the one that gives you the strokes talks to you gently and for a long time between each one.

Hally: I've heard enough, Sam! Jesus! It's a bloody awful world when you come to think of it. People can be real bastards. (13)

Both plays abound with this kind of specificity. The playwrights know the evils of their society. They do not need to exaggerate or distort. A simple, accurate and dense evocation of the reality of both societies is sufficient to make audiences squirm with discomfort.

It is interesting that both playwrights have had success outside of the limited milieu of their immediate society. They have been embraced by the commercial world of Broadway and honored with numerous prizes. Why are these plays appealing to predominantly white audiences? It can be argued that the theatre is essentially a liberal environment and that the playwrights are preaching to the converted. Certainly, it is intriguing that even during a time of extreme repression in South

Africa, when television was forbidden and films were brutally censored, Fugard's work flourished. Unlike Wilson, Fugard's early work was performed in small spaces and had none of the support of large professional productions. Yet, even though the work was presented to a very limited number of people, Fugard's voice was heard. Wilson, ably assisted by Lloyd Richards, has had a far more rapid assent into the realm of commercial theatre. Yet both playwrights have had an impact far beyond their immediate audiences. The works live and reverberate because they provide a poetic yet recognizable evocation of a particular place and time. They reveal inequity and corruption without becoming blatantly agitprop. The political thrust of the plays is central, but at the same time is subtle. The desire to effect change and to awaken the empathic bond in the audience is always subservient to the central life of the drama. The characters are real. They are not symbols or spokesmen, but breathing examples of the reality of societal prejudice.

One dimension that Wilson does possess that separates him from Fugard is his brilliant evocation of the supernatural. In all Wilson's plays there is a sense of a realm beyond the here and now which gives resonance to his work. In *Fences* the character of Gabriel brings into the world of Troy's domestic angst a perspective of another realm. Gabriel's condition can be simply explained away as the result of his war wound. But this rational explanation does not begin to account for the effect that the character has on stage. In the final moments of the play, as Gabriel blows ecstatically though his silent trumpet, and moves in a dance of bliss, the world of Troy, Rose and Cory is transcended, and Wilson gives us a glimpse of a absolute truth. Fugard has tried in some of his non-literal work, like *Dimetos*, to go beyond the world of South African reality. But he is far less successful. It is Wilson's special gift to be able to combine both realms and add to both in the synthesis. It can be argued that Wilson's ability to add this mythical dimension to the apparently naturalistic environments of his plays arises out of his desire to include the specifically African into his American world. In all Wilson's plays there is at least one character who embodies this anarchic free spirit and expresses the African soul unconfined by the strictures and limitations of the majority culture. White cultural and even epistemological expectations are exploded in these theatrical epiphanies.

It is at this point that the two playwrights part company. Fugard is by his own admission a typical white liberal, ultimately impotent in the face of the overwhelming inequity of the South African system. Yet, he is determined to witness the suffering and raise his voice against an easy conspiracy of silence. But, Fugard is not a revolutionary. Despite all the indignity he has suffered, Sam does not resort to violence. Fugard is not a violent man. He seeks desperately to make connections between black and white and bridge the vast chasm that separates the various peoples of his homeland. He dreams of a world without distinctions based on race. Wilson, in contrast, wants to assert the African in his characters. In trying to provide positive role models, Wilson needs to extort his fellow African Americans to reject the predominant culture and discover their own unique identity. Both artists write as a means to effect social change, but the society they long for is radically different. This distinction should not be used in assessing their value as artists. One need not necessarily agree with either playwrights' political convictions to appreciate the depth of their passion and the brilliance of their art.

WORKS CITED

Fugard, Athol. *Notebooks 1966–1977*. Ed. Mary Benson. New York: Knopf, 1981.

Savron, David, ed. *In Their Own Words: Contemporary American Playwrights*. New York: Theatre Communications Group, 1988.

Walder, Dennis. *Athol Fugard*. New York: Grove P., 1985.

Wilson, August. *Fences*. New York: French, 1986.

The B♭ Burden
The Invisibility of Ma Rainey's Black Bottom

Eileen Crawford

August Wilson came to Ma Rainey by way of St. Vincent DePaul and Bessie Smith. In what would seem to be either a bizarre combination or a just-right, only-in-America configuration, a secondhand store named for a 16th century French ecclesiastic provided a 20-year-old ninth grade dropout in search of a place to stand in the world with the discarded music of a "classic" blues singer of the 1920s. At this juncture, in 1965, that capability was not guaranteed to August Wilson—avid collector, voracious reader, and potential dramatist.

In libraries and in secondhand bookstores, Wilson had the freedom to explore and develop his mind in the Ellisonian sense of the "unstructured possibilities of Western culture and sensibility" (Ellison 30). Says Wilson, "I went to the library to read things I didn't know anything about; I read anything I wanted to" (Staples 111). He went to the St. Vincent DePaul store, too, because among its many discarded items was a veritable storehouse of popular music records of the 1920s and 1930s. Among them, a pirated, typewritten, yellow-labeled copy of Bessie Smith's "Nobody in Town Can Bake a Sweet Jelly Roll Like Mine." Wilson recalls what happened to him when he put the record on the turntable:

> For the first time someone was speaking directly to me about myself and the cultural environment of my life. I was stunned by its beauty, by its honesty, and most

important, by the fact that it was mine. An affirmation of
my presence in the world that would hold me up and give
ground to stand on. (Wilson 3)

From Bessie Smith, Wilson learned that all black people have a
song, a song of themselves to present to the world. For now, his
concern was the means by which black Americans had
established apparitions of control, economic stability, and
cultural affirmation, a true political dialectic born of a certain
autodidactic sensibility. His early writings would lead Wilson to
explore the economic exploitation endured by performers like
Ma Rainey and Bessie Smith at the hands of white studio
owners, producers, and other agents of control. Soon, however,
he realized that a focus on the economic exploitation of Ma
Rainey by the studio owner and her manager did not allow for a
full affirmation of this homespun heroine or for any examination
of her musicians as characters. Furthermore, as Wilson noted in
the liner notes to the recorded performance of *Ma Rainey's Black
Bottom*, "I didn't think of myself as a playwright then and the
idea of making the musicians characters did not occur to
me"(Wilson 3). He completed 20 pages of the project and then
dropped it. It took a 1978 exhibition of the art of Romare Bearden
to enable Wilson to have, like Bearden, "a clear vision of life's
compositions, to provide a vision of life in cultural, ritual and
sacred terms" (3). All of these half hesitant yearnings came to
fruition in October 1981, when, in need of a submission to the
Eugene O'Neill Center National Playwrights Conference, Wilson
took up his early project, revitalized by his awareness of the
complexity of Bearden. So that now, his drama could focus on
ideas, attitudes, lives, music and the "accumulated wealth of
knowledge of an entire people" as opposed to its previous
propaganda motif.

    Thus, August Wilson's *Ma Rainey's Black Bottom* is the first
in his ongoing series of cycle plays, each reflecting a decade in
the African American exploration of a time-space continuum
when blacks—post-emancipation—were responsible for their
own destinies and their own miseries.[1] What Wilson has termed
a "kind of four hundred year old autobiography" may also be
read as an ongoing series of character studies—Ma and Levee in
Ma Rainey's Black Bottom, Troy Maxson in *Fences*, Boy Willie in

The Piano Lesson, and Herold Loomis in *Joe Turner's Come and Gone.* Wilson places special emphasis on the boy/men who are misdirected, misunderstood and misbegotten by the society in which they hope to thrive and prosper but yet are incapable of being directed and guided by that black community. They are true asocial nonconformists who the community, in all its dignity and seriousness, has yet to figure out, especially how to challenge their destructive energies. More specifically, *Ma Rainey's Black Bottom* gives us two characters poised on the edge of either spiritual illumination or near tragedy, stunning in their ability to depict the despair and transcendant spirit of black people.

Additionally, Wilson so designs this drama that it is Greek in its tragic configurations and complexity, while remaining deceptively simple.[2] It observes the unities of time, place and action (one day's recording session, sometime in the 1920s in Harlem, New York). It focuses on the life of a person of significance (Ma Rainey). The band's role as off-bearer and signifier to Ma has the potential to act as the necessary choral element, a true chorus if they can realize their role. That is, if they (so, too, the audience in its catharsis) can face their true destiny with courage and dignity as supporters of one with the gifted, truly transcendental artistry of Ma Rainey. Finally, it is a set piece because thematically Ma Rainey's blues, too, is poised on the edge of either invisibility or spiritual illumination. As Ma Rainey would sing in "Screech Owl Blues":

> When a hog make a howl
> You know a storm is due
> When the screech owl holler
> You know bad Buck's
> Coming back once more

Gertrude Pridgett, "Ma Rainey," (1886–1939), is that "Screech Owl," one who acts as an omen for those who can hear her lyrics. One of the first blues women, she is as bragging, as arrogant, as bad as a man wearing State Street brogan shoes (Southern 323). Rainey first heard the blues in 1902 in a small town in Missouri where she was appearing in vaudeville tent shows. Rainey told of a girl from the town who came to the tent one morning and began to sing about the "man who had left

her." The sound of the song was strange and poignant; Ma
Rainey became so interested that she learned the song from the
visitor, used it soon afterwards and began to specialize in the
singing of such songs (Lieb 3). Rainey further claimed that it was
she who gave the songs the name "blues" after being asked time
and time again about the type of song she was singing and
finally answering in an inspired moment, "It's the blues"
(Southern 332).

This blues woman was a "heavy-hipped mamma" with
"great big legs, voluptuous, sensual, and as ugly as sin"
according to her friends who loved her with a singular devotion
(Southern 266). She relied upon African American adaptation
patterns of self-mockery and self-deprecating humor to bring
"tears to the eyes and laughter to the lips of all who beheld her
performance" (Southern 267). When she sang in that low, slow
cadence:

> Say, I'm gonna get drunk one more
> time cause when I'm drunk nothing
> don't worry my mind. ("Dead Drunk Blues" 1927)

> or

> You low down alligator, just watch me
> sooner or later, I'm gonna get you with
> your britches down! ("Black Eyed Blues" 1928)

No one was unmoved. Ma dressed for the part of blues legend
too. She often wore a necklace and earrings made of gold pieces,
diamond-studded tiaras, rings and bracelets. Her gowns were
always elaborate affairs of brocade, gold beaded satin, pearls and
furs. Ma Rainey's shows always included broad comedy skits
along the lines of chicken-stealing and watermelon-eating
episodes. After this general uproar, Ma Rainey herself made her
entree—telling ribald jokes about craving young "pig meat" men
and singing her trademark songs, "Memphis Blues," "Jelly Roll
Blues," "I Ain't Got Nobody," and "See See Rider." Ma Rainey
was a tremendous figure; she wouldn't have to sing words.
According to Sterling Brown, "she would moan and the
audience would moan with her" (as quoted by Lieb 17).

> ... An some jokers keep deir laughs a goin'in de crowded
> aisles, an some folks sits dere waiting wid deir aches an
> miseries, till Ma comes out before dem a smilin' gold-
> toofed smiles ... (as quoted by Lieb 27)

By 1923, Ma Rainey was the acknowledged fountainhead
of the "Classic" blues singers, defined as a female lead singer
with three backup instrumentalists: cornet, piano, clarinet or
saxophone player. As the Northern recording industry
"discovered" the untapped potential of these great blues singers,
moves were made to issue records to be sold in the black
community. Yet, Rainey was discovered by them in the full
throes of her career (Harrison 39). These early phonograph
records by women blues singers actually created whole new
styles of blues singing (Jones 102).[3] Through their songs these
singers became the principal spokespersons for black women in
the North and South, especially for those women who had left
field and farm for factory and tenement in the North. Traveling
alone, or with young children, this exodus of black women, in
advance of husband, friends and family, found the hostile urban
North lonely and without folk connections. The other side of the
paradigm saw these women in a world beyond the constraints of
small-town life. As E. Franklin Frazier notes, the cities offered
"comparative freedom from the religious constraints imposed by
rural church and community" (as quoted by Harrison 210) as
many of these women found themselves drawn to the new
dispensations—light industry and light living, the life of a "city
girl" as represented by cabarets, nights on the town, circuit rider
men and red-light districts. The blues they had heard in
Memphis and Birmingham could now be transplanted to the
North by such associations as TOBA (Theater Owners Booking
Associations)[4] which scheduled appearances of black acts in 67
theaters across the country.

Artists such as Ma Rainey became the troubadours for
African American folk culture, similar to what the Homeric
bards had been for Greek aristocracies. Wilson's drama, then, in
addition to being a tragedy, is an annunciatory set piece on the
theme of invisibility: the invisibility of race, the invisibility of art
versus philistinism, and the invisibility of the performer whose

values of the troubadour are in conflict with the opportunism of the short-con artist.

The immediate time and physical setting of *Ma Rainey* ... is the band room and recording studio of a Chicago record company whose race divisions puts out "race" records by black performers aimed primarily at black audiences. This event is an historic occasion, but no one present seems to realize it or to care. The studio owner and Ma Rainey's manager quarrel over money and Ma's general intransigence. Wilson describes the studio owner, Sturdyvant, as "unsensitive to black performers ... (whom) he prefers to deal with at arms length" (Wilson 17). Ma implies in her dealings with her manager that she views him variously as pimp, hustler and racial opportunist (1.1.76).

The play begins with the introduction of the four band members as they drift into the studio and engage in what would appear to be desultory rehearsals. Their very studied casualness is an indication of their command of the situation.[5] It becomes apparent that their songs represent their individual commitment to certain artistic goals in a society that denies them even a minimal chance for success. In fact, their very careers in this small musical world are a volatile anomaly. These men, now all mellowing toward middle age, are worn out by the battles they have engaged in during a persistent, lifelong quest for authenticity. Their group identity, as Ma's band, maintains whatever status is possible in the social structure. Their narratives, told in a vamp-until-ready motif as they await Ma's appearance disclose their encounters with America's virulent racism in the 1920s. Slow Drag's report of a torturous "dance" done by a black preacher for a white vigilante and Toledo's statement to Levee that "you just leftover from history; whites eat you in their stew" are a verbam sapiente of signs and sighs for the black community.

The symbolic acts of Toledo, for example, to educate himself and to make telling "comment" about the people and circumstances in which he finds himself are grounded in a system of perfectibility. Toledo, like many autodidactics, is fond of obtuse statements; he is, therefore, misunderstood. His problem centers around a critical aspect of cultural identity. Ralph Ellison's essay, "The Little Man at Cheehow Station," describes the American sense of identity wherein the individual achieves his potential unhindered by his ties to the past. "Here, theoretically, social categories are open, and the individual is not only considered capable of transforming himself; he is encouraged to do so" (Ellison 41). Toledo's cultural wholeness is not so easily arrived at as that of his Euro-American peers, but nevertheless, his mighty attempts to tame the chaos of his American dilemma and his mighty failures are evidence of his belief in his own American identity in its fullest sense.

So, too, the rich sensibility of the music these men play is an indication of their belief in culture-as-affirmation. The music gives audible expression to the inner dimensions of otherwise inarticulate men.[6] Individually, these men are harsh and profane, vulgarians for the most part. Yet, in Toledo's words, they exhibit a rich sensitivity toward their "art." Wilson envisions their playing ability as an aspect of their character. Cutler's guitar and trombone playing is solid and almost totally unembellished; his understanding of his music—read life—is limited to the chord he is playing at the time he is playing it. Slow Drag's bass is incorporated into his innate African rhythms which underlie everything he plays. Toledo, the piano player, is in control of his instrument; he understands and recognizes that its limitations are an extension of himself (1.1.20). Their music, then, is evidence of what Ellison describes as the "unstructured possibilities of culture" (30). What holds this successful, almost prosperous, band together is their understanding of the arcane ways of that American sensibility. They emerge (to paraphrase a 1960s popular music hit) from the drab camouflage of oppression into the gaudy plumage of jazz musicians: intense playing to exceptional lines, rhythms and melodies, ranges, voice like sounds and statements. Their personal stories are allegories of history.

For example, Levee is that individual who has yet to understand his own playing which reveals his bottomless anger—an anger generated by a father's agony, a mother's tragedy, which leaves him to make his way alone and confused. Because Levee is unable to internalize the lessons of the blues he plays, he can hear only their ambiguousness. Thus, his dual stance and name indicate, a dike, a stance against a tide of sheer music opportunism as well as one who would kill the fatted calf in his overly heated reception of the new music. When Toledo, whose playing closely parallels the resignation and defeat that he feels, tells Levee he is "just a leftover from history; whites eat you in their stew" (1.1.57), Levee's response is angry, frustrated: "I got lost in the [ingredients of] the stew" which indicates his alienation from both race and culture. He is losing the sardonic ability to laugh at that self-same pleasure, that self-same pain.

Levee believes that the "stew" of life has only one kind of ingredient, cannot be embellished and enriched over time. Levee's careerism leads him to jettison the core elements of the blues, its ability to make social commentary for justice, in favor of the new "real" music, as he calls it. He counters Ma's artistic statement:

> I always got to have some music going on in my head somewhere. It keeps things balanced. Music will do that. It fills things up. The more music you have in the world, the fuller it is. (2.1.82)

His own song of existential reality is a precursor to the next generation's form, to be called rhythm and blues:

> You can shake it, you can't break it
> You can dance at any hall
> You can slide across the floor
> You'll never have to stall
> My jelly, my roll
> Sweet Mama, don't you let it fall (2.1.80)

This vision reflects and further refines his character; Levee sees himself as outside history.

By contrast, Ma sees herself as history, steeped inside of history. For example, her arrival is perfectly informed, if a bit delayed by a traffic accident. Irvin has previously been told by Sturdyvant to "keep Ma in line . . . he is not putting up with any Royal Highness . . . Queen of the Blues bullshit" (1.1.18). Thus her entry with entourage (investigating policeman, Dussie Mae her love interest, and Sylvester, her unfortunate nephew) is a direct indication of her status: she carries herself in royal fashion (Wilson 48). The dialectic is set because Ma demands that due notice be given of who she is not only to the officious policeman but to the recording studio manager as well. When she says to Irvin, "Tell these people who I am" (1.1.48), Irvin's only response can be linear. For Ma the issues here have to do with the terms of control, mechanisms of professional choice and due recognition of her status as Queen of the Blues. Sturdyvant, on the other hand, can only react to her overbearing attitude. But as Thomas A. Dorsey would say of the historical Ma Rainey:

> Ma had the real thing. She just issued out there. It (her voice) had everything it needed. Just like somebody put out a plate of food and say everything is on the plate. And that's the way Ma handed it to 'em. Take it or leave it. (qtd. in Harrison 39)

Since Ma was "discovered" in the full throes of her career, she isn't beggin' for attention, recognition or the short-lived flattery of people like Irvin and Sturdyvant. This is at the heart of Ma's conflict with Levee. The values that inform her artistic integrity are the same that make her the troubadour-as-artist—her loyalty to friends and family and her independence from those that would subvert her art. Ma's concerns for Dussie Mae and Sylvester are easily apparent. She wants and supplies clothes and monies for them. She advocates that Sylvester send money home to his mother. But it is her insistence that Sylvester, whom she insists "doesn't stammer all the time" (2.1.74), be allowed to record the introduction to her song "Ma Rainey's Black Bottom" that is the telling character trait here. This is real independence, a "put it on the plate and eat it or leave it alone quality" that gives Ma her folk-poet assurance. As Ma tells Irvin:

> I ain't playing with you Irvin. I can walk out of here and go back to my town. I got plenty fans. I don't need to go through all of this. (2.1.74)

She is, of course, absolutely correct in her clear-sighted assessment of the source of her strength: her folk roots and its accompanying authority. While this may be used in most situations, the real basis of power comes with an assumption of grace. Ma's hubris, her inability to see a need to augment her musical style, will be the reason for the success of the threatening new musical dispensation. The blues is an aural music intended to take on shape and style during the performance. It also reflects the personal response of its inventor to a specific occurrence or situation. Thus, it has the potentiality for mutability. As a blues singer of note, Ma has more than a little responsibility to find a place for Levee inside history too, to share his experiences in one way or another. Of course, Levee goes out of his way to prevent her from doing so. Yet, as the troubadour, she must herald. Of concern is her propensity for the aggressive response, for the assertion of sheer power. While she is correct in her assessment that her band does not directly pay her due notice, the recording industry cares not about her, that she is truly being taken advantage of, she has the ability to be above all of this fracas. Thus when Levee requests "his song," Ma disappointedly responds with:

> What's all this about "the boys in the band say." I tells you
> what to do. I says what the matter is with the band. I say
> who can and can't do what. (2.1.77)

This can only bring on the point-of-attack incident.

Levee sees the very richness of the canvas of the blues as wild, primitive-tent carryings on. He would replace the country blues with mindless, jelly-roll sexuality. Traditionally, the sexual elements so apparent in the blues were a part of the memorable way of telling the story, of passing on information so that the essential element, the word wisdom, retains its emotional reference. Contained in Ma Rainey's statements are a philosophical system actually at work. Her emotional references are in time perspective—"I've been doing this a long time"—and are an answer for all situations in which she finds herself—"You sing because that is a way of understanding life" (2.1.82). Yet, the alacrity with which Levee disregards the "fullness" and "richness" of Ma's aesthetic, as well as the opportunism with which he subverts Ma's love interest, Dussie Mae, proves his disregard for his peers and for Ma and is an indicator of his essential nature—his is the personality of the philistine and short-con artist with the potential for a new idea. He wants his own band, "Levee Green and his Foot Stompers," and a different sound for the new modernity, *but* he places his future in the hands of Sturdyvant—the indifferent to blacks, preoccupied with money, white recording-studio owner.

Within this steamy microcosm, the drama emerges as a set piece on the theme of "The Blackness of Blackness": a dialogue concerning how black folk did and did not get over. With the advent of Ma Rainey in the recording session, all desultory playing stops and the avoidance strategies come to an end. The screech owl, that symbol of wisdom and bird of omen, has hollered. Ma says to Irvin, her manager, in response to his attempt to hurry her along, "We'll be ready to go when Madame says we're ready. That is the way it goes around here" (1.1.64). She ain't studying Irvin, Sturdyvant or Levee for that matter; her songs come from "the voice inside her" (1.1.63). Ma's stance with record company whites and others is one of aggressive assurance that "she knows more about her fans than they do" (1.1.63). Levee will not be able to alter her song with his new sound because she is quite able to, as she says, "carry my black bottom on back South to my town, cause I don't like it up here no ways" (1.1.63).

The issue here is will. As long as Ma Rainey has the power to enforce her will, all will acquiesce. Ma is not unaware of this situation. She is fully capable of using the old standbys of racial scars shared between her and the band members to enforce her authority. They know as well as she that if she had her way she, like Slow Drag, would tear this old building down. She uses this rage when she reminds the band, for example, that these producers and agents are rapacious subjugators of Black Americans. She is in effect asking for racial solidarity. She is reminding the band that she knows what the game is, that she is aware of whom they serve, and that she compromises with and tolerates these white promoters for the sake of sustaining their collective art:

> They don't care nothing about me. All they want is my
> voice. Well, I done learned that, and they gonna treat me
> like I want to be treated no matter how much it hurt
> them. . . . As soon as they get my voice down in them
> recording machines, then it's just like as if I'd be some
> whore and they roll over and put their pants on. (2.1.79)

The band members can only affirm her angry assessment of the real relationships in this industry. Denied real power by white society, Ma Rainey siphons it, forces it to the forefront in petty and not so petty ways. It is as if the small accumulations of each incident (a proper Coke Cola, rehearsals on her timetable, using her tongue-tied nephew to introduce her song, her petty hold over Dussie Mae) are her counter-strikes to being used in this grim visaged war of color. Her final paying of the score is her trademark song—you can kiss my "Black Bottom." Her entourage looks up to Ma—it copies her outrageous strategies, envies her behavior, emulates her mannerisms. Yet, as profane vulgarians they have failed to learn the real lesson of Ma's blackness. While they discuss in their many moving stories their suffering and tribulations, these narratives, in essence, must be seen as rituals of complaint directed primarily *at* the white man. Ma, on the other hand, does not do this because she understands the true "unstructured possibilities of culture" (Ellison 30). She knows that the incongruities of race and culture in America provide for maneuverability for one who is resolutely determined. Thus, Ma rules absolutely because art is her determiner. She allows for no other songs but her Black Bottom. Lacking this sense of direction, the band members, except for Levee, whose determination is based upon greed, must acquiesce. Levee, however, because Ma tends to intimidate and subdue him and others, confuses her artistic arrogance with what he can only understand as selfishness about what is blues art. Essentially, this power struggle is the age old one between the philistine as the cheap exponent of whatever sells at the moment and the artist for whom art is a way of life. Levee's essential character flaw is his misunderstanding of what oppression is all about. Ma truly knows that subjugation at the hands of the white power structure is what black artists have in common. It does not, cannot, differentiate them from each other. Levee hopes for a separate peace with the white man. His hamartia is that he can listen to neither Toledo, Ma, nor the blues lyrics to tell him differently.

Thus each artist responds to the common experience called racism, most often as a member of the ensemble, because of the racial investment therein. Unfortunately, the controlled anarchy of the group means that the perceived weakest member can be thrown into the forest of a thousand demons to die if he is perceived as not adhering to the group's mores. In other words, if the group begins to feel that a member has risen above his station, they become weary and capable of shunting him aside. Levee, the band members, and occasionally Ma cannot see Toledo as a man of strength, as a potential warrior to lead them out of their dilemmas. He is their resident man of thought. Unfortunately, his expressiveness is seen as an attempt by a "great big windbag" to do nothing more than show off (1.1.42). They see his playful sense of language as an effort to make them feel dissatisfied and restless. They see his commitment to the exploration of ideas as a prodding to do more when what they desire to do is complain and obey. When he chastises the band that they essentially wish to be "continually killed by the good times," they are certain that this is arrogant foolishness. This is apparent in Slow Drag's response to Toledo's lecture on Africanisms in Black American language: "I ain't no African" (1.1.32). Even Levee, who really does wish to do "more than just have a good time" (1.1.42), responds to Toledo's remarks with a snide putdown, calling them "highfalutin' ideas about making a better world for the colored man" (1.1.42).

The theme of the "Blackness of Blackness" is at the heart of the conflict couched within the artistic palaver between Ma and Levee. While Toledo can warn the group about terminal self-hate and short-term materialistic advantage, due to his own intellectual limitations, he cannot tell them of the whole truth: that they are on the verge of trading in their spiritual assets. For instance, he says:

> "I'll tell you something, as long the colored man look to the white folks to put the crown on what he say . . . as long as he looks to white folk for approval . . . then he ain't never gonna find out who he is and what he's about. He's just gonna be about what white folks want him to be about." (Wilson 37)

Toledo's warning is unintelligible because he does not have the insight to realize that his most effective pupil could be the one with the most drive and energy: Levee. Toledo repeatedly calls him ignorant, "ignorant without a premise" (1.1.32). While this is an absolutely correct assessment of Levee's intelligence, as he does possess an irate aggressiveness which is a barrier to his ability to apprehend life and benefit from time spent with

Toledo, Toledo succumbs to the band's assessment that Levee is a fool—a fool about his blue suede Florsheims, a fool to attempt to woo Ma's girl and an even bigger fool for reckoning without his hostess's consent to change her song.

Toledo can play and read and decode some of the complex messages in human relationships in many of the same manners as blues narratives. What Levee sees as "philosophy bullshit" (1.1.68) are Toledo's insights tinged with self-mockery. His rhetorical analogues, "spooked by the white man," "leftovers from history," lead him to use his warrior spirit in the only way he knows how. Toledo, casting his hard-earned wisdom before such sycophants as Slow Drag and rebellious youths such as Levee, finds himself mocked in return by such putdowns as "you read too many goddamn books"(1.1.25). The fact that he has not escaped in spite of some abilities is indicative of his status as black American. After all, what else is he to do? Become yet another black intellectual sorting mail in the post office? Become another overly competent, bored-crazy taxi driver? Become another Sunday afternoon preposterously dressed-up parader down Lenox Avenue? The best place for Toledo is in some way protected from blatant racism, within the group as their resident man of ideas. And furthermore, caught in the comforting web of racial identity, he cannot do any differently.

August Wilson so designs this drama that it is Greek in its tragic configuration. The tragic moment occurs within the unities of time, place and action. The audience is well prepared for a death; all has moved toward that end. The question is whose? Both Ma Rainey and Toledo are of sufficient stature to talk of tragic dimensions, replete as they are with their individual indicators of hubris and a perceived loss of dignity. There will be no real recognition scene, however. The real figure with tragic potential is, of course, Ma Rainey. Given her historical status, however, Wilson cannot allow the drama to yield to the inevitable. Instead Wilson wisely focuses on the single motivation of Ma Rainey, Toledo, and Levee: the concern with the direction of one's artistic life and how to use this art of the blues to inform that life. Thus Wilson's characters are myopically disposed toward pushing their fate to the brink of disaster due to their personalities. For instance, Ma Rainey is a bragging, difficult woman quite capable of bringing tragedy to other people's lives. Additionally, she is independent, sexually adventurous, and refuses to be intimidated by her lack of formal education. As she says, "I have my own way of doing things" (1.1.32). On the other hand, Levee's method of decoding the racial messages given by whites, like the other members of the band, is to engage in primal screams down the laughing barrel of anger, rage and dignity. Slow Drag determines to hide his innate intelligence for profitability and protection, while Cutler deals with the here and now, expecting and asking for nothing and getting out of life what little he can. This essential accommodation by all except Ma will ultimately prove the group's undoing. It becomes, then, a group loss, the black community's tragedy at the loss of an historical tradition. When Cutler reminds Levee that in his just-concluded subversion of Ma's song to the interests of Sturdyvant, he reminds Levee that he has been unnecessarily obsequious. Cutler continues, "You talking out your hat—that man comes in here, call you a boy, tell you to get off your ass and rehearse, and you can't say nothing to him, except Yessir!" (1.1.67); he has in his characteristic fashion unknowingly provoked the final incident.

This will occur as a result of Levee's pursuit and eventual conquest of Dussie Mae. At the moment of Levee's exultation and triumph, when he declaims, "Good God! Happy birthday to the lady with the cakes" (2.1.84), the audience's catharsis is underway. Our anticipation of what this infidelity will mean to all involved (a certain loss to Ma, eventual rejection of Dussie Mae by Levee, and Levee's gloating references whenever possible) commits the audience to sorrow and pity for Ma, as she will surely see this as a rejection of the deepest part of herself, one that is beyond her art. Tempered as it is now by Sylvester's achievement—he speaks without stuttering—Dussie Mae's rejection of Ma will surely mean that Ma knows that Dussie was taken by the virile man she cannot be and this was due in part to her distraction and support of Sylvester, an ironic dilemma. Ma will soon know that Sylvester's last chance in life at clear speaking was not recorded; Ma is soon to know that it was caused by Levee's careless indifference directed at Ma's triumph over Sturdyvant and Irvin, and finally Ma is soon to know that what may appear ancient with licentiousness and lewdness is not.

When Ma sings her trademark song, "I want to see the dance you call the black bottom, I want to learn that dance" (2.1.85), the audience is finally aware that to know her dance is to know Ma Rainey. Levee can never learn the dance. At best, Levee's misdirected opportunism finally finds the avenue it seeks in the acceptance of his song in place of Ma's, but it is a dufus jingle set to a sophisticated rhythm. So, too, the audience fully understands that while Ma may endure on the circuit a bit longer, the blues will now fast become another cultural artifact in the black community, a realization for the audience that is almost as unendurable for them as it is for Ma.

The stage is set for the final action. When the controls Levee has counted on and needs so badly are finally severed, Ma must—to save the whole—fire him. He has rebelled against her sovereignty, but set adrift, he knows no where else to turn but upon the group. While it may seem that the incendiary device for this conflagration is that moment when challenged by Ma and concerned about potential revenue losses, Sturdyvant callously dismisses Levee, Levee's frustration is actually due to his loss of certainty and his inability to act independently of the white man. Toledo's admonition that "as long as colored folks look to white folks for approval . . . they ain't never gonna find out who they is . . ." (1.1.37) turns out to have been the prophetic moment. Inherent in Levee's pleading that a new music is called for by the people who "wants something different, that's gonna excite them" (2.1.96) is the idea that they want a different music. In the end, we see that this is not necessarily so. As the artist troubadour figure, Ma Rainey offers to the band the challenge of history. The band members, however, are workers/craftsmen. Ma Rainey's example is to move inside of history; for them it is just a job. The additional dramatic irony is that Toledo doesn't recognize that this lesson applies more specifically to him than any other individual in the group. He commits the unforgivable insult, steps on Levee's brand new Florsheims; the audience and the band too are impaled on that footprint. Levee's anger and helplessness must find its outlet. His "see what you done" (2.1.109) is both absurdly incongruous and a metaphor for all.

Yes, see what you done done.

The irony is that this line resonates from Ma's song "C. C. Rider."

Here are those who accepted the burden of race. Here are those whose inclination is to endure the slow, painful evolution of the race. Each generation revels even in the company of race, and in the company of the race.

NOTES

1. While anchored in time, Wilson's plays are not chronicles in the classic sense. Because they are anchored in one time frame—the late l9th and 20th century—they are not concerned with historical figures or with historical materials but with characterization.

2. See reviews by Brendan Gill, Harold Kissel, Clive Barnes, Frank Rich and others. These critics have all tended to base their analysis on extraliterary criteria. Seldom have they concentrated on any aspect other than the "searing inside account of what white racism does to its victims." Unfortunately, this superficial nod toward literary analysis will form the pattern in their approaches to much of Wilson's dramatic efforts.

3. Daphne Harrison notes that through the blues, Ma Rainey (and others: Bessie Smith, Mamie Smith) became the principal spokespersons for black women in the North and South (20). They effectively changed the existing folk traditions of work, field hollers and chants done primarily by men to the new situations of the city, creating an urban blues, "apt to be more sophisticated in tone than the country blues" (Southern 335–336).

4. Also known colloquially by its black performers as "Tough on Black Asses," their busy circuit traveled the barbarous South from one Jim Crow town to another, beset by haphazard schedules, deplorable managers, inadequate housing, accommodations and a humiliating uncertainty about when, and if, they would be paid (Harrison 23).

5. Duke Ellington's band was famous for its casual approach to rehearsal—sauntering in late usually, yet, being allowed to witness this process was a signal honor prized by white critics.

6. This concept is also explored to great advantage by James Baldwin in "Sonny's Blues."

WORKS CITED

Baraka, Amiri (Leroi Jones). *Blues People*. New York: Morrow, 1963.

Barnes, Clive. "'Ma Rainey': The Black Experience." *The New York Post* 12 Oct. 1984.

Buford, John. "Plight of 1920s Blacks—Superbly Portrayed in New Wilson Drama." *The Christian Science Monitor* 16 Oct. 1984.

Ellison, Ralph G. *Shadow and Act*. New York: Random House, 1978.

Gill, Brendan. "Hard Times." *The New Yorker* 22 Oct. 1984.

Harrison, Daphne Dural. *Blues Queens of the 1920s: Black Pearls*. New Brunswick, NJ: Rutgers University Press, 1980.

Kissel, Harold. "Ma Rainey's Black Bottom." *Women's Wear Daily* 12 Oct. 1984.

Lieb, Sandra. *Mother of the Blues: A Study of Ma Rainey*. Amherst: University of Massachusetts Press, 1981.

Ma Rainey's Black Bottom. The Original Broadway Cast. Hollywood, Columbia Records, 1985.

Rainey, Ma. *Ma Rainey's Black Bottom: Original Rare Recordings by the Mother of the Blues*. Yazoo Records, Inc., 1986.

Rich, Frank. "Ma Rainey Opens." *Stage* Oct. 1984.

Southern, Eileen. *The Music of Black Americans*. New York: W.W. Norton, 1971.

Staples, Brent. "Spotlight: August Wilson." *Essence* May 1987.

Wilson, August. *Ma Rainey's Black Bottom*. New York: New American Library, 1985.

August Wilson's Folk Traditions

Trudier Harris

African American folkloric traditions have taken on many recognizable forms, ranging from the Brer Rabbit and John the Slave trickster tales to the blues, from legends and folktales to spirituals and gospels, from folk beliefs and ghostlore to preaching and folk expressions. Scholars studying such patterns have garnered their categorizations of the lore from a variety of collected sources, such as Zora Neale Hurston's *Mules and Men* and the seven-volume *Frank C. Brown Collection of North Carolina Folklore*. Patterns in the lore reflect patterns in African American history, including strategies for survival, ways of manipulating a hostile Anglo American environment, and a world view that posited the potential for goodness prevailing in spite of the harshness of American racism and the exclusion of blacks from American democracy and the American dream. African American folklore, as Ralph Ellison astutely pointed out, revealed the willingness of blacks to trust their own sense of reality instead of allowing the crucial parts of their existence to be defined by others.

In turning to examine August Wilson's plays and where they fit into this historical conception of African American folklore, it becomes clear that there is overlap as well as extension. Wilson's use of African American folk traditions approximates that of Henry Dumas and Toni Morrison. Certainly, he includes recognizable patterns of the lore in his dramas, but he is also about the business of expanding—within established patterns—what African American folklore means and what it does. Like Dumas and Morrison, he is as much a mythmaker as he is a reflector of the cultural strands of the lore he uses. His conception of "the shiny man" in *Joe Turner's Come and Gone* (1988) will serve to illustrate the point. "The shiny man" is an extranatural guide/seer who leads Bynum, one of the central characters, to discovery of the song that defines his being, his purpose in life, and his relationships with others. While there is no specific "shiny man" who can be documented in Hurston's work or any other collections of African American folklore, there are certainly references to unusual encounters with extra- or supernatural phenomena. Wilson adapts that pattern of human encountering otherworldly being from historical folklore; then, he riffs on the established pattern by naming the phenomenon "the shiny man." In imaginatively expanding traditional forms of the lore, Wilson shares kinship with Morrison, who also takes traditional forms, gives them new shapes, and bends them to her imaginative will throughout her novels.[1] Wilson's creation in *Joe Turner* of "the shiny man" and of powerful songs that define the essence of human significance and his creation in *The Piano Lesson* of a piano that evokes ghostly presences link him to the same creative folkloristic vein as Dumas and Morrison.

The references to "the shiny man" begin Wilson's transformation of traditional supernatural and religious phenomena into African American folkloristic phenomena. Jesus is obviously the supernatural being usually slotted into black folk religious encounters, yet Wilson argues that "the shiny man" serves the same purpose of rebirth or conversion. He will similarly reclaim rituals, such as baptism, for the African American folk tradition, for it is by resorting to rituals informed by their own culture and history that black people can save themselves. Songs, which play a large role in traditional conversion processes, become equally important for Wilson in relocating the power of conversion within Afrocentric forms. The process Wilson employs constantly encourages a rewriting of history and folklore as it relocates religious expectations and patterns firmly within folkloric traditions.

Wilson creates folklore, therefore, that is recognizable even in its surface unfamiliarity. It writes the history of a people tied to the South, to racism and repression, but simultaneously to a strength that transcends those limiting categories. Like Morrison, Wilson encourages a willing suspension of disbelief about the nature of the lore he presents. He does not establish the possibility of the existence of certain phenomena; he simply writes as if they are givens. We might say that his plays begin "in medias res." A world exists; Wilson invites viewers into it. Instead of going to meet the audience by trying to *prove* belief in supernatural phenomena, Wilson unapologetically invites the audience to come into his world, to rise to his level of belief. Wilson's willingness to receive black cultural phenomena into his creative imagination is reflected in his characters' willing immersion in those same traditions and in the power they have to influence audience participation in the worlds in which they live. *Joe Turner's Come and Gone* will make these points clearer.

Wilson begins the play with a striking reversal, the first signal that his treatment of folk traditions will have an individualistic signature. The play opens with the conjure man, Bynum, publicly conducting a voodoo ceremony in the backyard of the boarding house in which he rents a room. This public spellcasting (although it is offstage, it is clearly visible to the characters onstage) places Bynum in a category unlike that of most conjure men and women. Throughout their history, most of them have retained an element of secrecy about what they do, for their very reputations have depended upon an aura of mystery. Consider, for example, Aun' Peggy in Charles Chesnutt's *The Conjure Woman* (1899) or M'Dear in Toni Morrison's *The Bluest Eye* (1970). Both women, like most conjure people historically, live *apart* from the communities upon which they exert their power. Rumors about them are an integral part of how they function within their communities, and such rumors are absolutely crucial to the power they wield. The fact that conjurers come from an area apart from the community into the realm of the belief in their power gives them a grander, more psychologically effective appearance; the spatial distance also serves to prepare recipients mentally for the power about to be exerted in their behalf. M'Dear's appearance at Aunt Jimmy's house, for example, is a little like the parting of waters; there is awesome respect, respectful distance from her person, and respectful adherence to what she says. If she were around Aunt

Jimmy's house or the community every day, the familiarity would not only lessen her power but would reduce the fear and respect people hold for her.

Wilson's improvising on this tradition is twofold. First, it reveals the difference in spatial demands on Southern and Northern territory. Cities such as Philadelphia, New York, and Chicago, to which blacks migrated, even in 1911 had far less space for isolation than the South. A consequence of black migration to the North might have been the transformation of folk traditions to the extent that a formerly private conjure ritual can become public because the Northern public is more accustomed to advertisements about such activities.[2] This Northern/Southern clash, with its attendant attitudes toward belief in folk traditions, is also reflected in the characters of Bynum and Seth, the owner of the boarding house. Placing Bynum and Seth in the same space, with Seth constantly making disparaging comments about Bynum and his rituals, comments on the inability of those who attempt to escape their folk heritage to do so in reality. Secondly, *where* Bynum performs his ceremony might be a function of genre. Stage confinements on space might require that actions be in proximity to each other. That explanation does not really suffice, however, because we could simply just *hear* of Bynum's activities and thus assume the historical mystery surrounding conjure people.

Publicizing Bynum's actions is the beginning of Wilson's revision of the function of African American lore to the people it has served over the years. By making folk traditions central instead of peripheral, public instead of private, Wilson assigns them more power and potential to influence the life view of their practitioners as well as that of the supplicants. Seth and his wife Bertha might not approve of Bynum's actions, but they cannot ignore them. And his interactions with them are so normal that they cannot say definitively that he is some kind of crackpot. Though what he does might not have specific meaning initially, it has general value; that value will be realized later in the play.

Wilson alters, slightly but perceptively, our expectations of African American tradition by similarly redefining the audiences toward whom tellers direct their narratives. Storytelling occurs at significant points in the play, one of which is shortly after

Bynum performs his initial ceremony with the pigeons. He relates the tale of "the shiny man," that spiritual, otherworldly being who has determined his path as a conjure man. Although we have been introduced to Seth and Bertha, they are not the primary audience to whom Bynum directs his story; indeed, Seth is offstage at that point. He selects Selig, the white peddler/"People Finder" instead; he has earlier sent Selig in search of "the shiny man."

This choice is an intriguing one, for if we were to adhere to stereotype, we might assume that the white Selig would be less inclined to respond favorably to Bynum's tale of having encountered a shiny man and that Seth, a black man, and Bertha, a black woman, would be more receptive. So the question immediately arises as to why Wilson would have made this choice. Obviously there is the functional reason of conveying information to the viewing audience. That information immerses them in a world view that equates knowing the self with the meaning of life and that equates the meaning of life with an individual song that in turn defines the self. This circular interrelatedness of one human being to another links Bynum to "the shiny man" for whom he has hired Selig to search, and it further links the audience to the action onstage. The story of Bynum's encounter with "the shiny man" therefore begins the process of "Africanizing the audience"[3] that is inherent in Wilson's presenting the lore as a given rather than arguing for its acceptance. I use the phrase "Africanizing the audience" to encompass the white viewers who undoubtedly made up the majority of the viewing audience for Wilson's play; of course African Americans in the audience would simply have their beliefs reinforced, or—in the case of those upwardly mobile (like Seth) who have forgotten their roots—reclaimed. The immediate audience (Selig) and the viewing audience are thus simultaneously encouraged to a different way of perceiving reality, to understanding that it is possible to see around corners, as the Invisible Man would say. Selig's skepticism might mirror that of those viewing the play, but neither can erase from memory Bynum's tale of "the shiny man." Wilson thereby gives whites no choice but to become immersed in a black reality.

The tale of "the shiny man" introduces the idea of journeying toward the full potential of self by recognizing the nascent value inherent within the self. The pattern is legendary and familiar in that a stranger assists the narrator to a new level of understanding; as a result, the narrator receives a mission that he in turn must pass on to another lost soul. With its overtones of religious conversion, Bynum's encounter with "the shiny man" places new emphasis on folkloristic material by suggesting that it indeed functions *as* religion. Bynum's travels with "the shiny man" are not unlike those of the penitent who meets Jesus, and the encounter results in a beatific transformation. When Bynum is told to rub his hands together and to wash himself with the blood that issues forth, echoes of being "washed in the blood of the Lamb" certainly come to the minds of those knowlegeable about the African American folk religious tradition. The image of the sparrow and the flash of light to which Bynum is exposed continue these parallels. When the stranger departs from him and Bynum meets his long-dead father, other echoes of traditional and religious journeys are evoked. Bynum's father, in the role of helper, leads him to an ocean (in contrast to the River Jordan of religious tradition), shows him visions, and teaches him how to find the song that enables him to bind people to each other. The "Binding Song" (reflecting his name—"bind them") is the essence of who he is. Legend and myth, then, have practical purposes in the world in that they directly influence people's lives. With this entertwining of the secular and the sacred, Wilson suggests that the secular *is* the sacred. That equation is certainly a significant expansion from perceived ways of viewing African American folk traditions.

Wilson's use of "the shiny man" is the primary part of his rewriting of the savior motif in religious practices; another part is his use of the "bones people." Loomis' vision of the "bones people" similarly interweaves Christianity with mythology. That the bones people walk on water without sinking certainly evokes Jesus, but the phenomeonon more immediately evokes for Wilson's characters African American history and the enormity of the loss of lives and human potential during the middle passage. In the biblical tradition of Ezekiel 37:3 ("Son of man, can these bones live?") and the popular African American sermon where various bones are connected to each other to stand on their own as a result of "hearing the word of the Lord," the bones Loomis observes take on flesh and move forward from their dehumanized states; they stand on their own feet in ways that Herald Loomis is currently unable to effect. Thus Wilson uses the tale not only to "Africanize the audience," but to "Africanize" or signify on Judeo-Western Christian myths by adapting them to black history. The vision, which Bynum has apparently also seen because he can "respond" to Herald's "calling" forth of the story, is another representational level of the need to liberate the self, to find the best in the self and move forward with it. The story is a creation myth, reshaped to suggest that human beings can stand in in the role of god in shaping their own destinies; for black men to do so, they must also reshape the dehumanizing myth of the middle passage and move toward mental freedom. When Herald Loomis is able to stand on his own, that forward progress will be available to him.

Wilson further inverts Western mythology by denying that white men are altruistic or that they are the ultimate center of the universe around which everything else revolves. Joe Turner, the legendary white man who has shaped Herald Loomis's life, epitomizes this point; he enables Wilson to rewrite history even as he is in the process of redefining the meaning and function of folklore. Turner could rightfully be viewed as the devil, or even worse than that, for if he merely took people's souls, that would be an end to their misery.[4] By stealing their lives and their potential—without killing them—he consigns them to the fate of zombies. Men like Loomis become automatons, destined to live out the fate that others have prescribed for them, existing because they lack the imagination or the will to take their own lives. Loomis has committed the sin that Grange Copeland accused his son Brownfield of having committed; by blaming the white man for everything, he has made him into a god. Long after Loomis has been granted freedom several years ago—on Joe Turner's birthday—he still belongs to that man's definition of black male human beings. Lacking the will to extricate himself from his own history, or to change his life from the single-minded purpose of finding his wife, Loomis is so out of touch with the best in himself that he could not possibly have been a good father to the daughter he has paraded around for seven years in search of her mother. In order for Loomis to become a shiny man, he must lift himself from the pages of the ink that Turner has used to inscribe his life.

Turner looms over Loomis's past, his present, and his future. As an archetypal symbol of racism and repression, he is not simply a man, but a force. He represents the evil that takes away all the potential identified with black men, whether that evil historically took the form of slavery, sharecropping, or convict labor as a result of being jailed without any semblance of due process. He represents the collective failure of American democracy for all black people, the dismissal of the race from the American dream. It is not necessary for Turner to appear as a character in the play for the destructive history of his collective representation to be felt. As long as Herald Loomis lives, so will Joe Turner. As long as Bynum sings songs about this black male snatcher, he will live. Memory is stronger than experience, and as long as Joe Turner has captured the memories and imaginations of the men he jailed, he remains a part of their lives. His significance can obviously be diminished, however, in direct proportion to Loomis' ability to find the power and path to exorcise from the recesses of his being the negative effects of his encounter with Turner.

It is noteworthy that Loomis equates Martha and Joe Turner as the "stopping points" in his life, the time at which the fire of his potential was reduced to embers and when his mere existence began. He needs to find Martha in order to get "a starting place in the world" (72). It is almost as if he wishes to perform a rite of exorcism, one that can be accomplished when he hands over his daughter Zonia to Martha. Martha becomes a negative as well as a positive symbol in the text. By equating her with Turner as halting his life, Loomis evokes comparison to characters such as Bigger Thomas and Silas in Richard Wright's works; both blame black women for their plights and both link black women to a conspiring white oppressive system. Stereotypically, therefore, in answer to the question, "Who oppresses black men?", the response is "black women." This substitution of Turner with Martha and of the psychological effect of Turner with Martha's departure enables Loomis to make legends of both of them. In neither instance has he arrived at the state of being willing to take personal responsibility for his own future in the world. If we view Martha as more representative than human, however, her last name—Pentecost—and her ties to Christianity place her in the position of another unhealthy binding force from which Loomis must extricate himself.

The story that Loomis tells of having been caught in Turner's net reveals the extent of his continuing mental imprisonment. He relates the narrative almost in a trancelike state, as if he were re-experiencing the horrors of being under Turner's control. His narrative reveals the tranformative power Joe Turner has held over him, for his entrapment has forced him to wander "a long time in somebody else's world" (72). As Bynum recognizes, because Loomis has lived his life according to the directives of someone else's script, or their impact, he has forgotten his song. Exorcising Joe Turner from the essence of his being, the initial stage of which is turning his daughter Zonia over to her mother, will enable Loomis to move forward as a healthier, saner human being. Certainly Zonia is an innocent being, but she is tied to the Christian heritage that Martha represents; she thereby becomes more representational than individualistic. Giving her to her mother is another indication of Loomis' moving away from the confines of Western mythology—a painful process, but one that he and black people generally must nonetheless undertake.

Joe Turner, Bynum posits, captures black men because he wants their song, their souls. That song encompasses whatever black people can use to survive oppression. If Joe Turner takes it away, or represses black men so much that they become too stupefied to retain a will to survive, then he has won. What Loomis needs is comparable to what Hurston describes in her essay on High John the Conqueror; he needs the transcendant spirit of laughter and song, broadly interpreted, that will enable him to survive. Hurston identifies that spirit with a song and with the flying Africans who were able to lift up from their oppressive American burdens and fly back to Africa. If Joe Turner can suppress that alternative vision, that innate sense of trusting one's own reality, that singing spirit, then he can destroy a race of people without killing a single one of them.[5]

Singing and song in the play, then, have historical, folkloristic, religious/spiritual/metaphysical connotations. Not only do they represent the blues essence of the experience someone like Herald Loomis has undergone, but they also represent the voicing of the African American presence in the world—unchained physically and psychologically. Bynum's songs ("The Healing Song" and "The Binding Song") and the one that Loomis will shortly receive are pre-blues and post-gospel; they were there at the beginning of black presence in America and will transcend all the limitations of the early American experiences. In his presentation of African American folk forms, Wilson suggests that there is something almost preternatural about black people. When unburdened by societal repressions, they uncover or recover the sources of strength that guided their African and American forebears. Songs are literally and figuratively a claim for unfettered being in the world, one for which each individual must bear the weight of his or her own physical and spiritual health. Communities of black people can offer assistance, but the ultimate responsibility belongs to the individual.

The redefining functions of history and folklore enter when Loomis can rewrite his personal history and move into the collective mythical possibilities of black manhood.[6] In finally giving voice to the fact that "Joe Turner's come and gone" (91), Loomis begins to understand that the past must be laid to rest; the negative effects of his past life should be "gone" or certainly going. The future is available to him only when he can realize, like Sethe Suggs and Ralph Kabnis, that the pain of the past can finally have no claim on new lives. In rejecting traditional Christianity and bleeding for himself, Loomis achieves ultimate responsibility for his being in the world, which may be viewed as a state of godhead. Wilson uses our understanding of folk traditions to move Loomis to the level of myth and legend. As a designated shiny man, stories will surely develop about him as the stories have about the man Bynum encountered. And as a person with a newly discovered song of self-sufficiency, he will have the power to influence other people's lives.

Wilson's most conspicuous adaptation of African American history and folklore occurs in his bringing Joe Turner from the confines of song to the flesh of villainy. Wilson also collapses color consideration in the play. While Joe Turner might have been reputed in legend to have been a horrible *white* chain gang captain, the *documentable* history is that Joe Turner was a *black* blues singer as well as the title of a song. Eileen Southern, the African American musicologist, identifies Turner with Jimmy Rushing and others of the Kansas City ("Kaycee") school of blues singers and musicians.[7] The song, "Joe Turner," has been recorded in a single extended stanza:

> They tell me that Joe Turner's come and gone,
> Oh, Lord!
> They tell me that Joe Turner's come and gone,
> Got my man and gone.
> He come with forty links of chain,
> Oh, Lord!
> He come with forty links of chain,
> Got my man and gone.[8]

Wilson has managed some ingenious overlapping with the use of "Joe Turner." Since the original blues singer was male, and the original singer of the song itself was obviously female (lamenting in classic blues fashion the separation from her man), Wilson has incorporated both genders into the traditions that he presents just as effectively as he manages to work his themes across generations in the play.

Believed to be one of the—if not *the*—earliest blues songs, "Joe Turner" voices the susceptibility of black males to life on Southern chain gangs (a recurring theme in blues and work songs). Reduced in its published version to its essential elements, the song recounts how Joe Turner (obviously white by virtue of his full name and the action he effects) has removed a black man (obvious by the blues labeling, "my man," and the anonymity characteristic of white rule over generic black lives) through force ("forty links of chain") to a place that the plaintive tone suggests will be worse than hell. The word "gone" speaks volumes in its uncertainty in reference to condition and in its finality in reference to chronology.

By making Joe Turner a living white, legendary villain, Wilson gives flesh to the force that has historically separated black men from black women, that is, the white man—whether he did so through the sharecropping system or lynching black men or locking them away in jails with little possibility of escape. Joe Turner, as the characters in the play recall him, therefore personifies the *state* of the blues that has historically been imposed upon black people externally and the conditions that gave rise to the *singing* of blues songs. If the conditions that define some portions of the blues are white-derived, then black people have a conscious target at which they can direct actions for ending that blues state. It relocates power within them as they revitalize the forces within themselves that can destroy a Joe Turner. Simply singing about him in the blues form provides only temporary relief through the act of singing itself or through the cathartic function of the blues, as Langston Hughes so graphically presents that function in "The Weary Blues." The personification of Joe Turner as the state of the blues leads to a permanent way of exorcising that condition from black lives. This is not to eliminate blues *singing*, but the state that has led to the *need* for that singing. The songs can remain an art form without the attendant oppression, in this case, that has made them necessary. Joe Turner, in the last analysis, emblematizes the end of the state of the blues for Herald Loomis. By negating the potential that others have to capture his mind, body, and spirit, he can now turn to the best possibilities for creativity *within* himself, whether that creativity takes the form of singing (blues songs or otherwise) or something else.

This rewriting of the history and the song also places Wilson in league with other black writers. In writing about his experiences in Oklahoma City, ones that influenced his composition of *Invisible Man*, Ralph Ellison has commented on hearing Jimmy Rushing and other blues and jazz musicians perform (even at the Sunset Club in Kansas City).[9] In capturing the essence of the blues in the novel—not only in its compositional form, but in its ethos as well—Ellison included a blues song entitled "Peetie Wheet Straw." Some researchers claim that there was a historical figure of this name, and others identify the baggy pants black man with the wheelbarrow full of blueprints as "Peetie Wheet Straw." As a part of his bantering interaction with the Invisible Man, the little man says: "I'll verse you but I won't curse you—My name is Peter Wheatstraw, I'm the Devil's only son-in-law, so roll' em!"[10] The original song consists of these lines:

> I am Peetie Wheet Straw, the high sheriff of hell,
> I am Peetie Wheet Straw, the high sheriff of hell,
> And when I lock you up, baby, you're locked in a
> dungeon cell.
>
> I am Peetie Wheet Straw, the devil's son-in-law,
> I am Peetie Wheet Straw, the devil's son-in-law,
> The woman I married, old Satan was her paw.[11]

"Peetie Wheatstraw" was a blues signature; any bluesman could sign off with that name and therefore exhibit his ties to a history and a community of singers and songs, to a collectivity of experiences. The point is that transformation of blues, blues character, and form precedes Wilson and claims him for a tradition of such transformation in African American texts.

While Wilson's characterizations of Loomis and Bynum redefine the value of blues history and song, he debunks the romantic myth of the traveling blues man in the character of Jeremy. Black traveling blues men, so the mythology goes, strung their guitars and a small bundle of clothing over their shoulders and left the rural South for better territory in the urban centers of the South and the North. Langston Hughes offered an earlier version of the type in *Not Without Laughter* (1930), and Albert Murray immortalized the character in the person of Old Luze in *Train Whistle Guitar* (1974). Old Luze might hop a freight train and disappear for months on end, but he has high moral values, including encouraging his young would-be imitators to pursue their education. Jeremy, by contrast, has the country aura and a fast-talking desire for women, but he is lacking in values. He plays his guitar more out of a love for money than a love for music, and there is never any clear indication of how good a musician he really is. Jeremy, then, becomes local color for the migration north instead of a character who engages us because of some heartfelt tie to his music or to the history out of which the music evolved. Wilson strips the type of his romantic veneer and delivers him up as the superficial, unscrupulous womanizer that he is.

Such developments indicate again that Wilson is constantly revising the folklore, reinscribing it with features that enhance his own purposes. While Molly is on the scene ready to be the woman stealer of traditional blues, Mattie is there waiting for Loomis to get beyond his living blues and into a healthier male/female interaction; they thereby trade superficial romance for a deeper engagement with blues phenomenon, one that affirms cohesion rather than separation, and one that operates like Bynum's "Binding song." By transforming the blues from connotations of opression to connotations of liberation, Wilson can thus make the tradition elastic enough to achieve his goals without distorting it beyond a recognizable folk form.

Loomis' symbolic and literal transformation from the clutches of Joe Turner and Bynum's encounter with "the shiny man" are the major folkloristic occurrences in the play, but Wilson also saturates his drama with the richness of other African American folk traditions. In addition to the blues—and the history that spawned the blues—he textures the play with ghostlore and fetish animals, as well as with folk beliefs such as sprinkling salt to ward off bad luck and with the characters engaging in Juba, "a call and response dance" (52). We can certainly say that Bynum's encounter with "the shiny man" is a ghostly experience of sorts. And Loomis' relation of the story of the "bones people" similarly has its ghostly aura. Wilson cuts across generations, however, to suggest that the entire community is heir to these kinds of occurrences. One of the children in the play, Reuben, sees the ghost of Miss Mabel, Seth's long dead mother. She instructs him to release the pigeons he had promised his dead friend Eugene that he would release. He relates the occurrence to Zonia, who, after an initial incredulousness, rather quickly believes in the ghost. The ease with which they accept this incident (they move from discussing Miss Mabel's appearance to sharing their first kiss) points again to the texturing of the culture with folkloristic forms. It is not unduly scary or unusual for these children to see something supernatural, just as it is not unusual for their adult counterparts—Bynum and Loomis—to have extranatural experiences.[12]

The major fetish animal in the play is really a bird: the pigeon. Bynum sacrifices pigeons in the binding ceremonies he performs in the back of the boarding house. While flight motifs are endemic to African American culture, ranging from tales of flying Africans to stories of pilots at Tuskegee's flight school during World War II to Morrison's *Song of Solomon*, pigeons are not omnipresent characters in the lore. African American folktales frequently include buzzards—as Hurston does in *Their Eyes Were Watching God*—but pigeons do not appear with any regularity. Wilson's inclusion of them, therefore, reflects another expansion in his use of folk materials.

So the question becomes, "What kinds of connotations do pigeons carry for spell-casting ceremonies?" As a "binder," Bynum ties the lives of his clients to the persons for whom they are searching. He has tied Zonia to Martha, thereby making it inevitable that Loomis and Zonia will eventually find their way to the boarding house. Even as he pays Selig to assist in this effort, he knows that his magic is stronger. By pouring pigeon blood into the ground, the power of flight inherent in the bird is reversed, grounded so to speak, in a way that will ensure the eventual gathering of the separated mother and daughter at the boarding house. Loomis is almost coincidental to the binding that Bynum has effected with Martha and Zonia, but Bynum nevertheless has him under a spell to the extent that he feels obligated to bring his daughter to her mother. Bynum repeats his ceremonies more frequently after Loomis and Zonia arrive and while Selig is looking for Martha.

Pigeons, devoid of the message-carrying function usually associated with them[13] (or that function has also been transformed), become themselves the message in the case of Miss Mabel's demanding that they be freed. Eugene, she says, is waiting for them. Releasing the pigeons would mean that Reuben is honoring the friendship he had with Eugene and recognizing—in a healthier fashion than keeping the pigeons locked up—the ties he has to his dead friend. The incident becomes a microcosmic expression of the influence of the past upon the present, the dead upon the living, that is being acted

out with the grown-ups in the play. Releasing the pigeons will
enable Eugene, a part of the past, to rest in peace, just as
delivering his daughter will become part of the process of
Loomis' settling of the past and claiming of peace. Releasing the
pigeons becomes a transformative metaphor for the path away
from stagnation, away from holding on to Eugene *as he was;*
realizing that Eugene is not bound to the frozen point at which
Reuben remembers him enables Reuben to move to a different
psychological space. When Loomis realizes that he is not bound
by Joe Turner's definitions, he in turn can move to a different
mental territory. That the incident with the children precedes
Loomis' transformation illustrates again the circularity of the
drama that moves events and beliefs across younger and older
generations.

The circularity is in itself indicative of African American
folk traditions, for scholars long studying the culture have
emphasized that blacks prefer circularity to linearity. Circularity
in children's games, such as "Little Sally Walker," allows for
more cooperation than competition and for greater inclusion in
the telling of tales or with other activities among adults. The
circular imagery also suggests a return to the best in the self as
well as a return to the African cultural forms that underlie
African American existence. Only by returning to the possibility
he saw in himself *before* Joe Turner snatched him can Loomis
move beyond his incarceration and the dead years that he has
allowed to follow it.

It is of note, as well, that Wilson is not squeamish about
the sacrifice of pigeons in his play. His willingness to have Seth
describe Bynum's ceremonies so graphically indicates that he has
not acquiesced to any contemporary societal mores about proper
decorum. As a part of nature, as a part of a world where Joe
Turner can claim men's souls, it is not a significant trespass that
pigeons pay the price for the reuniting of a mother and daughter
or for the reclaiming of one of those lost souls. Taking the culture
as it is, not sanitizing it to placate the potentially hostile or
antagonistic, is a conscious creative decision on Wilson's part.

In transforming history and reclaiming/revitalizing
culture, Wilson outlines the process for Loomis to redefine
himself as a man. African American folk belief, then, becomes

the bridge over which Loomis walks to his manhood. It is also the road by which he finally travels to freedom. When Wilson uses secular mythology as the source of religious conversion and overwrites Christianity with African American folkways, he merges the secular and the sacred in ways that few African American authors have attempted. Centering Loomis' evolution into a shiny man upon his own blood as a cleansing agent, Wilson brings the hoodoo man into the pulpit, allowing him to become the sermon that those merely baptized in the blood of the Lamb can only imagine. His own blood enables Loomis to stand on his own two feet, like the bones people, and shape a future unfettered by traditional Christianity and its attendant themes of suffering and repression.[14]

NOTES

1. For an extensive discussion of this phenomenon in Morrison's work, see my *Fiction and Folklore: The Novels of Toni Morrison* (Tennessee, 1991). In creating myths of sentient islands in *Tar Baby* (1981) and of the dead returned to life in *Beloved* (1987), Morrison joined Dumas, who created myths of many otherworldly phenomena, including an "ark of bones," in his stories. Wilson's counterpart is a tale of the "bones people."

2. Consider, for example, the Prophet David in Ann Petry's *The Street* (1946). David is a Northern version of a Southern phenomenon and reflects the segment of folk belief that would eventually lead to advertisement by business card and newspaper ads, the kinds of things that would eventually be manifested in faith healers.

3. I coined the phrase "Africanizing the audience" to discuss authors I am treating in my latest book project, "In the African Southern Vein: Narrative Strategies in the Works of Zora Neale Hurston, Gloria Naylor, and Tina McElroy Ansa."

4. Charles Johnson includes a character called the "Soulcatcher" in *Oxherding Tale* (Bloomington: Indiana University Press, 1982). That character and idea epitomize what Wilson intends in *Joe Turner*. I am

grateful to Keith Clark and Valerie Matthews for pointing out this connection.

5. What Joe Turner wants is also comparable to what Alice Walker describes in her short story, "1955," or "the Elvis story." A white male singer records a song from a black woman. Although it is successful and he makes a lot of money from it, he returns to her again and again looking for the indescribable something that he believes is missing from his rendition of the song. That something represents the core of her blackness, the innermost part of her will and spirit that he can never co-opt but that he continually tries to harness. If he can harness it, then he achieves not only the monetary success but the spiritual aura that stands behind that success. He is similar to Octavia Butler's Doro, sapping the energy of those upon whom he preys to the point that they are figuratively lifeless.

6. Compare to Milkman Dead at the end of Morrison's *Song of Solomon* (1977) or Son Green at the end of *Tar Baby* (1981).

7. See *The Music of Black Americans: A History* (New York: Norton, 1971), 390, 401.

8. Included in Langston Hughes and Arna Bontemps, *The Book of Negro Folklore* (New York: Dodd, Mead & Company, 1958), 392.

9. See Ellison's "The Golden Age, Time Past" in *Shadow and Act* (New York: Vintage, 1964), 206.

10. Ralph Ellison, *Invisible Man* (1952; Rpt. New York: Vintage, 1972), 134.

11. Muriel Davis Longini, "Folk Songs of Chicago Negroes," *Journal of American Folklore* 52, (1939): 108.

12. Wilson continues to show his kinship to Dumas ("Ark of Bones" and other works), Toni Cade Bambara (*The Salt Eaters*, 1980), Morrison (*Beloved* and other works), and Tina McElroy Ansa (*Baby of the Family*, 1989) in the naturalness with which he treats interactions between the world of the living and the world of the dead.

13. Keith Clark suggests that killing the pigeons may be another way for Wilson to signify on white culture. The whole idea of transmitting messages has been used to "bind" black people to a certain position and a certain role ("nigger") in the society. Killing these symbolic messengers negates the power of white American culture to shape black lives.

14. I want to thank Keith Clark for reading this essay and providing several excellent suggestions for refinements, elaborations, and clarifications.

WORKS CITED

Bambara, Toni Cade. *The Salt Eaters*. New York: Random House, 1980.

Chesnutt, Charles. *The Conjure Woman*. 1899; Rpt. Ann Arbor: University of Michigan Press, 1969.

Ellison, Ralph. *Invisible Man*. 1952; New York: Vintage, 1972.

———. *Shadow and Act*. 1964; Rpt. New York: Signet, 1966.

Harris, Trudier. *Fiction and Folklore: The Novels of Toni Morrison*. Knoxville: University of Tennessee Press, 1991.

Hughes, Langston, and Arna Bontemps. *The Book of Negro Folklore*. New York: Dodd, Mead & Company, 1958.

Hughes, Langston. *Not Without Laughter*. 1930; Rpt. New York: Macmillan, 1969.

Johnson, Charles. *Oxherding Tale*. Bloomington: Indiana University Press, 1982.

Longini, Muriel Davis. "Folk Songs of Chicago Negroes." *Journal of American Folklore*, 52 (1939): 108.

Morrison, Toni. *Beloved*. New York: Knopf, 1987.

———. *The Bluest Eye*. New York: Holt, Rinehart, and Winston, 1970.

———. *Song of Solomon*. New York: Knopf, 1977.

———. *Tar Baby*. New York: Knopf, 1981.

Murray, Albert. *Train Whistle Guitar*. New York: McGraw-Hill, 1974.

Southern, Eileen. *The Music of Black Americans: A History*. New York: Norton, 1971.

Walker, Alice. "1955." In *You Can't Keep a Good Woman Down*. New York: Harcourt Brace Jovanovich, 1981.

Wilson, August. *Joe Turner's Come and Gone*. New York: Plume/New American Library, 1988.

Ghosts from "Down There"
The Southernness of August Wilson

Patricia Gantt

Audre Lorde, speaking of the impetus for her poetry, says, "I cannot recall the words of my first poem/ but I remember a promise/ I made my pen/ never to leave it/ lying/ in somebody else's blood" (39–40). August Wilson appears to have made a similar aesthetic vow of experiential fidelity: using what he himself calls "the blood's memory as my only guide and companion," Wilson has filled his five major dramatic works with characters whose psyches are rooted in the realities of the African American past, especially its complex Southern component (*Three Plays* xii). These plays constitute an investigation of that southern past and a substantive testimony to its legacies to twentieth-century experience, wherever it is lived.

As produced under the direction of Lloyd Richards and as published, the sequence of Wilson's plays begins with *Ma Rainey's Black Bottom* (1984) and concludes with his most recent success, *Two Trains Running* (1993), with *Fences* (1985), *Joe Turner's Come and Gone* (1986), and *The Piano Lesson* (1990) created in between.[1] Significantly, Wilson focuses on a different decade in each play: *Joe Turner* takes place in 1911; *Ma Rainey*, in the late 1920s; *Piano Lesson*, in the Depression; *Fences*, in 1957; and *Two Trains Running*, in 1969. To examine the African American historiography that the works create together, it is intriguing to approach them not from their actual order of composition, but as viewed from the playwright's chosen chronology. Doing so enables us to see how the plays express Wilson's artistic vision of the African American search for identity, as transfigured through generations of individuals and their memories.

At first glance it may seem peculiar to speak of the "southernness" of Wilson's drama. The playwright was, after all, born in Pittsburgh, Pennsylvania, and has lived most of his life there or in St. Paul, Minnesota. Nor do his plays take place in the South: Wilson sets all of them in Pittsburgh, except for *Ma Rainey*, which is set in Chicago. Yet each is replete with vestiges of a mysterious, fascinating locale characters have in common but often fear or reverence so much that they refuse to name. It is the South. Again and again they refer to the South as "down there" (a euphemism suggesting the forbidden locus of human sexuality as well as the geographic home of the slave past). This territory is for Wilson's characters variously a scene of slavery and sharecropping, of oppression and cruelty, of rejection, bittersweet yearning, and only restricted happiness. It lingers in memories and suffuses speech. It figures abundantly in each decade's play and is part of the "fabric of remembrance August Wilson summons up" (Wilde 74). Names (whether of characters or recalled places), music, art, vernacular expression, religion, food, folk wisdom, material culture, stories passed down in oral tradition, and often painful memories of incidents experienced there all serve as shadowy reminders of the South.

The first play in the historic cycle is *Joe Turner's Come and Gone*, a drama full of the sounds and memories of the South. Because the majority of the characters were born in the South or are only a generation away from it, it is no surprise that the texture of southern life is evident in much they say and do. Pittsburgh city people now, they still use a language laden with rural vernacular: a man is "hungrier than a mule"; a child who will not eat is "skinny as a bean pole"; a person on the edge of an action is "fixing to" do it; things beneath consideration are those a person "ain't studying" (5, 85, 13, 12). Characters' speech is often rich with folk lyrics, as when a man recalls John Henry's "ten-pound hammer" in bragging about his own sexual prowess (26). Folk belief and folk wisdom, too, are part of the play. One of the chief characters is Bynum, a conjure man skilled in the old ways of roots and potions. Consulted by a woman grieving for her missing man, Bynum gives her a packet to put under her pillow to "bring good luck to you. Draw it to you like a magnet" (24). Southern foodways, too, have made the northern journey, as folks gathered around the table share grits, yams, biscuits, or fried chicken. Out of the physical South themselves, *Joe Turner*'s people carry much of the South within.

The principal southern legacy they share, however, is their memory of the slave past, which Wilson brings into the play from its inception. The prologue places the action in the context of the diaspora—especially southern slavery—with a lyrical description of the migration of the "sons and daughters of newly freed African slaves" to the great cities of the north, where they hope to shape "a new identity as free men of definite and sincere worth" (iii). "Foreigners in a strange land . . . Isolated, cut off from memory . . . they arrive dazed and stunned" by all they have endured, mostly in the rural South (iii). The psychological baggage they carry is considerable: refused full access both to their African heritage and to modern financial and political power, they desire ways to "give clear and luminous meaning" to the as-yet unarticulated song they carry within, one composed of both "a wail and a whelp of joy" (iii). They arrive "carrying Bibles and guitars," symbols of old faith and new songs (iii). In this play, as in others, Wilson is not reluctant to explore the slave past, about which he says: "Blacks in America want to forget about slavery—the stigma, the shame. That's the wrong move. If you can't be who you are, who can you be? How can you know what to do?" (Freedman 40). For *Joe Turner*'s characters, the quest for identity and the pain of slavery's memories are inextricably bound.

The chief wanderer in *Joe Turner* is Herald Loomis who, after seven years' innocent entrapment on Joe Turner's Tennessee chain gang, wanders the country with Zonia, his young daughter. The seven years of Loomis' forced labor, according to Wilson, "can in fact represent the four hundred years of slavery" (Powers 54). Loomis searches for his wife Martha, whom he has not seen since his capture. He clings to the mistaken belief that if he can find Martha and bring her back into the ruptured family circle, he can be free of painful memories and construct a new identity for himself. Loomis longs for "a starting place in the world" (*Joe Turner* 73). "Got to find my wife," he says; "That be my starting place" (76). After almost four years of searching, he and Zonia arrive at Seth Holly's Pittsburgh boardinghouse, a microcosmic "community" in which various types can come together.

Seth, an independent craftsman besides owning the boardinghouse, is adamant about *not* having the recent Southern backgrounds several others share. When another character muses, "I reckon everybody done picked some cotton," Seth insists, "I ain't never picked no cotton . . . I ain't never even seen no cotton" (70). Son of free parents, he disdains "that old backward country style of living" he ascribes to southern immigrants "from the backwoods" (5, 6). He characterizes these travelers as "foolish-acting niggers" for naïvely believing they can find the good life in the city or its steel mills (6). "They got a rude awakening," Seth tells his wife Bertha; he has been in the North all his life and knows prejudice is not isolated below the Mason-Dixon Line (6).

A regular visitor at Seth's boardinghouse is Rutherford Selig, a peddler also known as the "People Finder" (6). When Loomis hears of Selig's ability to find people, he enlists his assistance in locating Martha. Selig reveals a sinister twist to his talent when elaborating his credentials to Loomis. A white man, he, too, is directly connected to the slave past: "[W]e been finders in my family for a long time. Bringers and finders. My great-granddaddy used to bring Nigras across the ocean on ships. . . . My daddy, rest his soul, used to find runaway slaves for the plantation bosses" (41). The irony of Loomis' requesting Selig's help is apparent.

Bynum, the rootworker and conjure man, is in many ways the most intriguing individual in the play, and figures significantly in Edith Oliver's characterizing *Joe Turner* as "the most mystical, most remote and dispersed of all Mr. Wilson's plays" (107). Bynum seems always "lost in a world of his own making" where metaphysics, rather than the clear reality which guides Seth, is the order of the day (Wilson *Joe Turner* 4). Like others in the play, Bynum is searching—but his search is a different kind: he is looking for his "shiny man," a person he has seen in a dreamlike vision experienced on the road one day (6). In Bynum's symbolically-laden vision, the stranger promises to show him the "Secret of Life," but instead leads him to a mystic place where everything is disproportionately sized and infused with a blinding light (9). There Bynum encounters the ghost of his father, who encourages him not to sing someone else's song, but to find one of his own. The ghost tells Bynum to find the "shiny man"; then Bynum will know his song has been "accepted and worked its full power in the world" (10). Bynum's vision is heavy with symbolic meaning for the African American search for identity. Forced for so long to sing others' songs, African Americans must find their own and sing them boldly. Bynum's father had a "Healing Song" which, although it might sound "no different than any other song" to its hearers, had curative power (61). Bynum chooses a "Binding Song," for he observes the lack of unity in his people and sees this forceful melody as a cure for their separation and mutual lack of power (10).

Song—particularly the significance of finding one's own song to sing—becomes a vital element in *Joe Turner* from the time Bynum recounts his vision. The music sought is Houston A. Baker, Jr.'s "long black song," one in which interconnections of past, present, and people spiral together into a unified whole (*Song* xi). Both dialogue and stage direction frequently depict the searchers who people this play in terms of their progress in achieving a personal or collective song, one "useful in making sense of this world" (143). When Jeremy, a young man who lives at the boardinghouse, enters, for example, stage directions depict him as one whose "spirit has yet to be molded into song" (Wilson *Joe Turner* 12). Later, when Bynum speaks with Mattie Campbell, a woman searching for a man she can feel a sense of belonging with, he tells her that she and her man are "lost from yourselves," but that "where you're supposed to be alive, your heart [is] kicking in your chest with a song worth singing" (22). Most importantly, Herald Loomis is said to be a man "unable to harmonize the forces that swirl around him" (14). Injustices suffered in Tennessee have robbed him of his song. "Herald" in name only, he cannot sing because he has no sense of self or belonging.

Act One culminates in Bynum's leading the people at the boardinghouse in an impromptu *Juba*, a dance/song of call and response, "reminiscent of the Ring Shouts of the African slaves," and interconnecting participants with the antebellum South and beyond to the African past (52). Loomis screams at them to stop, when suddenly he is overtaken by his own vision—one of bones walking on the water. The dance becomes a call-and-response folk sermon, with Loomis describing his vision and Bynum leading him on. This scene is full of what Clive Barnes calls the "verbal riffs and emotional cadenzas" that fill the play, and allows Loomis to begin articulating his song ("O'Neill"). Frantically he chants his vision about disunity and dispersion, in which dead bones walking across the water are impelled to stand and "get up on the road" toward healing (Wilson *Joe Turner* 56). Only by expressing their connection with the past can the boardinghouse residents attain what Frank Rich terms "a degree of unity and peace" ("Panoramic" C15).

Act Two finds Bynum repeating a disturbing song of the South—W.C. Handy's blues ballad which gives the play its title. The song tells the story of Joe Turner's notorious cruelty, which Loomis knows firsthand. Bynum hopes with this particular tune, a reminder of the past and its dominance by the white oppressor, to provoke Loomis into remembering his own song. He says, "Now, I can look at you, Mr. Loomis, and see you a man who done forgot his song. Forgot how to sing it. A fellow forget that and he forget who he is" (Wilson *Joe Turner* 71). If Bynum can help Loomis recall his song, he will salvage both their identities. He assures Loomis that his song—his sense of independent worth—has not vanished, just gone underground. But Loomis is resistant to Bynum's pleas.

Selig reappears, justifying his title of "People Finder" by bringing Martha with him. In revealing why she has not waited for Loomis in Tennessee, Martha recalls the demeaning weariness and the danger inherent to staying "down there" in the South (89). She explains: "They told me Joe Turner had you and my whole world split half in two. . . . So I killed you in my heart . . . then I picked up what was left and went on to make life without you. . . . I couldn't drag you behind me like a sack of cotton" (90). Martha expresses the griefs and troubles provoked in the South through a metaphor of the southern landscape. Even more deeply embittered now, Loomis turns on Bynum, who, along with Martha, is urging him to wrest his own meaning from life. Told he must be cleansed in "the blood of the lamb," Loomis rejects the Lamb of formulated Christianity (93). He perceives himself as the innocent sacrifice, rather than "Mr. Jesus Christ," who has looked on for generations without intervening while "enemies all around me picking the flesh from my bones" (92, 93). But if blood is required to achieve purity, he will oblige. "I don't need nobody to bleed for me," he says, "I can bleed for myself" (93). Loomis then takes out a knife and slashes himself, smearing blood from his lacerated chest onto his face in an inclusive, horrific ritual of death and rebirth as old as West African scarring *rites de passage* and as new as the victorious pronouncement he makes in that Pittsburgh kitchen. At that point Loomis is able to stand alone; he regains his song, one of "self-sufficiency . . . free from any encumberance other than the workings of his own heart and the bonds of the flesh" (94). Accepting responsibility for putting his world together, he is at last free. His northern migration has proved liberating in both physical and spiritual terms. Loomis, "shining like new money," is newly minted in the wholeness Wilson finds essential to his vision for modern African Americans (94). That wholeness can come only when, like Loomis, one looks squarely at the past, however painful, and moves resolutely forward, taking only those legacies which can help him on his way. Then he, too, will be "free to soar above tha environs that weighed and pushed his spirit into terrifying contractions" and can stand alone (94).

Ma Rainey's part in Wilson's "grand dramatic design of providing a panoramic view of the American black experience since the days of Lincoln" also relies on repeated echoes of the South (Barnes "O'Neill"). The play takes place in 1927 Chicago at a rundown recording studio on the Southside, where members of a blues band wait to record a session with Ma Rainey, legendary blues queen. The blues, *Ma Rainey*'s symbol of the African American heritage, could "instruct and allow [free men of definite and sincere worth] to reconnect" if it were truly heard as Ma herself hears it, as a personal song to be improvised and sung with fervor (Wilson *Ma Rainey* xvi). Ma values the blues as "life's way of talking . . . a way of understanding life . . . [and] keep[ing] things balanced" (82). Yet the blues does not function in this play as what Houston A. Baker, Jr., terms a "vibrant network . . . the multiplex, enabling *script* in which Afro-American cultural discourse is inscribed" (*Blues* 4). For Sturdyvant and Irvin, who have set up the session, the music is only a way to "make a bundle" (Wilson *Ma Rainey* 19). Ma's song has been stolen from her and claimed by another, thus making the blues a means of pointing out black victimization by societal racism.

Although once again basing the dramatic context in allusions to the South, Wilson's prologue indicates that southernness will not be so essential to *Ma Rainey's Black Bottom* as it is to his other productions, despite its being centered on music born in the South:

> Whether this music came from Alabama or Mississippi or other parts of the South doesn't matter anymore. The men and women who make this music have learned it from the narrow crooked streets of East St. Louis, or the streets of the city's Southside, and the Alabama or Mississippi roots have been strangled . . . (xvi)

The birthplace of the blues is just one entity in the racist culture that pervades America and dominates this play.

Nevertheless, southern cultural background is just as evident in *Ma Rainey* as it is in *Joe Turner*. The headnote to the play is a portion of a song by southern bluesman, Blind Lemon Jefferson. There are references to slavery, to farming in the rural South, and specifically to sharecropping; the city bluesmen's disgust for menial work in the city—emblematized through mention of an acquaintance who runs an elevator in St. Louis—is expressed as being "better than stepping in muleshit" (93). Wilson has received considerable praise for the "extraordinary acuity" of his ear—"a quality that has a black audience murmuring 'That's right' or 'Tell it' during his plays, as they might at a Jesse Jackson speech or a B. B. King concert"—and the playwright's "virtuosity with the vernacular" is a part of each page of *Ma Rainey*'s dialogue (Freedman 49). This authenticity, clear in the blues musicians' speech, marks such lines as "It sure done got quiet in here" (Ma Rainey), "Why you be asking?"

(Toledo), "She out for what she can get" (Cutler), "Ain't nothing wrong with hauling wood. I done hauled plenty wood" (Slow Drag), or "We's in Chicago, we ain't in Memphis!" (Levee) (Wilson *Ma Rainey* 82, 29, 22, 93, 38). The South, though background for most of the characters, is seen almost exclusively in pejorative terms.

The South's main detractor is Levee, *Ma Rainey*'s protagonist, who ironically takes his name from the embankments along the Mississippi; his name, according to Paul Carter Harrison, suggests an affiliation with the "new music soundings of jazz" and a possible rejection of the blues (308). The most frequent targets of Levee's abuse are Christianity and Toledo's philosophical talk about building a better life. He demeans Toledo's ideas as ineffectual nonsense, calling him "Booker T. Washington" and telling him he's "just a whole lot of mouth" with his "highfalutin ideas" and "that old philosophy bullshit" (Wilson *Ma Rainey* 41, 42). Levee feels that "if there's a god up there, he done went to sleep. . . . God don't mean nothing to me," and would agree that religion is only a "white man's palliative" (43, 46; Walker 18).[2] He becomes increasingly antagonistic towards Toledo, equating Toledo's frequent expressions of religious faith and his references to "making the lot of the colored man better for him here in America" with the oppressive life in the rural South, a backward place of horrific memories for Levee (Wilson *Ma Rainey* 41).

Alice Walker's characterization of rural Southern life would suit Levee well: "I can recall that I hated it, generally. The hard work in the fields, the shabby houses, the evil greedy men who worked my father to death and almost broke the courage of that strong woman, my mother" (21). Levee fixates on Toledo's rough shoes, symbol to him of what life might be like without music, and says, "Nigger got them clodhoppers! Old brogans! He ain't nothing but a sharecropper. . . . Got nerve to put on a suit and tie with them farming boots" (Wilson *Ma Rainey* 40). The racial brutality Levee has witnessed in the South fuels his relentless bitterness. When he was eight years old, he witnessed his mother's gang rape by eight or nine white men; trying to defend her, he was slashed across the chest by one of the rapists, and still carries the scar. Levee's father Memphis, whose hard work and savings earned him "nearly fifty acres of good farming land" in Mississippi, was away buying seed and fertilizer at the time (69). Upon Memphis' return, he "acted like he done accepted the facts" of his wife's rape, "smiled in the face of one of them crackers who had been with my mama . . . and sold him our land" (70). Pretending to leave, Memphis then doubled back and killed four of the rapists before the white establishment caught him, lynched him, and set his body afire. Levee learns from his father to handle whites by masking and waiting for his chance for revenge: "I can smile and say yessir to whoever I please," he tells the other bluesmen, "I got time coming to me" (70). This is a man who "cannot bear the weight of his own rage" (Smith 184). At the climax of the play, Levee's rage finally erupts into violence.

Much of Act Two consists of a series of debates between Toledo and Levee about the fairness of life and the powerlessness of blacks in white society. Finally Cutler, the leader of the blues band, brings the discussion home by pointing out how unimportant the band and their music are to whites: "[W]hite folks don't care nothing about Ma Rainey. she's just another nigger who they can use to make some money" (Wilson *Ma Rainey* 97). Cutler shares a bitter memory, in which the Reverend Gates, a black preacher, gets off a train at a small southern crossroads. In this place "the only colored rest room is an outhouse they got sitting way back two hundred yards or so from the station" (96). The train leaves before the minister can get back. A group of whites with guns torment him, tearing the cross from his neck, ripping his Bible, and making him dance. Hearing this story, Levee is incensed:

> "Why didn't God strike some of them crackers down? . . . 'Cause he a white man's God. That's why. God ain't never listened to no nigger's prayers. God take a nigger's prayers and throw them in the garbage. . . . In fact . . . God hate niggers! Hate them with all the fury in his heart. . . . God can kiss my ass." (98).

Hearing this, Cutler leaps to his feet and punches Levee in the mouth. Levee, overwrought, pulls a knife, but begins screaming—not at Cutler, but at God, demanding to know where God was when his mother was being raped and calling on

Jesus to have mercy: "Did you turn your back, motherfucker? Did you turn your back?" (99). His encounter with Cutler unleashes the wrath Levee has suppressed for so long.

Soon after this incident, Levee tries to interest Sturdyvant in his arrangements, hoping through his music to find the control over his life that is missing everywhere else. Sturdyvant rejects Levee's music and condescendingly dismisses him, and Levee then turns on the first person he sees. It happens to be Toledo, who accidentally steps on Levee's shoe with his "raggedy-ass clodhoppers" (110). Displacing all his pent-up frustrations from the racism he and the others have suffered North and South onto Toledo's heavy farmer's shoes, Levee again pulls his knife. Before he knows what he is doing, Toledo is dead. This recording session—not a rehearsal of music so much as of the evils of the American racist society—ends in further victimization. By killing Toledo, Levee "has not only desecrated a natural life, but also cut himself off from ontological continuity, a sort of cosmic suicide" (Harrison 311). He rejects the unity Toledo, through his philosophy, has tried to extend, just as he rejects all contact with Toledo's southern farm boots.

The southern heritage, the "whole solid past" which will not be rejected, but must be faced and dealt with, is strongest in Wilson's drama of the Depression years, *The Piano Lesson* (Welty 206). The "lesson" mentioned in the title is not merely one conducted on the actual keys of an upright piano which fills the Charles family's Pittsburgh parlor. The piano's lesson is also inscribed in the wooden carvings the upright bears, mask-like carvings reminiscent of African sculptures, "rendered with a grace and power of invention that lifts them . . . into the realm of art" (Wilson *Piano Lesson* xiii). Further, this lesson is dramatically foregrounded through the Charleses' confrontations about whether to sell the piano to finance Boy Willie's dream of land ownership "down there" in the South, or to hold onto it for what it represents to his sister Berniece of both their flesh-and-blood heritage and their proud spiritual legacy of reverence for family and the past (3). According to Frank Rich, "the disposition of the piano becomes synonymous with the use to which the characters put their ancestral legacy . . . somber shrine to a tragic past [or] stake to freedom" (C15). "The past has never passed" for this

haunted brother and sister, but exists in ghosts of their southern
heritage that are both actual and psychological (Ching 71). In *The
Piano Lesson* Wilson invites his audience to consider a number of
crucial questions: What is the place of tradition? of community?
of family? of the past? What do we owe them and memory? To
examine these questions, *Piano Lesson*'s people must look back to
their shared southernness, which pervades August Wilson's
imagination and theirs.

Boy Willie, part owner of the piano, is eager to go South
again. He sees his chance to own a piece of Mississippi farm land
as his chance to be somebody. He tells his uncle Doaker, "I ain't
got no advantages to offer nobody," but that if he had land,
"something under his feet that belonged to him," he could
"stand up taller" (91, 92). "I ain't gonna be no fool about no
sentimental value," Boy Willie proclaims (51). He does not
understand why Berniece will not play the piano if it means so
much to her, or at least pass its story on to her daughter Maretha
so she could "know where she at in the world" (91). Berniece,
however, would rather keep the piano in the parlor, dusted but
never played, as a momento of the sacrifice of their ancestors.
She remembers her late mother's playing the piano and saying
she could hear the spirits of her ancestors talking to her when
she did so.

Berniece is apprehensive, too, about the ghost of Robert
Sutter, the slave owner who laid claim to their family long ago,
and split them up to buy the piano for his bride. The first Boy
Willie, a slave with the gift of woodworking, is forced to carve
the images of his wife, the first Berniece, and their son into the
piano.[3] The master woodworker does not stop there, but goes on
to fashion a pictorial history of the entire family into the wood of
the piano. Eventually Boy Charles, father of the present Boy
Willie and Berniece, goes into the Sutter home and takes the
piano. Disturbed for years because the Sutters own it, Boy
Charles feels that whoever possesses the family's pictographs—
and therefore the stories of their past—somehow controls their
spirits. Vindictive whites burn Boy Charles alive in the boxcar
where he is hiding; he has given his life to reclaim the visual
symbol of the family's past. His ghost walks, too, mysteriously
dealing retribution to Mississippi whites. Berniece believes that if

she does not play the piano, she can avoid disturbing the troubled spirits, and, thereby, spare Maretha the burden of the past. At the same time, Berniece is convinced that "Money can't buy what that piano cost. You can't sell your soul for money. It won't go with the buyer. It'll shrivel and shrink" (50). But Sutter's ghost walks their house, and Maretha has already seen it. The burden of the past, as well as its beauty, belongs to all of them.

Wilson skillfully conducts the debate between brother and sister, with each confrontation adding more details to the family story and increasing his audience's tension at the lack of resolution. Wining Boy, Doaker's older brother, brings matters to a climax with his musical tribute to memory. All at once the presence of Sutter's ghost is felt, and various people gathered in the Charleses' home try to exorcise it, including Avery, a minister. All efforts are useless. Boy Willie wrestles with Sutter's ghost, but is thrown. Berniece then realizes that she must save them from Sutter's evil presence by playing the piano. She can neither ignore the past nor let it lie dormant nor sell it nor give it away. She must take it up and "play" it, make it a part of her. She sits at the piano and begins a powerful song, playing and singing her incantation to Mama Berniece, Mama Esther, Papa Boy Charles, and Mama Ola—the old ones who have kept the past from being forgotten—asking them repeatedly to help her preserve her loved ones from their common enemy. Her prayer is granted, and Sutter's ghost vanishes. Berniece, in whose name kinship is embedded, liberates her family by confronting the past she has steadfastly avoided throughout the play. She finds comfort in the confrontation. Berniece learns, as Wilson insists his people must, that she cannot suppress any portion of her selfhood if she and her loved ones are to move on with their lives, balanced and whole. At the conclusion of *The Piano Lesson* Boy Willie leaves for Mississippi, content for Berniece to keep the piano so long as someone will make use of it to bring music and meaning to the present. Through music, the piano's song reaffirms the stories of the past, transforming the ugly and awful, along with the beautiful and tender, into a joyous melody of hope.

By the decade explored in his 1950s play, *Fences*, Wilson's characters are more concerned with coping with the present than with looking to their southern past. Wilson makes this focus clear in his prologue: Unlike European immigrants and their descendants, he writes:

> descendants of African slaves were offered no such welcome or participation [in the city]. They came from places called the Carolinas and the Virginias, Georgia, Alabama, Mississippi, and Tennessee. They came strong, eager, searching. The city rejected them and they . . . [lived] in quiet desperation and vengeful pride . . . in pursuit of their own dream. That they could breathe free, finally, and stand to meet life with the force of dignity and whatever eloquence the heart could call upon." (xvii)

Reminders of the South are plentiful enough—in Troy Maxson's recollections of coming to manhood on his father's Alabama farm, in the collard greens and cornbread Rose Maxson serves up in her kitchen, in Troy's yearning for the exoticism of "one of them Florida gals . . . [with] some Indian blood in them" and Bono's longing for a woman "[g]ot them great big old legs and hips wide as the Mississippi River," or in a reference to Troy's storytelling ability as having "some Uncle Remus in your blood" (4,5, 13). *Fences* again displays the "authentic root" of Wilson's dialogue in southern dialect, noted in the discussion of earlier plays and evident throughout, as when Rose admonishes Cory, "Your daddy like to had a fit with you running out of here this morning without doing your chores" (Henderson 67, Wilson *Fences* 29). These southern echoes are secondary, however, to the main consideration of the play, the fences society builds up around us and those we construct, willingly or unwillingly, around ourselves.

The theme of this play, articulated so strongly before in Wilson's drama (particularly in *Joe Turner's Come and Gone* and *Ma Rainey's Black Bottom*) is the need to sing one's own song. The recurrent melody in *Fences* is a traditional folksong from Troy's childhood, about a dog named Blue that "treed a possum out on a limb" (99). On the day of Troy's funeral, when Cory Maxson comes home and confronts his connections with the past, including his embattled relationship with his dead father and his tie to his half-sister Raynell, he affirms his part "in a continuum that runs from Pittsburgh to the antebellum South and finally to Mother Africa" (Freedman 36). Cory and Raynell are able to sing the song together. It is at once theirs and Troy's and older than all of them, a melody of their interconnectedness. Inappropriate as the song of dog and possum may seem on such a solemn occasion, it signifies, as Ralph Ellison says of the blues,

> an impulse to keep the painful details and episodes of a brutal experience alive in one's aching consciousness, to finger its jagged grain, and to transcend it, not by the consolation of philosophy but by squeezing from it a near-tragic, near-comic lyricism. (90)

Threading backward through time, the song binds brother and sister to each other and to the mixture of pain and inarticulated love which is their common legacy. At the song's conclusion, they are for the first time truly a family.

In *Two Trains Running*, Wilson goes to the late sixties, "a turbulent, racing, dangerous, and provocative decade," and sets his drama in a Pittsburgh restaurant symbolically placed between life (Lutz's Meat Market) and death (West's Funeral Home) (Wilson *Two Trains Running* xviii). Vernacular language, southern place names, foodways, songs, and cultural customs are all as evident in *Two Trains Running* as in Wilson's earlier works and are as seamlessly incorporated as before. For this play, as in *The Piano Lesson*, the oral history of the southern past is focal. Restaurant owner Memphis, who has witnessed tremendous change since leaving the Jackson, Mississippi, farm where he grew up to settle in Pittsburgh, sees every occurrence as an occasion for a story. He keeps southern oral tradition alive. Memphis and his friend Holloway, a regular at the restaurant and something of a historian, constantly swap memories. Now Memphis faces the possibility that his restaurant will be torn down, a risk which provokes his recollecting the past with even greater intensity than he has done before.

Memphis has been out of the South for almost forty years, but intends one day to catch one of the two daily trains running there and go back, to flaunt his material successes in Jackson, where he was robbed of his land and run out of town. He believes in working hard and saving money, and has no use for

Wolf, who plays the numbers, or Sterling, a young man who will not or cannot keep a series of menial jobs, his only option since release from prison. When Memphis voices his opinion that Sterling is "lazy," he provokes a history lesson from Holloway:

> People kill me talking about niggers is lazy. Niggers is the most hard-working people in the world. Worked three hundred years for free. And didn't take no lunch hour. . . . If it wasn't for you the white man would be poor. Every little bit he got he got standing on top of you. That's why he could reach so high. (34).

Holloway goes beyond the slave past to the Middle Passage, then returns to present inequities. To him, Memphis needs the sense of perspective that history can provide. But Memphis does not seem to care about the long view: he has watched civil rights leaders come and go, and nothing seems to have improved much, as far as he can tell. "Malcolm X is dead," Memphis says (40). "They killed Martin. If they did that to him you can imagine what they do to me or you. If they kill the sheep you know what they do to the wolf. . . . Ain't no justice. That's why they got that statue of her and got her blindfolded" (41, 42). Memphis wants nothing to do with history or with politics. His credo is that God blesses the child that's got his own, and he intends to mind his own business and protect his property as best he can.

Memphis goes to the courthouse on the day city officials are planning to make a decision about taking his property, sure they will try to cheat him. According to his observations, "the only way to recover what has been lost or stolen is by following the dominant culture's tactics: robbery, burning buildings for insurance, carrying guns to assert power," or cheating someone out of control (Wilde 74). To his surprise, the city offers him thirty-five thousand dollars for his property, ten thousand more than he has declared himself ready to fight for. Confused at this sudden turn, Memphis looks for guidance. He goes to Aunt Ester, the local prophetess; she tells him he must "go back and pick up the ball" (109). Memphis interprets her advice as a mandate to return to the South, face things there, and reclaim his farm. By dealing with the past, he can be free to go forward. Thus *Two Trains Running* carries a question which resonates through all Wilson's plays: how can we know who we are and where we are going, if we do not face our past, struggle towards understanding it, and reconcile ourselves to its present legacy to us?

August Wilson's dramatic works, ranging freely across the decades of American history, perform what Addell Austin terms a "vital function of the black theatre" (89). Lyrical works of art, these plays operate on another level as well. They hold up a "live mirror for helping black people to see, to cope with, and to redefine their perceptions of their own humanity" (Bass 64). A very essential part of that humanity, Wilson suggests, comes directly from the influences and inheritances of the southern past.

The five major plays written so far—full of fresh, inclusive portraits of America—provide multiple opportunities for the redefinition and self-identification their creator has often expressed as being crucial for African Americans. Wilson elaborates his reasons for redrawing the American past, and in doing so explains his vision for his work: "The message of America is 'Leave your Africanness outside the door.' My message is 'Claim what is yours'" (Freedman 36). Recasting the past allows one to turn with clarified vision toward the future. By looking to the southern past and incorporating its knotty, conflicted legacy of language, custom, history, belief, and deep pain, Wilson seeks a reaffirmation which can inform, strengthen, and empower. His plays tell us that strength does not lie in avoidance of the past, even one as fraught with complexity as the southern past is. If we seek today to find "the real person, the whole person" within, we must look to *all* our yesterdays (Powers 52). Then we can find our own songs, vigorous and enabling. Acknowledging the vestiges of the past within ourselves, we can truly lay claim to what is ours.

NOTES

    1. References to the dates of Wilson's plays are to their publication in paperback, rather than to their earlier openings at the Yale Repertory Theater or to any appearance elsewhere.

    2. Wilson has commented several times on the failure of Christianity to serve African Americans. Ishmael Reed quotes him as saying, "God does not hear the prayers of blacks" (93). Wilson also told Kim Powers, "Your god should resemble you. When you look in the mirror you should see your god. If you don't, then you have the wrong god" (54).

    3. Names repeated in *The Piano Lesson* exhibit Wilson's talent for incorporating something Kimberly W. Benston notes as an important feature of Richard Wright's work, as well, the "shamanistic voice [that] keeps the ancestral names alive and resonant" (10).

WORKS CITED

Austin, Addell. "The Present State of Black Theatre." *Drama Review* 32.3 (Fall 1988): 85–100.

Baker, Houston A., Jr. *Blues, Ideology, and Afro-American Literature.* Chicago: University of Chicago Press, 1984, 1987.

——. *Long Black Song: Essays in Black American Literature and Culture.* Charlottesville: University Press of Virginia, 1972, 1990.

Barnes, Clive. "O'Neill in Blackface." *New York Post* 28 March 1988.

Bass, George Houston. "Theatre and the Afro-American Rite of Being." *Black American Literature Forum* 17.2 (Summer 1983): 60–64.

Benston, Kimberly W. "'I Yam What I Am': Naming and Unnaming in Afro-American Literature." *Black American Literature Forum* 16.1 (Spring 1982): 3–11.

Ching, Mei-Ling. "Wrestling Against History." *Theater* 19.3 (Summer/Fall 1988): 70–71.

Ellison, Ralph. *Shadow and Act.* New York: Random House, 1964.

Freedman, Samuel G. "A Voice from the Streets." *New York Times Magazine* 10 June 1987: 36, 40, 49, 70.

Harrison, Paul Carter. "August Wilson's Blues Poetics." In *Three Plays by August Wilson*. Pittsburgh: University of Pittsburgh Press, 1991.

Henderson, Heather. "Building *Fences*: An Interview with Mary Alice and James Earl Jones." *Theater* 16.3 (Spring/Fall 1985): 67–70.

Lorde, Audre. "To the Poet Who Happens to Be Black and the Black Poet Who Happens to Be a Woman." *Callaloo* 14.1 (Winter 1991): 39–40.

Oliver, Edith. "Boarding House Blues." *New Yorker* 64.8 (April 11, 1988): 107.

Powers, Kim. "An Interview with August Wilson." *Theater* 16.1 (Fall/Winter 1984): 50–55.

Reed, Ishmael. "In Search of August Wilson." *Connoisseur* 217 (1987): 92–97.

Rich, Frank. "A Family Confronts Its History in August Wilson's *Piano Lesson*." *New York Times* 17 April 1990: C13.

———. "Panoramic History of Blacks in America in Wilson's *Joe Turner*." *New York Times* 28 March 1988: C15.

Shannon, Sandra G. "From Lorraine Hansberry to August Wilson: An Interview with Lloyd Richards." *Callaloo* 14.1 (Winter 1991): 124–135.

———. "The Good Christian's Come and Gone: The Shifting Role of Christianity in August Wilson's Plays." *MELUS* 16.3 (Fall 1989–1990): 127–142.

Smith, Philip E. "*Ma Rainey's Black Bottom*: Playing the Blues as Equipment for Living." In *Within the Dramatic Spectrum* VI. Ed. Karelisa V. Hartigan. New York: University Press of America, 1986.

Walker, Alice. "The Black Writer and the Southern Experience." *In Search of Our Mothers' Gardens*. New York: Harcourt Brace Jovanovich, 1983. 15–21.

Welty, Eudora. *The Optimist's Daughter*. New York: Vintage Books, 1972.

Wilde, Lisa. "Reclaiming the Past: Narrative and Memory in August Wilson's *Two Trains Running*." *Theater* 22.1 (Winter 1990–1991): 73–74.

Wilson, August. *Fences*. New York: Penguin, 1986.

———. *Joe Turner's Come and Gone*. New York: Penguin, 1988.

———. *Ma Rainey's Black Bottom*. New York: Penguin, 1985.

———. *The Piano Lesson*. New York: Penguin, 1990.

———. *Three Plays*. Pittsburgh: University of Pittsburgh Press, 1991.

———. *Two Trains Running*. New York: Penguin, 1993.

Father, Son, and Holy Ghost
From the Local to the Mythical in August Wilson

Pamela Jean Monaco

If the Black Revolutionary Theatre of Amiri Baraka and Ed Bullins defined African American theatre of the '60s and '70s, then August Wilson and his Theatre of Experience can be said to define African American theatre of the '80s and '90s. This shift from a didactic drama reflects not only the change in the political and social climate of the decades but also the recognition of the need to attract and keep a national audience of African Americans. In order to develop this audience, the playwright has several choices in terms of subject matter.

One option is to write about the issues and concerns of the day. Certainly this is the case with Black Revolutionary theatre. The drawback to such an approach is that the material can become dated, limiting the long-term drawing power. When the political unrest of the '60s and early '70s gave way to the political passivity of the "me generation," this drama ceased to have contemporary relevance for its audience.

Another approach is to write about eternal conflicts or interests that will remain relevant. To do so is to write a ritualistic drama that Ron Milner defines for the African American playwright as being a reflection and projection "of a unique and particular way of being, born of the unique and particular condition of black people" (as quoted by Steele 31). Shelby Steele contends that the reliance on ritual ensures living drama because "patterns are established which have the function of reaffirming the values and particular commitment of the audience for whom the plays are written" (30). It is this method that August Wilson chooses.

Wilson favors drama of the interior setting that focuses on an individual and his or her family construct. Each play takes place in a specific decade, revealing the particular pressures endured by African Americans in this period. Taken together, his plays chronicle the experiences of the African American throughout the 20th century. Situating the protagonist within a familial organization, Wilson demonstrates the impact of political and social changes on the individual and the community.

Wilson acknowledges that he has found a creative inspiration for his writing in 20th-century African American history. The historical context supports what Jim O'Quinn suggests is Wilson's purpose: "to demonstrate the healing effect of self-empowerment that comes when people establish bonds with their own ancestry" (39). In all of his plays, he emphasizes the personal transformation that comes from venerating one's traditions and heritage. By embracing one's roots, one sheds the limitations imposed by others and achieves self-definition. As Wilson says, "It's largely a question of identity. Without knowing your past, you don't know your present and you certainly can't plot your future" (Devries 25). His plays illuminate the liberating effect of finding oneself by knowing—and accepting—one's past.

Wilson invites the audience to share this experience with his characters by writing about the local, the everyday lives of people just like themselves. His characters face the disappointments and challenges that his audience also knows. By showing the warrior spirit developed through identity with a culture, he confers to his characters, and likewise to his audience, a type of nobility. He reveals through his writing the beauty and nobility in the struggle to survive. By doing so, Wilson transforms drama from a spectacle observed to a ritual, a ritual that affirms a common vision, thereby elevating the story of local history to the mythical.

Four of Wilson's plays, *Joe Turner's Come and Gone*, *The Piano Lesson*, *Fences*, and *Two Trains Running*, illustrate the personal freedom that comes from recognizing and accepting one's cultural or personal legacy. These plays neatly fall into two categories. *Joe Turner's Come and Gone* and *The Piano Lesson* can be paired because they specifically address the need to embrace one's cultural roots and because the history that one must come to accept is clearly more distant and more African than American. In addition, each play realizes the living presence of one's heritage by presenting it on stage as a ghost that incites the protagonist into recognizing the power the past has in the shaping of our lives. Through his use of the specter as catalyst for redemption, Wilson reminds his audience that this vision is a shared experience.

Fences and *Two Trains Running*, on the other hand, share a concern with accepting one's own individual family or community. In each case, there is again an important offstage force that reminds the characters and the audience of the presence of the past. As with the other two plays, the focus is on the need to accept one's legacy, but Wilson's artistic lens has shortened from looking at the distant to looking at present. One might say that the dramatic question has shifted from "Who are we?" to "Who am I?"

Ma Rainey's Black Bottom stands beside these plays and offers a tragic illustration of the consequences of failing to discover one's identity within one's own community and heritage. Because this play offers "proof" of the validity of the assertions established in the other plays and because it serves as a contrast, I will discuss *Ma Rainey's Black Bottom* last rather than following the dramatic time sequences used to discuss the other plays. In all the plays, however, Wilson shows that it is only through the willingness to face and accept the forces of the past that the protagonists will be given hope, power, and ultimately, deliverance.

Set in 1911, *Joe Turner's Come and Gone* revolves around the character Herald Loomis, a man recently released after seven years of forced labor under Joe Turner. He has come to Pittsburgh to find his wife, Martha Pentecost, who, after being saved, left her home and family during Loomis's absence. By finding his wife, he believes he will find an identity. Before he finds his wife, however, Loomis discovers that self-identification will come, not through embracing the song of others, but through embracing the roots of his heritage.

The process of personal transformation begins when the boarding house members decide to Juba, which Wilson describes as reminiscent of the ring shouts of the African slaves. He specifies that the singing and dancing should be as African as possible and must include some reference to the Holy Ghost. When the Holy Ghost is mentioned, Loomis, a deacon of the church, responds in a frenzy, wanting to know what is holy about the Holy Ghost. Speaking in tongues and dancing, Loomis sees bones that rise from waters, walk across the waters, and become flesh and blood. The ghosts of his heritage visit Loomis, which he internalizes not as some distant myth, but as people. As he says, "They black. Just like you and me. Ain't no difference" (55). Finally, lying on the ground exhausted, he feels "the wind blowing the breath into my body . . . I'm starting to breathe again" (55).

The wind that blows through Loomis is that of a different spirit. The spirit of his African roots enables him to see himself as one with others who resisted oppressive powers and endured. He begins to authenticate himself not as a captured slave who failed his family but as a survivor. Allowing himself to question a spirituality handed down to him by those who have controlled him, Loomis finds a self-determination he did not know. Seeing the spirits of his roots renews his own spirit. Not surprisingly, Loomis no longer needs to re-establish a connection to his wife in order to find himself.

The final act of liberation comes when, reunited with his wife, she tries to save him. Loomis, however, is incapable of separating Christian belief from belief in the superiority of the white man. The philosophy of accepting this world as "just a trial for the next" equates to giving away control over one's destiny. This passive acceptance of injustices cripples the will to fight for change. Essentially calling Christ another white man looking for sacrifice, Loomis cuts himself with a knife and washes himself in his own blood. In his purification ritual, he unites himself firmly with his cultural roots through the scarification process.

One may wonder how such a play will make converts to the theatre out of a community whose backbone has been the church. Although some have taken issue with Wilson's depiction of Christianity, Wilson does not deny the important role religion has in bringing order and stability to the lives of many. One might note that Wilson assigns the raising of the next generation to those who espouse a Christian ideology. Although Loomis and his daughter love each other deeply, Loomis "presents her to Martha," saying "That she need to learn from her mother whatever you got to teach her. That way she won't be no one-sided person" (90). Rather than reading this as a gender choice, one should notice Wilson's acknowledgment of the potential value such ideology has in child raising. What Wilson does reject is the prioritizing of religious tradition over cultural traditions, particularly if the religious belief numbs one to this world.

The analogy between the scene of Loomis's vision and the Pentecostal commemoration of the visitation by the Holy Spirit to the apostles is obvious. By offering this analogy, Wilson demonstrates that the recognition of where one comes from can offer one a type of salvation parallel to that offered by Christian faith. Loomis's spirit and will to fight had been broken during his captivity. He had looked to his wife and religious faith for help instead of nurturing his own sense of self. Once Loomis embraces the vision of the past, he becomes rejuvenated by a life force that is painfully lacking in Martha. The Holy Spirit may have made Martha spiritually pure, but the reliance on religious faith has also offered her an escape from life in this world. Without the will to challenge the hardships of this world, she has become a mere shell. Wilson reminds his audience that one can find the power of deliverance in this world, too, by embracing the spiritual resilience of one's ancestors. As Paul Carter Harrison notes, "Inside the spiritual dynamism of the ancestors—perceived and made useful in the present as opposed to being arrested in the past—is the true song of redemption and liberation" (314).

Joe Turner's Come and Gone could be described as a play dramatizing the importance of discovering one's cultural heritage. *The Piano Lesson*, on the other hand, teaches the necessity of accepting one's family history. This history is symbolically represented by the piano that has been passed down to the siblings, Berniece and Boy Willie.

The piano was previously owned by Robert Sutter, a slave owner who had traded Berniece and Boy Willie's great-grandmother and grandfather for it. Their great-grandfather, Papa Willie Boy, remained on the plantation and later carved into the piano the whole family history. Papa Willie Boy eventually stole the piano because "it was the story of our whole family and as long as Sutter had it . . . he had us" (45).

The conflict in this play is how best to preserve the memory of a family's history. For Berniece, the piano has become a sacred relic; she will not sell the piano, nor will she embrace it and her history. As with Martha Pentecost, she has retreated from life by denying the past. She has fled her home in Mississippi after the death of her husband, finding sanctuary with her daughter in her uncle's house in Pittsburgh. Culturally uprooted, Berniece's life has become a ritual of denial.

That Wilson believes Berniece has become deracinated is evident in the conversation of Maretha, Berniece's daughter. Berniece has told Maretha no stories of her heritage nor given her any reasons to have pride in herself. Berniece believes that by teaching Maretha that she is "living at the bottom of life," she is teaching Maretha the truth (92). Berniece is Wilson's reminder of the dire consequences of allowing others to interpret one's own heritage. Rather than looking through the circumstances of her ancestors to the human traits that allowed them to endure the hardships, Berniece has allowed the white man to define not only her past but her present too. Only by becoming culturally grounded can she realize the truth of self-actualization.

Boy Willie represents the alternative approach to honoring one's past. For Boy Willie, the piano is the life blood of the family. He has come North to persuade Berniece to sell the piano so he can buy the land that their ancestors worked on as slaves. Selling the piano will continue to celebrate the family. He states: "When [my daddy] come along he ain't had nothing he could build on. His daddy ain't had nothing to give him. The only thing my daddy had to give me was that piano. And he died giving it to me. I ain't gonna let it sit up there and rot without trying to do something with it" (46). Boy Willie does not need a visual shrine to commemorate his heritage because he keeps the memory of his heritage alive. The piano is a gift bestowed that will allow him to follow in his father's footsteps but with a freedom and security his father was denied. Boy Willie's very actions will be the living remembrance of his family's past.

The spirit that awakens Berniece is not the ghosts of her parents or grandparents but the ghost of Mr. Sutter, whose land Boy Willie wants to buy. For a few days she is the only one in the house who sees this image. Boy Willie does not see this specter until the very end of the play when he and Berniece battle over the piano. The ghost of a dead white man does not haunt Boy Willie because he has looked at the story of his ancestors as a source of pride. Because he does not accept their attempts to define him, neither living nor dead white men control him. As with Loomis, he sees that his ancestors had a strength of spirit that refused to be broken. That he has taken this family legacy and incorporated it into his soul is reflected in his outlook on life: "Ain't me and the white man no different" (38). I'm living at the top of life . . . I'm in the world like everybody else" (92).

Berniece recognizes the empowering force that can come through embracing one's history when she sees the fearlessness with which her brother wrestles with Sutter's ghost. Finding the courage to join her brother in battle, she plays the piano and calls out the names of her ancestors in song. Only then does the ghost of Sutter dissipate. Having looked to her ancestors for strength, Berniece discovers the healing power of cultural and family pride.

The sheer drama of this play would keep an audience engaged, but Wilson provides a meaning that resonates beyond the theatre. In both *Joe Turner's Come and Gone* and *The Piano Lesson*, Wilson alludes to the African concept of Mantu, which is a belief that the spirits of the dead influence the living (Campbell 145). This African philosophy postulates that through "this interchange of life force, by which the departed give advice to and empower the living," the living shall in return bring honor to the ancestors (Campbell 145). The dramatization of this philosophy stimulates the viewer into recognizing the source of

strength that each person has in his or her family history as well
as in the traditions of the African American culture. In both plays
the spirits of the dead are not seen by the audience, allowing the
viewer to bring his or her own family spirits to the stage and to
become part of the ceremony.

Fences and *Two Trains Running* dramatize the next step of
the process towards self-actualization. Just as *Joe Turner's Come
and Gone* and *The Piano Lesson* demonstrate the need to honor
one's ancestors, these two plays show the necessity of accepting
the limitations of one's family or one's self. As the characters
struggle to find their identity, they discover that being
responsible for one's own destiny means being accountable for
one's past. In each play, the characters learn that the hope for the
future can only be found by turning to the family or family
construct.

In *Fences* Troy and Cory Maxson must learn to forgive the
sins of the father in order to find their own sense of self. This
father-son relationship at the heart of the play contributes to the
enthusiastic public response, invoking from many a comparison
to the classic *Death of a Salesman*. Such comparisons, however,
ignore some of the crucial aspects of this play that set it apart. As
Harrison points out, "Cory's confrontation with Troy is a rite of
passage which is often misconstrued as a struggle between father
and son for dominance when, in fact, there are no rights shared
by sons with their fathers in traditional African American
households" (304). The rite of passage in this play is the need for
an identity separate from that of one's father. Wilson shows that
this identity can only be achieved by first accepting one's father's
song.

In order to appreciate the necessity of accepting this part of
one's self, one must first look at another father-son relationship,
that of Troy and his father. In one of the longest speeches in the
play, Troy describes growing up with "[a daddy] sometimes I
wish I hadn't known" (50). After a final confrontation over a
young girl that left Troy severely beaten, Troy decided that the
"time had come for me to leave my daddy's house. And right
there the world suddenly got big. And it was a long time before I
could cut it down to where I could handle it. Part of that cutting
down was when I got to the place where I could feel him kicking

in my blood and knew that the only thing that separated us was the matter of a few years" (52–53).

Troy solved his identity problem by running away from that which challenged it. Rather than confronting who his father was and reconciling that knowledge with his own concept of self, Troy tried to deny the existence of this part of himself. As Troy's words indicate, one can't leave the baggage behind when beginning the journey of selfhood. Trying to do so severely compromises the search for self. Troy has found himself becoming his father in spite of his best efforts.

The consequences of this evasion multiply as Troy builds his own life. As the title indicates, barricades exist in the various relationships. Troy has inherited the legacy of fear of emotional commitment. Because his primary relationships were truncated, Troy has never learned to receive and give true love. The unsettled business upon which he built his own identity leaves him feeling defensive. As he holds his sons and Rose at arm's length, he forces them to form a relationship that excludes him. He does not have the stability of self to look at Cory's aspirations and possibilities as belonging to Cory, separate from him. Troy cannot let Cory find his own song because Troy is still trying to authenticate himself.

Like *Joe Turner's Come and Gone* and *The Piano Lesson*, *Fences* also contains an unseen presence that haunts the protagonist. The difference between this play and the other two is that this presence never is experienced by the audience. Even though we do not see the specters in the two earlier plays, their presence was made tangible for us because of the dramatic reactions of the other characters. In *Fences* the unseen presence is that of Death, which Troy reports to us and the other characters.

Troy "encounters" the presence of Death three times during the course of the play. The first time we hear of this specter is when Troy tells Bono of his encounter when he had pneumonia, which taught him that "I got to keep watch" (11). The two other occurrences are not reported but happen when Troy stands alone on stage and speaks directly to Death. These meetings follow confrontations, first with Rose and then with Cory, during which Troy manages to kill the love from those he loves the most. In his rage, he tells Death, "I'm gonna build me a fence around what belongs to me. And I want you to stay on the other side. . . . This is between you and me" (77).

The fact that Death is the specter signifies several things. Obviously, Death symbolizes the death of these particular relationships. More importantly, Wilson reminds us that the past is never dead. At the very moments when Troy has failed with his wife and son, Death appears to him, reminding him, and us, that his failed relationship with his father has not died but continues to haunt. Rather than trying to put a fence between his present and his past, Troy needs to construct a bridge. Without making this attempt, Troy will continue to repeat the mistakes of the past he desperately tries to escape.

Cory's relationship with Troy supports this contention. Like Troy, Cory resolves his self-identification by leaving home and the threat to his concept of self. The intergenerational conflict seems to continue with the same unhappy results.

When Cory returns home after Troy's death, he tells his mother that he cannot go to the funeral because "I can't drag Papa with me everywhere I go. I've got to say no to him" (96). Like his father, Cory believes that denying his father is the "way to get rid of that shadow" (97). When Cory finally decides to go to the funeral, he does so because he has come to accept his father's faults and looked to the man himself. Singing the song of Blue, the same song that Troy sang, Cory demonstrates that he can embrace the song of his father without becoming his father. Because he has recognized that he can only be his own man by first acknowledging the foundation laid down by his father for him to build on, Cory, unlike his father, will not be haunted by the past. Continuing to sing the song about his father's dog ties him to his father and to those who came before.

Unlike the other three plays discussed so far, *Two Trains Running* does not center on a single protagonist. Likewise, in keeping with the changes in society that eroded the nuclear and extended family, the play presents a new concept of family. Although the patrons of Memphis's restaurant are not tied by blood, they are tied by the desire for connection and community. As such they represent a new concept of family that allows all to participate. By extending the definition of family, Wilson affirms the value of a culture that can unite and nurture in the same way the traditional family has. By choosing to use community as the family construct, Wilson again highlights the value of a cultural connection.

Another difference between this play and the others is the narrowing perspective with respect to taking control over one's own destiny. *Two Trains Running* builds on those that precede, just as Wilson shows that future generations must. From the embracing of the distant past illustrated in *Joe Turner's Come and Gone* to the embracing of one's legacy of one's parents in *Fences*, we arrive at the necessity of embracing the circumstances of one's own life that have brought one to this point in time. The character of Sterling exemplifies this final step.

In a talk Wilson gave at the John F. Kennedy Center for the Performing Arts in Washington DC, in November of 1991, Wilson stated that he named the character Sterling because of his sterling personality. Like a little kid, Sterling approaches life with an enthusiasm unhampered by life's hardships. Although just released from prison after serving a sentence for armed robbery, he has not allowed circumstances to stop him from dreaming. What he learns in the course of the play is how to define himself in terms of his community.

Like Boy Willie, Sterling has not allowed the white man to define who he is and what he is capable of doing. As he says, "I can do anything the white man can do. If truth be told . . . most things I can do better" (52). He robbed the bank because he had no money and "figure[d] I'd get my money where Mellon got his from" (46). Unlike Boy Willie, however, Sterling does not see himself in connection to others. Boy Willie pursued his dreams because of his awareness of his heritage. All of Sterling's get-rich-quick schemes arise from the desire to line his own pockets. In order to find all the happiness he desires, he must first accept his place within the community. He learns this lesson from Aunt Ester.

Aunt Ester is another of Wilson's unseen but fully realized forces that remind the characters and audience of the importance of cultural and familial commitment. Reported to be 322 years old, making her birth date 1647, Aunt Ester clearly represents one of the early generations of African slaves brought illegally to this country. This physical description reminds us of the African aspect of the African American identity, but Aunt Ester also teaches lessons of how to reconcile oneself to one's circumstances. Her words of advice to Sterling, "I cannot swim does not walk by the lakeside," are translated by Sterling as "Make better what you have and you have best" (98). Sterling comes to see that he will not find happiness by always looking at what others have and trying to be better, but by making the circumstances he finds himself in better. To do so means looking at how to benefit the community and not just himself.

Wilson points out that "In *Two Trains Running*, there are three ways in which you can change your life in the community. Two of them are dead—the Prophet Samuels and Malcom X. Aunt Ester is the third way" (Barbour 14). This third way connects the individuals to the essence of their existence, to that which makes them uniquely African Americans. The message that Aunt Ester offers resembles advice given by Memphis earlier in the play, but advice from Aunt Ester takes on the function of sacred teachings. As Holloway says, a visit to Aunt Ester "get my soul washed. She don't do nothing but lay her hands on your head. But it's a feeling like you never had before. Then everything in your life get real calm and peaceful" (24). Aunt Ester's answers to "Who am I" connect her visitors to "Who we are": the personal and the communal become fully integrated.

The dramatization of this integration occurs in the last moments of the play. After nine and a half years of reminding Mr. Lutz of his obligation, Hambone has died without ever receiving his ham. Never stooping to receiving second best, Hambone pleaded his case in the best way he could according to the white man's rules. When Sterling runs on stage, bleeding from his hands and face, with a ham he stole from Lutz to put in Hambone's casket, we witness the transformation of Sterling from a man seeking self-aggrandizement to a man seeing himself as part of a family. The dripping blood symbolizes a purification process similar to that of Loomis, as Sterling finds himself through his willingness to sacrifice for others. Building on the tradition of Loomis, Boy Willie, and Troy and Cory, Sterling symbolizes the ultimate liberation possible from a self-actualization based on one's cultural traditions. As Wilson says of Sterling, "There is a new black man you're going to have to deal with, who is not just going to wait for his ham" (DiGaetani 278).

If the characters just discussed illustrate the positive potential that comes from finding one's identity through the bonding of oneself to one's heritage and community, then the character of Levee in *Ma Rainey's Black Bottom* warns us of the possible tragic outcome of failing to do so. Although Wilson wrote this play before the others, it underscores the points raised thus far through its cautionary message.

Like *Two Trains Running, Ma Rainey's Black Bottom* has the focal characters who have formed a familial bond based on the need for community. Unlike *Two Trains Running*, however, the threat to this "family" is present on stage, allowing the audience to witness and recognize the menace to the African-American community. Instead of an unseen force that reminds us of the importance and power of the past, Wilson presents on stage the greatest obstacle to this force: those who turn their backs on the African American community.

Cutler, Toledo, and Slow Drag share a common history that extends over a period of time. The stories they share and the incidents and people they all know illustrate that their bond is long-lasting and solidly formed. Although Levee is only described as younger than the other men, his lack of knowledge about how the group works together and his ignorance of the histories of the other men suggest he is a newcomer to this group that he does not wish to embrace. Ma Rainey has her own extended family, but even she has a deeper familial bond to these men than Levee does. Levee's overwhelming desire is to separate himself from Ma Rainey's group and form his own band.

The search for self-identification necessitates a detachment from others in order to define oneself as different. However, the success of this process depends on the retention of the values and beliefs of one's heritage or community. Unlike Berniece or Troy, Levee has not tried to deny his family's past. He proudly carries the scars of his family's brutalization on his body and attempts to follow his father's examples of defiance of the white man, but he has failed to recognize that true strength comes when individuals work together as one. As Toledo says to Levee, "What you think . . . I'm gonna solve the colored man's problems by myself? I said, we. You understand that? We. That's every living colored man in the world got to do his share . . . I'm talking about all of us together" (434).

Levee's failure to see himself as one of a tribe has led him to constantly compare himself to others according to what he does or does not have. Unfortunately, the standards Levee strives to attain are those set by the white man. Because his dreams are controlled by the white man, Levee must play the role assigned to him if he hopes to realize his goal. Toledo suggests that doing so is like selling one's soul to the devil, which is a form of slavery. "We done sold ourselves to the white man in order to be like him. Look at the way you dressed. . . . That ain't African. That's the white man. We trying to be just like him. We done sold who we are in order to become someone else" (468). Levee cannot see this, proclaiming, "I ain't no imitation white man. And I don't want to be no white man. As soon as I get my band together and make them records like Mr. Sturdyvant done told me I can make, I'm gonna be like Ma and tell the white man just what he can do" (468). Yet Levee's very words indicate how dependent he is on the white man.

This is not to say that Levee is a type of Uncle Tom. Like Herald Loomis, he recognizes that Euro-centered Christianity too often becomes an ideology of control over the African American. Levee and Loomis both recognize that praying to a white God is like praying to the white man. The pent-up rage Levee feels towards the white man comes spilling out when he calls on God to come save Cutler, whom he threatens with a knife. This scene does not end in an epiphany like that of Loomis, for Levee has no ideology with which to replace Christianity. Because Levee has no belief in anything other than himself, he has nothing to sustain this fight. He continues to measure himself against the white man instead of with the African American. Toledo reminds us of the consequences of this: "As long as the colored man looks to the white folks to put the crown on what he say. . .as long as he looks to white folks for approval . . . then he ain't never gonna find out who he is and what he's about" (431).

Of Wilson's five plays, this is the only one to end in tragedy instead of triumph. Unable to see the salvation offered by finding an identity through one's heritage and community, Levee slays the one who offers him this message of hope. The only one to embrace his African roots, Toledo was also the only one with the ability to read, making him the least dependent on others. When Levee kills Toledo as a proxy for the white man who has spurned him, Wilson demonstrates the insidious control still held over African Americans who fail to unite. For those who remain unconvinced of the self-empowerment offered through an identity with one's heritage and community, *Ma Rainey's Black Bottom* illustrates the slavish effects of failing to find this unity. Toledo may have found that he can't convince the other musicians that music is spelled with a "c" if they don't know right from wrong, but Wilson finds a way of convincing his audience of his truth. Taken together, his plays dramatize, through both positive and negative resolutions, that the true liberation of self-actualization only comes from knowing and accepting one's culture and community.

Wilson calls himself a cultural nationalist, which he defines as believing "that blacks have a culture, and that we have our own mythology, our own history, our own social organization, our own creative motif" (Moyers 54). He firmly believes that "If black folks would recognize themselves as African and not be afraid to respond to the world as Africans, then they could make their contribution to the world as Africans" (DeVries 25). August Wilson proves to his audience the wondrous possibilities that come from establishing bonds with one's ancestry. Holding up to his audience the struggles and triumphs of the ordinary men and women who have come before, he demonstrates how tradition can sustain one through any hardship and challenge. He proves that the African heritage is a repository of both values and survival skills. While writing about the local, he restores the knowledge about the sacred—one's mythical ancestors—to his audience. For celebrating the history of a race as sacred knowledge, Wilson earns the title of mythmaker.

Works Cited

Barbour, David. "Interview: August Wilson." *Stagebill*. The Kennedy Center. November 1991: 10+.

Campbell, Jane. *Mythic Black Fiction*. Knoxville: University of Tennessee Press, 1986.

DeVries, Hillary. "A Song in Search of Itself." *American Theatre*. January 1987: 22–25.

DiGaetani. *A Search for a Postmodern Theatre: Interviews with Contemporary Playwrights*. Westport, CT: Greenwood Press, 1991.

Fabre, Genevieve. *Drumbeats, Masks, and Metaphor*. Trans. by Melvin Dixon. Cambridge: Harvard University Press, 1983.

Harrison, Paul Carter. "August Wilson's Blues Poetics." *August Wilson: Three Plays*. Pittsburgh: University of Pittsburgh Press, 1991. 291–318.

Hill, Errol, ed. *The Theatre of Black Americans*. New York: Applause Theatre Books, 1980.

Moyers, Bill. "August Wilson's America: A Conversation with Bill Moyers." *American Theatre* June 1989: 13–17, 54–56.

O'Quinn, Jim. "The Light in August." *Stagebill*. The Kennedy Center. November 1990: 34+.

Steele, Shelby. "Notes on Ritual in the New Black Theatre." In Errol Hill, ed. *The Theatre of Black Americans*. New York: Applause Theatre Books, 1980, 30–44.

Wilson, August. *Ma Rainey's Black Bottom. Plays from the Contemporary American Theater*. Ed. Brooks McNamara. New York: NAL, 1988. 410–480.

———. *Fences*. New York: NAL, 1986.

———. *Joe Turner's Come and Gone*. New York: NAL, 1988.

———. *The Piano Lesson*. New York: NAL, 1990.

———. *Two Trains Running*. New York: NAL, 1993.

Approaches to Africa
The Poetics of Memory and the Body in Two August Wilson Plays

Gunilla Theander Kester

> Time and space have no meaning in a canefield.
> *(Jean Toomer in* Cane*)*

In different but possibly analogous ways, August Wilson's plays *Fences* (1985) and *Joe Turner's Come and Gone* (1986) highlight the metaphoric relationship between African American history and the black body. In both plays Wilson extensively explores static and dynamic relationships to that history and, by refocusing on the black body as a locus for a new and dynamic metaphorics of African American history, he attempts to reformulate the African American poetics of memory. Tracing both personal and racial history, the poetics of memory functions as a dialectic of recalling reminiscent of the African American tradition of call and response.[1] Bringing the past into the present as a vivid and active component of people's daily lives, it also attacks the linearity of time and, as a result, often leaves people trapped in a sense of futility. Troy's frustrated rage that eventually made him whip his father as a young boy leads, in adult life, to his endless cataloguing in his stories of imaginary and real abuse of himself and his people. The generational pattern of abusive parenting increases the impression of repetition and paralysis. In *Joe Turner's Come and Gone* this paralysis is further concretized in Loomis' inability to stand up. His nightmare vision of the bones people expresses the horror of the middle passage and the anguish of a dislocated African American identity all too firmly shaped in response to an exploitative alien white culture. In both plays the fabric of memory is stitched together by domestic details such as Bertha's biscuits and Rose's chicken, Seth's pots and Troy's fence, the changing of sheets in the boardinghouse, and the carrying out of trash, which Troy's son often neglects. Hermeneutically, these details indicate the various protective limits which the characters attempt to draw around their lives. The constant focus on the importance of a home—a house, a room, a roof, a fence—indicates how difficult the characters' struggle for a decent existence in America has been; it also suggests a spatialized metaphorics. In both plays, but particularly in *Joe Turner's Come and Gone*, the spatial, at times even geographical, view of history traps the characters in a nostalgic and static metaphorics of history. On the one hand, in contrast to a temporal sense of return, the spatialization of history strongly suggests that the distance as well as the need to approach Africa is equally vital for each new generation of African Americans. On the other hand, it contains a warning that, to become a dynamo of change, each such approach must involve a fresh revision of the metaphoric relationship between the black body and its history.

The recurring dialectic in the poetics of memory between a static and a dynamic presentation of the black self develops into a strong metaphorics which is both referential and self-reflexive. It belongs both to "life" and to "art." In this way, Wilson's plays keenly illustrate what Linda Hutcheon terms the politics of postmodernism and defines as a mode which

> juxtaposes and gives equal value to the self-reflexive and the historically grounded: to that which is inward-directed and belongs to the world of art (such as parody) and that which is outward-directed and belongs to 'real life' (such as history). The tension between these apparent opposites finally defines the paradoxical worldly texts of postmodernism. (2)

Hutcheon emphasizes the contemporaneousness and newness of the postmodern mode which, in her view, constitutes a break with the introvert modernist mode in the earlier part of the century.

But the dual quality of worldliness and artistry in Wilson's plays does not so much constitute a break with an earlier literary mode as it represents an ongoing, strong characteristic of the African American literary tradition. This tradition is too complicated and too many-faceted to discuss in detail here, but I would like to mention two pervasive aspects which might indicate the range of complexity involved. On the one hand, the consistent lack of historical data about the fate of the African American people before, during, and after the middle passage has necessitated a unique attention to the creation of imaginary "artistic" supplements of historical events. On the other hand, historical documentation of, for example, the brutality of slavery such as in the genuine slave narratives, has produced a respectful silence or a tenuous resistance against efforts to recreate that history in art.[2] The metaphorics of Wilson's plays partake in this complex tradition. It clearly places the plays in the world (as Edward Said would say), and it ties them to the history of the African American people. It also strengthens the notion that African American postmodernism will contain features specific to its tradition.

The metaphorics of Wilson's plays is worldly, historical, and contingent. It illustrates the inexpugnable reality of history and the, in our minds, inextricable relationship between histories and stories, life and art. In "White Mythology: Metaphor in the Text of Philosophy," Jacques Derrida supplies a description of metaphor within the Western tradition of metaphysics as a palimpsestic layering which reveals its root-system and its history. A metaphor, Derrida argues,

> implies a *continuist presupposition*: the history of the metaphor appears essentially not as a displacement with breaks, as reinscriptions in a heterogeneous system, mutations, separations without origin, but rather as a progressive erosion, a regular semantic loss, an uninterrupted exhausting of the primitive meaning: an empirical abstraction without extraction from its own native soil. (215).

This description eloquently captures the value and function of Africa as native soil and empirical abstraction, as geographical and metaphorical space, in African American literature. The poetics of memory and the various notions of homecoming present in Wilson's plays are so many metaphorical versions of that space and of various approaches to Africa.

In both *Fences* and *Joe Turner's Come and Gone* Wilson strengthens the spatial metaphorics by flattening and conflating the time continuum so that the past is continuously present in the now. *Fences* flattens the dimension of time by bringing to the surface of the present an acute sense of the closeness of personal experience and by drawing a parallel between past and future generations. Situated in the yard outside of Troy Maxson's house, the play creates an intense tension between a sense of unchangeability in life coupled with a pervasive restlessness which demands more than status quo. Troy becomes the central focal point of this tension as he, more than any other character, denies the possibility of change in life for him and his people; yet he becomes the most active agent of change both at the workplace and at home. Trapped in a situation which in so many ways resembles that of his father, Troy works hard to provide for his family but gets little or no pleasure out of his life. His main concerns are the condition of the roof of his house and the fence he wants to build around the yard. At the same time, he raises the question why he, as a black man, is not permitted to drive the garbage trucks, and he fathers a child out of wedlock. These changes of his social and familial situations are both vitally connected to his body. Symbolically, the tension between status quo and change ultimately seems projected in the juxtaposition of Troy's house and Troy's body, which to both his wife and his son seems too large for the house.

The play opens with a curious little anecdote that also focuses on the body of a black man and the big watermelon that man tries to hide from a white man. Troy recalls a scene that took place between a black man with a watermelon and the white overseer at Troy's workplace. Troy tells his friend Bono that a "nigger had a watermelon this big" and refused to understand the white man, Mr. Rand, who asked him about it. The play indicates that Troy shows the size of the watermelon with his hands. This way the play starts off with an *Unbestimmtheitsstelle* or a place of indeterminacy; a moment when each director, actor, or reader must decide how big they want to make the watermelon and the discussion it raises.[3] It is quite clear, however, that for Troy, who describes the watermelon as "sitting there big as life" (105), the importance is immense. In Troy's story, the man with the watermelon pretends ignorance and answers Mr. Rand with a question: "What watermelon, Mr Rand?" Troy interprets Mr. Rand's silent response to the black man as an indication that he figures that "if the nigger too dumb to know he carrying a watermelon, he wasn't gonna get much sense out of him. Trying to hide that great big old watermelon under his coat. Afraid to let the white man see him carry it home" (105–6). The symbolic connotations of the motif of the watermelon and the androgenic image of a man who tries to hide it under his coat are strong. However we interpret the watermelon, that short story projects the vulnerability of the body and introduces the need for a home as one of the main themes of the play. Since the two men respond to each other's behavior, it also highlights the contiguity of racial difference and the relative nature of self-identification.

The relative nature of self-identification is particularly emphasized in the intertwining of generations and the stories of fathers and sons in *Fences*. Similar to *Joe Turner's Come and Gone*, it also recreates a movement from a spatial, more restrictive metaphorics toward a metaphorics of the black body as a dynamic and progressive force. The play focuses on Troy—the man with a name which, in the Western tradition, is full of fateful historic connotations of war and destruction—as a central character and sets up his body as an icon of strength for himself and the people around him. The initial description of Troy focuses on his body: "a large man with thick, heavy hands; it is this largeness that he strives to fill out and make an accommodation with. Together with his blackness, his largeness informs his sensibilities and the choices he has made in his life" (105). Rose's ambivalent account of her first impressions of her future husband echoes the same feeling. She saw him as a man who could "fill all them empty spaces" and who was so big that he filled up the house leaving little or no space for her (189).

Similarly, when he holds his newborn daughter, there is "an awkward indelicateness about the way he handles the baby. His largeness engulfs and seems to swallow it" (172). The play establishes the size of that body to measure its strength and vulnerability against a constant overflow of cultural "leftovers"—memories, babies, trash—which that body seems unable to control or stop. Symbolically, the uncontrollable force of this cultural flow overpowers Troy's frozen attitude and shows him as both a producer of change and a product of it.

Troy's changing situation at work further emphasizes the distance between his personal sense of powerlessness and his ability to claim new space and new responsibility for black men. Both at work and at home he seems unable to overcome the historical reification of the black body. Bono and Troy are clearly exploited at a job where they are allowed only to lift and carry trash, but not to drive the garbage trucks. They in turn reproduce the pattern of reification of the black body in their private lives where they use female bodies to provide them with moments of desire and liberation. Describing the body of "that Alberta gal" (106), for example, gives the two men great pleasure.

> Troy: "You can look at her and tell she one of them Florida gals. They got some big healthy women down there. Grow them right up out the ground. Got a little bit of Indian in her. Most of them niggers down in Florida got some Indian in them."

> Bono: "I don't know about that Indian part. But she damn sure big and healthy. Woman wear some big stockings. Got them great big old legs and hips as wide as the Mississippi River" (108).

Describing the girl's body as a geographical place passively waiting for the male explorer, Troy and Bono narrate the female body as a space, and they partake in an ancient male stereotyping of the female body. The spatialization of the female body and Troy's negative reaction to his son's wish to play football in school enforce the impression that Troy sees the black body as incapable of change. The sense of stasis he experiences pervades all spheres of life. When Troy hears that Cory got recruited by a football team, he doesn't like it. "I told that boy about that football stuff. The white man ain't gonna let him get nowhere with that football. I told him when he first come to me with it. . . . It ain't gonna get him nowhere" (111). Even the prospect of death doesn't change Troy's view of himself. "I ain't worried about Death. I done seen him. I done wrestled with him" (113). Troy's views of himself, his lover, and his son are quite static. Rose tries to tell him that times "have changed from when you was young, Troy. People change. The world's changing around you and you can't even see it" (138). But Troy does not believe in a possibility of change.

> Woman . . . I do the best I can do. I come in here every Friday. I carry a sack of potatoes and a bucket of lard. You all line up at the door with your hands out. I give you the lint from my pockets. I give you my sweat and my blood. I ain't got no tears. I done spent them. We go upstairs in that room at night . . . and I fall down on you and try to blast a hole into forever. I get up Monday morning . . . find my lunch on the table. I go out. Make my way. Find my strength to carry me through to the next Friday. (138)

Troy's depressed account of everyday life is juxtaposed to his stories in which he freely mixes fact and fiction and in which he creates his own poetics of memory.

The juxtaposition of fact and fiction, past and present, tends to erase the validity of such distinctions in the poetics of memory. This becomes evident, for example, from the stories Troy tells about his house. He says that if his brother Gabriel hadn't suffered a severe head injury during the Second World War and hadn't been paid 3000 dollars because of it, Troy, in spite of his hard work, "wouldn't have a pot to piss in or a window to throw it out of" (128). He claims that, even though he was working every day, he couldn't get any credit to buy some furniture until one day a white man offered him furniture on interest. "Man what drove the truck give me a book. Say send ten dollars, first of every month, to the address in the book and everything will be alright. Say if I miss a payment the devil was coming back and it'll be hell to pay. That was fifteen years ago" (117). The people around him don't believe his story, but they appreciate his Remus-ability to fabulate. Anthony A. Bibus III describes Troy as "an expert storyteller" who "uses stories to demonstrate his love for his wife, to teach values such as fair play and responsibility to his sons, to pass on his philosophy for coping with adversity—'you got to take the crooked with the straights' (37)—and to preserve family history and instill dreams for the future" (21). In his stories, Troy also turns the poverty of their race into something as large as a battle between good and evil. The battle between good and evil returns in Gabriel's and Rose's visions of a life after death. In *Joe Turner's Come and Gone* a young boy gets a message from a ghost. In a similar way Gabriel's tales of St. Peter and the gates of judgment, as well as Rose's song about Jesus as a fence, add a transcendental level to the poetics of memory.

Troy's poetics of memory has its origin in a dual sense of abandonment and commitment. Troy owes both his feelings of homelessness and his pride over taking responsibility for his own family to his father. A poor, hardworking man who raised his eleven children picking cotton for a Mr. Lubin, Troy's father was trapped in a circle of debt and deprivation. He saw his children mainly as helpers: "Sometimes I wish I hadn't known my daddy. He ain't cared nothing about no kids. A kid to him wasn't nothing. All he wanted was for you to learn how to walk so he could start you to working" (147). Troy's memories are regretful, yet he seems proud of his father for having stayed with his family instead of "searching out the New Land" (146). Troy finally rebelled against his father when he was fourteen and the father caught him fooling around with a girl instead of working. Troy first thought that his not working was the main reason for the abuse, but when he realized the father wanted that girl for himself, Troy fought back. He started whipping his father the way the father whipped him. At that moment the father turned toward Troy "and when my daddy turned to face me, I could see why the devil had never come to get him . . . cause he was the devil himself" (148). As a man who has faced the devil, Troy is opposed to Gabriel and Rose. His story of that moment draws the perimeters of his existence as clearly as Gabriel's belief in St. Peter and Rose's belief in Jesus identify them. Abruptly cut loose from his home, Troy spends his life trying to recreate a sense of home and to relive that moment when he lost that sense through the poetics of memory. As a father, Troy very much repeats his father's behavior, especially toward Cory. Troy seems determined to give his son the same sense of loss of—and desire for—a home. When Troy and Cory fight, however, the focus remains on Troy's inability to get beyond that moment by the creek when he saw the devil. Looking at his son some thirty years later, he repeats himself when he tells his son "You got the devil in you" (180). The poetics of memory in *Fences* illustrates the strong influence of a past which remains a vital or even controlling part of the present.

The poetics of memory functions in the same way to erase the passing of time in Cory's feelings about his father. When Cory returns home for Troy's funeral, he doesn't want to go to the funeral because he feels that he "can't drag Papa" with him everywhere (188). He fears that the presence of his father has inescapably located itself in his own body.

> Papa was like a shadow that followed you everywhere. It weighed on you and sunk into your flesh. It would wrap around you and lay there until you couldn't tell which one was you anymore. That shadow digging into your flesh. Trying to crawl in. Trying to live through you. Everywhere I looked, Troy Maxson was staring back at me . . . hiding under the bed . . . in the closet. I'm just saying I've got to find a way to get rid of that shadow, Mama. (188–9)

Cory corroborates his father's identification with the house he once lived in, but he subtly moves the focus from the house which was once so important to his father, to a discourse about the body. Cory's mother enhances this shift when she emphasizes that Cory must "grow into" the shadow or "cut it down to fit" him. "But that's all you got to make life with. That's all you got to measure yourself against that world out there" (189). Ultimately, the body becomes the primary locus for the poetics of memory and the struggle to change. The play ends with Gabriel's soundless and terrifying dance which is both "eerie and life-giving" (192). In a silent pantomime Gabriel presents his version of the intolerable yet dynamic relationship between the poetics of memory and the body.

In an analogous way, *Joe Turner's Come and Gone* exposes the movement from a spatialized poetics of memory toward a dynamic one which centralizes the black body as the main metaphor for change. In this play, Wilson builds up a comparison between two parallel systems of meaning. Seth Holly, the if-not-prosperous-yet-solid owner of a boarding house and maker of pots and pans which he sells for a profit, is a man who tries to make it in America and who upholds American values and means of existence. He is making fun of Bynum, who is out in the garden preparing a chicken for voodoo slaughter and burial. He does not care for "that old mumbo jumbo nonsense" (205), "all that heebie-jeebie stuff" (206). Instead he thinks of his vegetable garden, and when Bynum begins a ritual dance outside, Seth gets worried that he will step on his plants. His fear indicates how strongly the old stuff can still threaten Seth; it shows how closely the past is woven into the present. The closeness to the past is also strongly connected to the absent person in this scene, the young man Jeremy, who has spent the night in jail for drunkenness. Seth complains about his backward behavior too: "These niggers coming up here with that old backward country style of living. It's hard enough now without all that ignorant kind of acting. Ever since slavery got over with there ain't been nothing but foolish-acting niggers" (209). In his attempts to separate himself from fellow men like Bynum and Jeremy, Seth really tries to drive a wedge between the past and the present so that he can go on with his life without the burden of the past. The play shows, however, that in viewing the past as a burden and a hindrance Seth is wrong. The deeply rooted ability to overcome linear time is a gift which Bynum got when he found his song; it is a source of power that neither Seth nor anyone else would desire, or could afford, to lose. For most of the characters in the play, the regaining of that power involves a reformulation of the spatialized metaphorics in the poetics of memory.

When he introduces his search for the shiny man who once showed Bynum the Secret of Life, Bynum strengthens the spatial metaphorics of the play. He tells how the two men walked together until they came to a bend in the road. "Got around that bend and it seem like all of a sudden we ain't in the same place.

Turn around that bend and everything look like it was twice as big as it was. The trees and everything bigger than life! Sparrows big as eagles!" (212). In this unusual place Bynum met his father, who showed him around and taught him how to find his song. The image of the father as a teacher of history indicates how personal and unavoidable a confrontation with the past is; partly, it is also a lesson in spatial historiography, for the father takes him into the strange land.

> Then he carried me further into this big place until we come to this ocean. Then he showed me something I ain't got words to tell you. But if you stand to witness it, you done seen something there. I stayed in that place awhile and my daddy taught me the meaning of this thing that I had seen and showed me how to find my song. (212–3)

By excluding any description of the ocean and what actually took place there, Bynum seems able to heighten the terror of what he saw and to create a mystery around the birth of his song, which is born in suffering like all living things. At the same time, he pays tribute to the suffering of the people who actually lived that history in real life. Also, by representing history as a space, as a place one can traverse, Bynum flattens time in order to emphasize the closeness of the past.

Bynum also represents personal relationships within the spatial metaphorics of the plays. When talking to Mattie Campbell, who wants her lover back, Bynum makes it clear that those who live without a sense of time are lost. He tells her that he can bring back her lost lover, but that not all people are supposed to come back.

> And if he ain't supposed to come back . . . then he'll be in your bed one morning and it'll come up on him that he's in the wrong place. That he's lost outside of time from his place that he's supposed to be in. Then both of you be lost and trapped outside of life and ain't no way for you to get back into it. Cause you lost from yourselves and where the places come together, where you're supposed to be alive, your heart kicking in your chest with a song worth singing. (223)

To Bynum, time and space are contiguous. He does not need Heisenberg and the laws of quantum physics to explain the nature of a universe where time and space are inseparable. Yet, his descriptive terms reinforce the spatial metaphorics of the plays. Later, when he tries to make Jeremy think a little before he takes up with Mattie, Bynum uses a geographical imagery that clearly enhances the spatial metaphorics of the plays.

> Now, you take a ship. Be out there on the water traveling about. You out there on that ship sailing to and from. And then you see some land. Just like you see a woman walking down the street. You see that land and it don't look like nothing but a line out there on the horizon. That's all it is when you first see it. A line that cross your path out there on the horizon. Now, a smart man know when he see that land, it ain't just a line setting out there. He know that if you get off the water to go take a good look . . . why, there's a whole world right there. A whole world with everything imaginable under the sun. Anything you can think of you can find on that land. (245)

The geographic imagery of Bynum's poetic vision of the way people meet strengthens the spatial metaphorics complementing it with a spatial vision of personal relationships.

Spatial metaphorics also contributes to the understanding of death as can be seen in Reuben's experience with Miss Mabel's ghost and Loomis' vision of the bones people. Through the untimely death of his "bestest friend," the young neighboring boy Reuben has learned an early lesson about the linearity of human time. The return of Miss Mabel's ghost teaches him, however, that in some mysterious way the dead are alive. For him the fate of his dead friend becomes a locus of desire as he wishes that his dead friend might return so that they can play together again. But as soon as he contemplates the possibility of a return, it attracts a sense of lack and insatiability as Reuben envisions the return not only of Eugene, but of all dead people, who then will make the world grotesquely crowded. The horror of that vision makes Reuben all the more keen on listening to Miss Mabel's message from Eugene: "She say Eugene was waiting on them pigeons. Say he couldn't go back home till I let them go" (276). The introduction of a notion of a kind of "homespace" after death, a clear indication of the end of dislocation, also functions to reinforce the spatial metaphorics of the play.

Bynum, too, labors to end the sense of dislocation which has become so strong as to virtually paralyze Loomis. Even though Bynum continuously participates in and strengthens the more static poetics of geography and spatial historiography, he privileges the dynamic image of the black body as the vehicle for each person's song and a metaphor for change. In the second half of *Joe Turner's Come and Gone,* the fate of the black body becomes the strongest sign for the spatialization of time and history in the play. When Loomis hints that he has seen "some things he ain't got words to tell you," (250) Bynum begins to pull the story out of him. Slowly, Loomis describes his meeting with "the bones people": "I come to this place . . . to this water that was bigger than the whole world. And I looked out . . . and I seen these bones rise up out the water. Rise up and begin to walk on top of it" (250). A wave washes the bone people up on land and they have flesh and skin. "They black. Just like you and me. Ain't no difference" (252). Loomis shares with Reuben the horror of the return of the dead, but his image changes the focus from the geographical space where history occurred, the ocean of the middle passage and the coastline of the new continent, to the black bodies that walk away from that space. The two men share a short coming together during this transitional moment in the play when Loomis tells Bynum that he is one of the bones people.

Bynum tries to make Loomis formulate his experience in terms of language or song rather than in spatial imagery. Loomis describes how after he was freed by Joe Turner he's been looking for his wife to get "a starting place in the world. The world got to start somewhere. That's what I've been looking for. I been wandering a long time in somebody else's world. When I find my wife that be the making of my own" (269). The spatial master trope that carries the play is forged out of the experience of the Diaspora. It reproduces the experience of dislocation and its effects, which are clearly seen in the people who gather in Seth's boardinghouse. Troping on the landscape of the Diaspora, Wilson's characters spatialize history in order to maintain its presence. In an odd way, though, this very technique of keeping history alive distances history from the people it affects the most by placing it outside of the black body. Bynum's attempts to relocate the historical focus from a geographical metaphorics of sea and coastline to a bodily focus of bones and black skin suggest a different metaphorical relationship to history and can possibly explain the absence of the spatial metaphorics in the climactic finishing scenes of the play which, instead, center on the bodies of Zonia and Herald Loomis.

Since many people have responded negatively to Wilson's portrayal of black women, it is particularly important to notice the focus on Zonia's body. Sandra G. Shannon, for example, raises this issue in her interview with Lloyd Richards, the Yale Repertory director who has produced many of Wilson's plays. In his response, Dean Richards points to *Joe Turner's Come and Gone*.

> I know that August, at one point, was concerned about including more women in his work, which I think he has made a conscious attempt to do. But now in terms of his understanding or appreciation, I think he has written some of the most wonderful speeches about women in his work. In *Joe Turner's Come and Gone*, Bynum has a beautiful speech about women. There's a wonderful appreciation and understanding there that enter into the action of the play and is very dependent upon what the play chooses to be about. (130)

In making Zonia and the black female body a central agent of change in the final scenes of *Joe Turner's Come and Gone*, Wilson has gone further in his attempts to rehabilitate his portrayals of African American women than he did when he let male characters give beautiful speeches about them.

The young girl Zonia fears the future and the changes it will bring. She wants to continue walking down dusty roads with her father in an endless quest for the absent mother. Bertha asks Zonia how she can "expect to get any bigger" if she doesn't eat and she points out that there is something very unusual about Zonia's eating habits: "I ain't never seen a child that didn't eat" (281). By avoiding eating Zonia is fighting against change and trying to arrest her physical development. But even if she tries very hard to deprive herself of nourishment, her bones are growing; they betray her coming womanhood no matter how skinny she tries to stay. Her final outburst reveals that her body is the space where change is inscribed, and it will take place outside of her control: "I won't get no bigger! My bones won't get no bigger! They won't! I promise! Take me with you till we keep searching and never finding. I won't get no bigger! I promise!" (286). Zonia's relationship with her body reflects the metaphorical relationship between the black body and change as it is portrayed in the play. As long as Zonia wants her life to remain the same, she is forced to look upon her body with suspicion and distrust. Loomis, too, has come to see his body as his chief enemy, the main source of exploitation and evil: "My enemies all around me picking the flesh from my bones. I'm choking on my own blood and all you got to give me is salvation?" (288). When he turns the knife on himself, Loomis combines gestures of self-hatred and liberation; freeing him from guilt, this ambiguous act returns him to the black body and to a self-image untainted by Joe Turner's ilk.

The story of Loomis shows that history, when it is seen as a spatialized metaphor, can entrap people in a futile nostalgia for the moment of transformation itself. This moment of transformation, which occurred during the cruel days of the beginning of the Diaspora, was initiated with the enforced deracination from one continent and the arrival at the other. Bynum suggests that the trope of the Diaspora prolongs the process of dislocation by trapping the mind in the moment of transformation; the black body, he suggests, may be the alternative route which might finally provide the path to Africa, a direct link home beyond the moment of dislocation. In *Joe Turner's Come and Gone* the black body then becomes the utopian homespace, the suggestive new image for change, the mobile body which ultimately transcends the static metaphorics of a spatialized history.

Fences and *Joe Turner's Come and Gone* testify to Wilson's attempts to inspire a recoding of the African American poetics of memory in various ways. In the overall realistic plays, the poetics of memory introduces many different kinds of literary styles and levels of discourse. These stylistic shifts juxtapose the mimetic and the metaphoric, and they disturb the pervasive realistic impression of the plays. They also constitute a major contribution to the postmodern qualities of the plays. The recoding of the poetics of memory shifts the attention from a spatialized, often static, metaphorics of the past toward a dynamic metaphorics of the black body. By centralizing the black body as mainly unexplored and unknown metaphorical space in *Fences* and by opposing the metaphorics of the black body to a spatial historiography in *Joe Turner's Come and Gone,* Wilson certainly participates in the poststructural movement which makes the writing of the body a central locus of difference. Simultaneously, and more importantly, he opens a fresh avenue to a progressive revision of the African American poetics of memory where each approach to Africa is of vital significance.

NOTES

1. John F. Callahan discusses the pervasive power of call and response in African American contemporary fiction and culture. He argues, among other things, that "African-American writers use the act of voice as metaphor for the process of change" (17).

2. In an article on *Oxherding Tale,* William Gleason notes Charles Johnson's "loud silence" when he "chooses not to out-narrate the [authentic slave] narratives" (721).

3. In discussing the intentionality of the work of art, Roman Ingarden argued that the literary work of art differed from real and ideal objects in that it contained many of these places of indeterminacy. On stage, in any production of a play, these places of indeterminacy provide the actor and director with concrete choices which will in some way determine the tenor of that production. For a readily available discussion of Ingarden on this issue, see Wolfgang Iser (1708).

WORKS CITED

Bibus III, Anthony A. "Family Metaphors in Three Plays by August Wilson: A Source of Deeper Cultural Sensitivity." *Social Work in Education* 14 (1992): 15–23.

Callahan, John F. *In the African-American Grain: The Pursuit of Voice in Twentieth-Century Black Fiction*. Urbana and Chicago: University of Illinois Press, 1988.

Derrida, Jacques. "White Mythology: Metaphor in the Text of Philosophy." *Margins of Philosophy*. Chicago: University of Chicago Press, 1982. 207–271.

Gleason, William. "The Liberation of Perception in Charles Johnson's Oxherding Tale." *Black American Literature Forum* 25 (1991): 721.

Hutcheon, Linda. *The Politics of Postmodernism*. London: Routledge, 1989.

Iser, Wolfgang. *The Act of Reading: A Theory of Aesthetic Response*. Baltimore: The Johns Hopkins Univrsity Press, 1980.

Shannon, Sandra G. "From Lorraine Hansberry to August Wilson: An Interview with Lloyd Richards." *Callaloo* 14 (1991): 124–135.

Wilson, August. *Three Plays*. Pittsburgh: University of Pittsburgh Press, 1991.

Ma Rainey and the Boyz
Gender Ideology in August Wilson's Broadway Canon

Kim Marra

Having won a catalogue of prestigious national awards for his five major plays—*Ma Rainey's Black Bottom* (1984), *Fences* (1985), *Joe Turner's Come and Gone* (1986), *The Piano Lesson* (1987), and *Two Trains Running* (1990)—August Wilson has attained the stature of premier theatrical mythographer of the African American experience. His achievement has been seen as analogous to that of Eugene O'Neill, Arthur Miller, and Tennessee Williams in white America (e.g., Hornby, 1988). While many theatre artists and critics, most notably Lloyd Richards, Frank Rich, Clive Barnes, Jack Kroll, and William A. Henry III, have lauded his poetically realistic methods of dramatizing African American racial struggles, the gender ideology endemic to the construction of race in his plays remains a largely unanalyzed facet of his dramaturgy. This critical blind spot is a noteworthy aspect of Wilson's accession to the canon of American playwrights and one which offers an entree for a feminist critique of his work.

Two possible explanations for the blind spot will help delineate issues which I, as a middle-class white feminist critic, am challenged to pursue. Like most of his canonized predecessors, Wilson writes in a predominately realistic mode whose narrative structure posits a male protagonist and constructs female characters as Other. As feminist theorists have shown, this representational strategy naturalizes power relations of sexual difference rooted in biological essentialism which perpetuate male dominance.[1] It has not served the interests of the male-dominated critical establishment which confers canonical status to unmask gender's ideologically inflected socio-cultural construction.

A second possible explanation for the critical blind spot with regard to gender in Wilson's plays is more specific to his position as African American mythographer. Writing of the relationship between Wilson's life and work, Samuel G. Freedman notes that the playwright came into artistic and political consciousness amid the civil rights and black nationalist movements of the 1960s, suggesting that "if he had written *A Raisin in the Sun*, the Younger family would not have moved to the suburbs, it would have joined either the Blackstone Rangers street gang or the Nation of Islam" (49). Among the black artists and intellectuals who influenced Wilson during this formative decade, according to Freedman, who interviewed the playwright for a 1987 biographical sketch, were Ishmael Reed, Amiri Baraka, and Malcolm X. These influences locate Wilson in a tradition of African American activists who have advanced the cause of their race through the reclamation of African cultural roots and the assertion of black manhood. By self-consciously authoring a history of his people in America and by focusing chiefly on the plight of African American male protagonists, August Wilson has followed a trajectory charted by his influential predecessors. His efforts have brought him to a summit of dramatic achievement never before reached by a member of his race.[2] A feminist critique foregrounding dynamics of gender ideology in the work of a male artist widely heralded for success in overcoming racial oppression risks being construed as counterproductive to the cause of black racial advancement.[3]

However, the high profile and intellectual genealogy which may insulate Wilson from feminist criticism also mandate a rigorous gender analysis of his work. Precisely because he has achieved the stature of premier African American theatrical mythographer, the perceptions of women disseminated in his plays have influential power and thus merit critical attention; traditionally, presumptions of universality by canonized male authors have indicated inscription of oppressive gender ideology. Female characters written, according to Samuel G. Freedmen, from a sensibility "fired in the kiln of black nationalism" (40), warrant particular scrutiny. Along with its many positive achievements for African Americans, the black nationalist tradition is one which black feminists identify as fiercely sexist (e.g., Wallace 1978). As Audre Lorde and others have pointed out, fighting racial oppression with gender oppression only perpetuates oppression itself and, by pitting black men and women against each other, can lead ultimately to the destruction of the race (Lorde 120; Collins 188; hooks 100).

Because of Wilson's stature and heritage, the gender ideology inscribed in his representations of women has implications for the larger American culture as well. bell hooks has argued that leading contemporary African American image-makers working in film and television, like Eddie Murphy, Arsenio Hall, Chuck D., and Spike Lee, have succeeded with white as well as black audiences in part because their products reinforce the sexist values of white supremacist capitalist patriarchy (102). hooks writes: "commodification of blackness that makes phallocentric black masculinity marketable makes the realm of cultural politics a propagandistic site where black people are rewarded materially for reactionary thinking about gender" (109). Although Wilson's earnings may not rival those of his electronic-media contemporaries, his *Fences* ranks as one of the top-grossing straight plays in Broadway history. His unprecedented popularity among black but mostly white middle- and upper-middle-class audiences begs the question of whether and to what extent his plays perpetuate a gender ideology which oppresses American women across lines of race, ethnicity, class, and sexual preference.

To address this question, I begin by outlining a theoretical paradigm derived from leading exponents of black feminist thought for analyzing African American gender constructs. Critics such as Audre Lorde, bell hooks, Michelle Wallace, Angela Davis, Mae C. King, Bonnie Thornton Dill, Barbara Sizemore, Sondra O'Neale, and Patricia Hill Collins have analyzed the ideological forces informing representations of women by black male authors working under white oppression.

I will then apply this paradigm in a critical examination of the female characters in Wilson's Broadway canon: *Joe Turner's Come and Gone* (1988), *Ma Rainey's Black Bottom* (1984), *The Piano Lesson* (1990), *Fences* (1987), and *Two Trains Runnng* (1992).[4] Each play is considered in turn according to Wilson's self-imposed historical chronology to assess his vision of how perceptions of women and gender relations have changed over time.

I

Many black feminist critics relate the construction of black womanhood in works by black male authors to the mythohistorical crisis of black manhood in a white supremacist patriarchal capitalist culture. Given August Wilson's focus on the quest of the African American male hero to self-actualize, the impact of this crisis on his representation of women is highly relevant. Barbara Sizemore capsulizes the root cause of the crisis which dates from the period of slavery in America and still ghosts black male consciousness: ". . . the black man wants to be like the white man. There is only one destiny, and it is white" (8). Following the standard mythohistorical narrative, the black man internalizes the dominant cultural injunction to become a man on white terms but is prevented from achieving this manhood on the basis of skin color. So torturous is the resulting conflict that it may induce insanity as well as anguish.

Significantly, under slavery, the chief instruments of white oppression of black men were economic and sexual as well as racial. The black male slave, being property, could not own it and gain material control over his own destiny, a chief mark of white manhood. White slave masters sexually oppressed black men by torturing them in specifically emasculating ways, including literal, bodily castration and the psychological castration of raping their mothers, wives, sisters, and daughters whom they were powerless to defend. White supremacists' use, of these economic and sexual tools of emasculation have compelled black men to compensate by pursuing sexual conquest and material acquisition as the chief sources of manhood (Davis 12–13; King 14–15; Wallace 1990, 151). Because of racial barriers, the black male quest to self-actualize is thought to be even more dire than that of white men seeking to emulate the patriarchal ideal (hooks 96–97).

The impact of the crisis of black manhood on the perception of black women is complex and multi-faceted. Most pertinent to this essay are ideological forces constructing the figures of the mother and the female sexual partner *vis-a-vis* the black male quest to self-actualize.

Black feminist analyses reveal a highly ambivalent ideology—one encompassing virulently negative and idolatrously positive extremes—inscribed in constructions of black motherhood under white supremacist capitalist patriarchy. In relation to black manhood, negative connotations have accrued to African American mothers through the black mammy stereotype which Patricia Hill Collins contends "represents the normative yardstick used to evaluate all black women's behavior" (71). Originating in the slavery era, the faithful, obedient domestic servant was prized in white families because she was deemed sexually undesirable to the patriarch and therefore a safe, self-sacrificing nurturer of his children, one who could do the "dirty work" of child rearing beneath the dignity of the WASP wife. Collins adds: "By loving, nurturing, and caring for her white children and 'family' better than her own, the mammy symbolizes the dominant group's perceptions of the ideal Black female relationship to elite male power" (70). For the black youth aspiring to manhood, the impact is negative on at least two counts. First, the mammy privileges white children over him, depriving him of the maternal nurturing necessary to launch him on the path to self-actualization. Second, by accepting and profiting from her subordination in the white household, she ingests white racist values with which she then infects her own home in the black community (Dance 125).

Additional negative connotations accrued to black women through the black mammy stereotype in the 1960s with the emergence of the so-called black matriarchy thesis. This construct derives largely from Daniel Patrick Moynihan's 1965 government-sponsored study of the black family undertaken during the "War on Poverty" launched by the Johnson administration.[5] The thesis holds that, as primary wage-earners in their families, black mothers spend too much time away from home and fail to provide proper guidance for their children. Further, black mothers' earning power places them in the aggressive, "unwomanly" position of dominance in the household, which allegedly emasculates their black male family members. As a result, husbands and lovers flee the domicile and abdicate responsibility for their children. Collins observes, "From an elite white male standpoint, the matriarch is essentially a failed mammy, a negative stigma applied to African American women who dared violate the image of the submissive, hard-working servant" (73). The Moynihan Report cited black matriarchy as the primary reason for a supposed absence of patriarchy in the black family and resulting African American cultural inferiority (Collins 75).

Authored by a member of the white supremacist patriarchal elite, the black matriarchy thesis gained ascendancy in both the African American and Euro American communities. As Mae C. King wrote in 1973: "Notwithstanding the refutation of the stereotypes [e.g. by Robert Hill], the black woman still bears the brunt of the negatives associated with such images" (16). These negatives have been leveled against black women by black and white male leaders alike. Of the 1960s nationalist movement, Pauli Murray observes: "the black militant's cry for the retrieval of black manhood suggests an acceptance of this stereotype, an association of masculinity with male dominance and a tendency to treat the values of self-reliance and independence as purely masculine traits."[6] Indeed, the internalization of the castrating black matriarch stereotype is so pervasive as to prompt Haki Madhubuti's analysis of black nationalist misogyny: "The 'fear' of women that exists among many black men runs deep and often goes unspoken. This fear is cultural."[7] "Even though," notes bell hooks, "individual black nationalists like Haki Madhubuti speak against sexism, progressive Afrocentric thinking does not have the impact that the old guard [internalized white supremacist patriarchal] message has" (107).

The cultural ascendancy and continuing resonance of the black matriarchy thesis strikingly demonstrates the implications of white and black oppression of black women beyond as well as within the black community. Cheryl Townsend Gilkes has pointed out that "the public depiction of Black women as unfeminine, castrating matriarchs came at precisely the same moment that the [middle-class white female dominated] feminist movement was advancing its public critique of American patriarchy" (296). Moynihan's thesis served the socio-political and economic agenda of white supremacist capitalist patriarchy against white as well as black women, Collins observes:

> The image of the Black matriarch emerged at that time [1960s] as a powerful symbol of what can go wrong if white patriarchal power is challenged. Aggressive, assertive women are penalized—they are abandoned by their men, end up impoverished, and are stigmatized as being unfeminine. (75)

Moreover, the black matriarchy thesis has been used for conservative, anti-feminist ideological ends by constellating that primal fear of white middle-class America, the dissolution of the patriarchal nuclear family. Collins remarks that "maintaining the mythical norm of the financially independent, white middle-class family organized around a monogamous heterosexual couple requires stigmatizing African American families as being deviant, and a primary source of this assumed deviancy stems from allegations about Black male sexuality" (165). Following Collins' and Gilkes' arguments, contemporary representations of African American women which perpetuate the castrating black matriarch stereotype are complicit in gender oppression across racial lines.

Countering the negative aspects asscribed to black matriarchy are aspects constructed as positive in relation to black manhood. Appropriating a white Christian dialectic in "Black Eve or Madonna?: A Study of the Antithetical Views of the Mother in Black American Literature," Daryl C. Dance outlines some of these positive aspects. In contrast to those authors like Amiri Baraka "who apparently view the Black woman as the fallen Eve who must be destroyed before she corrupts others," Dance stresses the work of other black writers like Maya Angelou and George Jackson who "have paid tribute to the Black mother as a Madonna bringing salvation to her Black children" (125). Behavior attributed to black mothers which many black men, fearing castration, have seen as negative, Dance argues should be appreciated for its positive effects, namely the survival of the black race under white oppression. If the black mother, "cognizant of the slave master, the lynch mob, the present-day legal system," had not taught her son "to mask and repress his normal masculinity and aggressiveness . . . , the country's lynching statistics would be even more horrifying and our mental institutions would be even more crowded (127). . . . That is indeed a kind of love—the deepest and strongest kind—the kind that must require a mother to hide her natural emotions and punish her child to save his life" (129). Dance concludes that the black mother is "unquestionably a Madonna," "a strong Black bridge that we all crossed over on, "whose love, strength, endurance, and "ability to survive in the most ignominious circumstance . . . [have] made possible the new militant . . ." (130–131).

Dance's argument, though attempting to counter the negative aspects attributed to black matriarchy, is problematic for black feminists. Collins argues that adulation of black women for archetypal maternal qualities of devotion, self-sacrifice, and unconditional love inscribes them in another oppressive stereotype, the "superstrong Black mother" (116). Citing Barbara Christian's research, she adds: "In many African American communities so much sanctification surrounds Black motherhood that 'the idea that mothers should live lives of sacrifice has come to be seen as the norm.'"[8]

From a white feminist perspective, Dance's argument is problematic as well, because it reflects essentialist assumptions which reinscribe dominant gender ideology. Unlike Moynihan, Dance displaces the blame for emasculating black matriarchy from black women onto white oppression, but she agrees with Moynihan in implying that this form of womanhood is perverse and "unnatural." Dance assumes that if black women did not have to contend with white oppression, they would channel their innate maternal impulses into rearing sons to manifest "normal masculinity," which is the prescribed role for mothers in dominant American patriarchal culture. Structurally, Dance's argument proceeds from a bipolar Eve/Madonna model which reifies the essentialism inherent in both positive and negative aspects of black matriarchy. Locked in diametrical opposition, each pole reinforces the other by contrast. Thus, feminine representations which romanticize monolithic black matriarchy, no less than those which revile it, perpetuate gender ideology oppressive to both black and white women.

The bipolarity informing the construction of black motherhood also informs the construction of the black woman as a sexual partner for the black male struggling to self-actualize in American society. The negativity ascribed to the black female derives from the dominant culture's representation of her since the slavery era as the antithesis of desirable white femininity; "Blue-eyed, blond, thin, white women could not be considered beautiful without the Other—Black women with classical African features of dark skin, broad noses, full lips, and kinky hair" (Collins 79). To constellate the bourgeois WASP domestic goddess by contrast and further racial oppression, the black woman was constructed as physiognomically unrefined, sexually animalistic, unclean, and impure (O'Neale 152). Black feminists have labeled the racist stereotype of the sexually aggressive black woman the Jezebel (Collins 77) or the "depreciated sex object" (King 17). Collins notes pithily, "black 'whores' make white 'virgins' possible" (176).[9] Black feminist critics also emphasize that this construct continues to govern representations of black women by both black and white male authors (O'Neale 143; hooks 62).

The notion of black female antitypes of desirable femininity has had particular impact on women's self-perceptions and relations between the sexes in African American culture. Under white supremacist capitalist patriarchy, the chief mark of manhood is to possess a culturally desirable feminine icon. Given the stigmas historically attached to black women, Barbara Sizemore observes "white women are preferred by all men" (4) and notes the significant number of prominent black men who have married white women (8). Consequently, as Collins writes, ". . . African American women experience the pain of never being able to live up to externally defined [white] standards of beauty—standards applied to us by white men, white women, Black men, and, most painfully, one another" (80). The ideology of black female anatomical and moral deficiency which justifies black women's degradation is thus internalized and perpetuated by blacks as well as whites, male and female.

This widespread cultural denigration of black women has become the signal factor informing portrayals of intersexual relations. In a racist society which puts white virgins on a pedestal and mythologizes black sexuality, black and white men are given license to use degraded black women as throwaway sex objects. In the case of black men, for whom economic opportunities for asserting manhood have often been denied, this exploitation of black women becomes the primary means of demonstrating phallocentric masculinity. By this ethos, notes hooks, the black male, to become a man in America, need not hold a steady job, own property, and be head of a household; "he was a man simply because he had a penis. Furthermore, his ability to use that penis in the arena of sexual conquest could bring him as much status as being a wage earner and provider" (94). In some prominent representations of black masculinity, e.g., by Robert Staples, George Jackson, and Amiri Baraka, sexual exploitation of black women is further justified as a response to black male rage at emasculating black matriarchs (hooks 97; Collins 188; Lorde 1984, 120). "Although the attitudes expressed by Baraka and Jackson appear dated," writes hooks, "they have retained their ideological currency among black men through time" (99).

As with the white Christian virgin/whore dichotomy, the black Jezebel has her positive counterpart. Positive aspects of the black woman as a sexual partner for the black man coincide with those of the black matriarch in the mythos of Mother Africa. Archetypally, the mother symbolizes origins or connection to one's heritage and racial regeneration. Barbara Christian observes, "There is no doubt that motherhood is for most African people symbolic of creativity and continuity."[10] This symbolism transfers to the African American context where actual, surrogate, and potential black mothers are credited with racial uplift and nurturing black community development (Collins 1987, 6). In embracing a black madonna (as opposed to the WASP feminine icon valued in the dominant culture), the black man embraces his own cultural origins.

Like the positive aspects inscribed in black matriarchy, however, this positive dimension of the black woman as a sexual partner for the black man remains problematic from a feminist perspective. A black Madonna/Jezebel dichotomy simply supplants the white Virgin/Whore paradigm and reiterates the oppressive dynamics inherent in bipolar stereotypic constructs in another context. The oppressive effects of this gender ideology are particularly evident in the black nationalist movement which, according to Barbara A. Sizemore, is characterized by extremely dichotomous thinking regarding black women. Sizemore contends that implicit in Elijah Muhammed's *Message to the Blackman in America* is "the warning that women are evil and given to sin."[11] Further, "[Muhammed] perpetrates the untruth that black women make higher salaries than black men and he denigrates the black woman by seeing her as immoral and ignorant" (6). Consequently, black women, rendered abnormally powerful under white oppression, must be forcibly kept under guard, veiled, and restored to the "natural" feminine state of purity, submission, and devotion to male advancement. As Baraka writes in *Mwanamke Mwananchi*, "Nature has made woman submissive—she must submit to man's creation in order for it to exist."[12] Given this influential African American male value system, representations of black female sexual partners and wives as "naturally" submissive, self-effacing, and unquestioningly devoted to their men can perpetuate a particularly virulent sexism, an oppressive gender ideology exacerbated by socio-economic inequities under white supremacist capitalist patriarchy.

As mentioned above, Wilson's ties to the black nationalist tradition in African American thought and activism are particularly significant in light of black feminist critiques of the movement's preoccupation with black manhood and bipolar views of black women. Though Wilson's plays are set in various decades from the 1910s to the 1960s, all are written from a contemporary post-civil rights, post-nationalist perspective. The ensuing discussion explores the means by which his Broadway representations of women perpetuate, subvert, and/or deconstruct the sexist gender ideology inherent in culturally pervasive positive and negative black female stereotypes.

II

Joe Turner's Come and Gone

Wilson begins his history of the African American experience in 1911, the year of the action of *Joe Turner's Come and Gone*. At this historical juncture, the playwright tells us, "the sons and daughters of newly freed African slaves" wander northward into the city of Pittsburgh, Pennsylvania "seeking to scrape from the narrow, crooked cobbles and the firey blasts of the coke furnace a way of bludgeoning and shaping the malleable parts of themselves into a new identity as free men of definite and sincere worth" (xv). The quest for identity is focused chiefly on the hero, Herald Loomis, a thirty-two-year-old deacon struggling to emerge from white oppression vividly symbolized in the demonic white bounty hunter, Joe Turner. Loomis, says Wilson, "is driven . . . by his search for a world that speaks to something about himself. He is unable to harmonize the forces that swirl around him, and seeks to recreate the world into one that contains his image" (13).

The primary female characters in the play are constellated according to needs dictated by the male quest. As Bynum, the play's chief philosopher, says to young Jeremy in a man-to-man talk:

> . . . when you grab hold to a woman . . . You got a whole way of life kicking up under your hand. That woman can take and make you feel like something. . . . it's a blessing when you learn to look at a woman and see in maybe just a few strands of her hair, the way her cheek curves . . . to see in that everything there is out of life to be gotten. It's a blessing to see that. You know you done right and proud by your mother to see that. (45–46)

Like Jeremy, Loomis searches for the right woman on whom to project the new life he is forging for himself. He begins by looking for the wife who left him after his capture by Joe Turner: "I just wanna see her face so I can get me a starting place in the world. . . . I been wandering a long time in somebody else's world. When I find my wife that be the making of my own" (72).

Loomis does indeed find his wife, but his journey also takes a different turn. Wilson charts his hero's quest for self-discovery through key images of black womanhood.

The first feminine image Loomis encounters is Bertha, the forty-five-year-old wife of Seth Holly, the owner of the boarding house in whose kitchen most of the visible action of the play transpires. Bertha is virtually a fixture in this room of the house; six of the play's nine scenes begin with her at or heading for the stove area to cook or clean up. A dedicated, hardworking, boundless source of maternal strength, sustenance, and comforting, sage advice, she is the nurturing matriarch *par excellence*. Wilson transfers the black matriarch's bounteous resources from white kitchen to black to benefit her own family and race. A property owner, Seth is the most prosperous black man in the play, and his prosperity is linked to the beneficent self-sacrifice and fortitude of his wife. If Loomis were to have such a woman behind him, he, too, might find himself and prosper. Bertha thus becomes the alpha and omega of the black hero's search for selfhood.

Loomis next encounters Mattie Campbell, "a young woman of twenty-six whose attractiveness is hidden under the weight and concerns of a dissatisfied life [but who] still believes in the possibility of love" (21). Mattie needs a man and a family to make her life meaningful, and she clings to this dream in spite of having been deserted by her lover and having lost two children. Her man left her because she failed to help him realize his vision of selfhood. After telling Mattie her husband's departure was fully justified under these circumstances, Bynum asserts: "You got to let him go find where he's supposed to be in the world" (23).

Wilson's characterization of Mattie locates her within the stereotype of "depreciated sex object" (King 17). Her drama of desertion, of being passed over by her black lover for a woman more desirable in dominant cultural terms, is played out in her ill-fated relationship with Jeremy. Her fierce need for a man prompts her instantaneously to accept his sexual overtures, but the demands of her need soon alienate him and inspire nightmarish visions peppered with metaphors of castration. Jeremy tells Bynum: ". . . Ain't nothing worse than a desperate woman. . . . They get to cutting up your clothes and things trying to keep you staying. Desperate women ain't nothing but trouble for a man" (18–19). Following phallocentric dictates, Jeremy drops Mattie the minute a more "attractive" woman comes along.

Mattie's need for a man and family to nurture in order to find fulfillment render her a potential matriarch. Though she is not, ultimately, attractive to Jeremy, she is to Herald Loomis. By the middle of the second act, he is moved to tell her, "It's been a long time since I seen a full woman . . ." Then, writes Wilson, ". . . He touches her awkwardly, gently, tenderly. Inside he howls like a lost wolf pup whose hunger is deep. He goes to touch her but finds he cannot" (77). The hero's need for black maternal nurturing to emerge from the horrors of white terror and oppression overpowers Mattie's need for male companionship, which renders her attractive and not threatening to him.

In addition to selfless nurturing, Mattie represents a new faith for the former church deacon. Her spiritual beliefs remain rooted in Afrocentric religious tradition; she attributes the loss of her two babies to the infliction of a "curse prayer" (22). To embrace Mattie would be to renounce his white-dominated religious as well as familial past.[13] Before he can self-actualize through consummation with this personification of Mother Africa, however, Herald must reckon with other constructions of black femininity marking stages of his journey.

Herald, along with Jeremy, encounters Molly Cunningham, the chief foil to the beneficent nurturing and powers of salvation inscribed in the mammy figures. Like Mattie, Molly is twenty-six years old and lonely, but there the similarity ends. Where Mattie supports herself with an ironing job, Molly brazenly thwarts the mammy's burden by refusing to do domestic work, which she claims killed her mother, in either white or black homes. Moreover, she attempts to assert control over her own destiny by refusing ever fully to trust men and by taking precautions to ensure that she not become pregnant. The playwright, however, neutralizes the subversive potential of this character by inscribing her in the oppressive ideology of the Jezebel, the sexually aggressive black woman who has eaten the forbidden fruit of dominant cultural values and threatens to poison those who lie down with her. In contrast to Mattie's humble, downtrodden aspect, Wilson implies Molly is seductive and dangerous, "the kind of woman that 'could break in on a dollar anywhere she goes.' She carries a small cardboard suitcase and wears a colorful dress of the fashion of the day" (47). Taking money conspicuously from her bosom, Molly announces she is looking for a room and would like some male company.

Marking these female characters with positive and negative stereotypical feminine aspects, Wilson defines heroism according to the representations of women his male characters choose. Significantly, Molly holds little appeal for Wilson's hero, Herald Loomis. Jeremy, on the other hand, is totally smitten; Wilson notes that his "heart jumps out of his chest when he sees her" (47). The fact that Molly eschews the domestic work traditionally ascribed to black women and wears a fashionable dress makes her more of a sexual trophy in dominant cultural terms than Mattie. By rejecting Mattie in favor of Molly, Jeremy becomes an anti-hero, a sell-out to the material and sexual aspirations of the dominant culture.

Through Herald Loomis' choice of women, Wilson articulates a more Afrocentric, though perhaps no less sexist, vision of heroism. Appearing only in the last few pages of the play, the woman for whom Herald is initially searching, his wife Martha Loomis/Pentecost, figures more symbolically than physically in his quest for selfhood. She represents the past with which he must reckon and then leave behind. Formerly, Herald was a church deacon, but his subsequent capture and torture at the hands of Joe Turner have caused him to question his faith. In his hour of need, both God and his wife deserted him. Though Martha offers legitimate reasons of self-preservation for her actions, in Herald's mind, she abandoned him to make a new life for herself serving the white man's God. The betrayal is such that he cannot go back, either to her or the church. In restoring their daughter to her mother, Herald relinquishes his ties to a religious and familial past rooted in white domination.

Fearing her husband has gone to the devil, Martha tries to woo him back to Christ. But Herald lays bare his chest and wounds himself, claiming he can only be washed clean by his own, black blood. Brandishing his self-inflicted stigmata, he becomes the "shining man," shimmering with his own sense of spirituality and freedom from Martha, Christianity, and Joe Turner. He crosses the threshold into the new century and a new sense of selfhood, but precisely the kind of man he will become remains a mystery. The final action is that of Mattie rushing out after him, the Afrocentric mother figure destined to nurture this new man. Whereas the playwright grants his hero the freedom to forge himself anew, he leaves this primary female character indelibly inscribed in an oppressive stereotype.

Ma Rainey's Black Bottom

Where *Joe Turner* ends on a hopeful note with the symbolic birth of a new black savior, the portrayal of black male heroism in relation to white oppression and black womanhood grows considerably more ominous in the next play in Wilson's chronology, *Ma Rainey's Black Bottom*. The play is set in Chicago in 1927 at the height of material prosperity for middle-class white America. Executives of Paramount Studios are profiting from the "race" division of their enterprise by co-opting black artists and capitalizing on the new market of black consumers. In so doing, white oppressors have corrupted the blues, a source of African American cultural knowledge and sustenance, into an instrument of racial exploitation and abuse. Under white supremacist capitalist patriarchy, whites control the means of blues production, obligating black performers to please studio executives before their own black audiences. In this larger context of racial oppression in which values and senses of identity are distorted, the black male hero, Levee, pursues his quest for manhood. To prove himself to the white bossess, he must assert his will over that of a formidable matriarch, the legendary Ma Rainey.

Like Herald Loomis, only more literally, Levee defines the achievement of manhood in terms of "finding"—and recording—"his own song." The attitudes and means by which he pursues this goal have been forged from his tortured personal history of white supremacist economic and sexual abuse. As relatively anonymous members of Ma Rainey's back-up band, he and his fellow black musicians have been excluded from the material prosperity conspicuously enjoyed by the dominant culture. We learn of Levee's sexual victimization when he vividly recounts the childhood horror of having to watch helplessly while white men gang-raped his mother. Having been economically and sexually oppressed, Levee now seethes with ambition to prove himself by recording and selling hit songs to a new generation of black consumers and by pursuing an ethos of sexual conquest.

Though invested with the ambition needed to fight oppression, Levee lacks the vital perspective on his quest provided by his more literate and philosophical bandmate. Toledo cautions him: "As long as the colored man look to the white folks to put the crown on what he say . . . He's just gonna be about what white folks want him to be about" (469). In particular Levee has ingested white supremacist capitalist patriarchy's phallocentric ideal. The more his efforts to pursue opportunities for economic advancement are thwarted, the more he focuses on his genitals as the primary signifier of his manhood. His phallic preoccupation distorts his view of women by reducing them to "your next piece of pussy" and constellating profound fears of castration, such as those surrounding his experience in a New Orleans bar. He tells his fellow musicians:

> Man, they got some gals in there just don't wait! I seen a man get killed in there once. Got drunk and grabbed one of the gals wrong . . . I don't know what the matter of it was. But he grabbed her and she stuck a knife in him all the way up to the hilt. He ain't even fell. He just stood there and choked in his own blood. (481)[14]

These gender perceptions render Levee's struggle with Ma Rainey more one of sexual power politics than of artistic or generational differences. Deluding himself that Sturdyvant is genuinely impressed by his talent, Levee has written his own arrangement of a popular song in Ma's repertoire, "Ma Rainey's Black Bottom." Because the song explicitly references female buttocks, Levee's attempted rearrangement and playing of it becomes, symbolically, a phallic gesture. His venture echoes that of white male authors throughout Western history who have asserted phallic supremacy by taking possession of the female body and molding it according to their vision. But the metaphoric manipulation of Ma Rainey's buttocks acquires particular racial and sexual significance. As Sandra Shannon has noted, Ma's black bottom and her flagrant use of it in performance were viewed as instances of black female sexual transgression, a defiant "mooning" in the face of still prudish Anglo-America. (140) For Levee to dictate the rearrangement of this song would be to slay a socially corruptive hydra of fallen, licentious womanhood, a signal heroic act marking accession to manhood in the dominant culture. Conversely, by this same phallocentric logic, for Levee to succumb to Ma Rainey's manipulation of her own black bottom would be an abdication of male sexual power tantamount to castration.

In relation to Levee's phallocentric heroic quest, Ma Rainey, one of only two female characters in the play, is constructed as a caricature of the emasculating black matriarch. Wilson describes her as "a short, heavy woman" (476). In dominant cultural terms, her physique marks her an antitype of desirable femininity. According to Shannon, this, in addition to her music, was a major part of her audience appeal; "Her down-home, earthy style, her naughty lyrics, and her rugged looks were welcomed by weary Southern blacks, no longer impressed by the deceptive glamour of the North" (137). However, incarnating an opposite of idolized bourgeois WASP womanhood also enables the white studio executives to exploit and degrade her. Seeing herself as their whore and playing the role for all she can get, Ma becomes complicit in this process. She knows that as soon as she gives them what they want, which ultimately she will, "they roll over and put their pants on" (497). When she lies down with the white man, she ingests the poison of his oppression and then passes it on to the "family" of her back-up band over which she rules with an iron hand.

Ma's antifeminine aspects are drawn to such an extreme that she threatens not only to emasculate the male hero but to appropriate the phallus herself. She uses her voice like an instrument of pleasure, teasing with the promise of performance and then witholding satisfaction until she gains maximum manipulative power. Her prowess is evidenced by the presence of Dussie Mae, whose "greatest asset," Wilson tell us, "is the sensual energy which seems to flow from her" (476). Seeing the New York production, reviewers Frank Rich, Jack Kroll, Howard Kissel, and Gerald Weales referred to this character variously as Ma's "lover," "lesbian lover," "slim, sexy mistress," and "girlfriend." Levee even attributes to Ma his own—albeit distorted and deluded—standard of masculinity. He asserts: "I'm gonna be like Ma and tell the white man just what he can do. . . . Make the white man respect me!" (508). Having masculinized Ma, he engages in a macho rivalry with her for Dussie Mae's affections. He attempts to prove that by virtue of having "a red rooster" to introduce to Dussie Mae's "brown hen," he is more of a man than Ma is (499).

Ma's most castrating action occurs when she brashly demonstrates that she is fully able to use her manipulative power to advance a black man's career after having expressly denied Levee that support. Angering white management and annoying her band, she prolongs the recording session so that her stuttering nephew can deliver the introduction to her song. Unlike Sylvester, a physically large but socially crippled mama's boy, Levee has tried to assert an autonomous authorial and entrepreneurial will. Ma stifled this gesture of manhood with her emphatic declaration, "I'm singing Ma Rainey's song. I ain't singing Levee's song. Now that's all there is to it" (486). She now adds insult to injury by favoring one manifestly less capable than her young trumpet player. This castrating blow is dealt Levee in full view of the white bosses and Dussie Mae. After the session, Sturdyvant retracts his offer to record Levee's songs, claiming that Ma's records will sell more, and Dussie Mae rejects the trumpeter to exit with her mistress, acts which confer the ultimate "manhood" on Ma.

Not surprisingly, the pain and frustration of this public emasculation push Levee into a volatile rage. The seemingly small provocation of Toledo scuffing one of his fancy new Florsheim shoes, signifiers of his thwarted economic aspirations, moves him to plunge a knife into his fellow band member. Because he kills the insightful Toledo, the only one capable of understanding the oppressive dynamics causing his suffering, the act is tantamount to Levee's self-destruction and, in a larger sense, to race suicide.

Frank Rich, currently the most influential of white male reviewers, pronounced this play "a searing inside account of what white racism does to its victims." From a feminist perspective, however, Wilson's representations of women undermine this powerful message. Rather than subverting or deconstructing black female stereotypes, Wilson in this play pushes them to extremes. Ma assumes monstrously castrating matriarchal proportions, ones, in fact, reified in Rich's review where she is described as being "at the height of her fame. A mountain of glitter and feathers, she has become a despotic, temperamental star, complete with a retinue of flunkies, a fancy car, and a kept young lesbian lover." Dressed like a Jezebel, Dussie Mae, the only other female character in the play, is reduced to an opportunistic pawn in Levee's futile struggle with Ma to prove his manhood. Ma becomes such an overpowering and at times gratuitously manipulative matriarch—capable of bringing even Irwin to his knees—that she and not the white-dominated music industry comes across as the primary or at least the most immediate cause of Levee's demise. In this respect, the play, rather than offering new insight into the dynamics of white oppression, reinscribes the black matriarchy thesis in a Broadway context.

The Piano Lesson

As with *Ma Rainey*, Wilson's portrayal of the 1930s turns on a central conflict between two combatants of different genders: a male hero striving to achieve manhood and a castrating female matriarch who thwarts his endeavor. The dynamics of the struggle, however, differ from those in the earlier play because the two characters are siblings, and the stakes for survival are even more dire, given the Depression era context. The older sister, Berniece, is widowed and the mother of a nine-year-old daughter. Her brother, Boy Willie, as his name suggests, is less mature and still a roving bachelor. Each has inherited an equal share of the principal family heirloom, the piano into whose legs their great-grandfather, born a slave, carved icons of their ancestry, and each has distinct and seemingly irreconcilable plans for this legacy. Berniece vows to retain the piano as a totem of her familial and racial past; Boy Willie is determined to sell it and parlay the profits into buying his own farm and fulfilling the Jeffersonian vision of the American Dream. By taking the piano from Berniece, Boy Willie deprives her of a cultural legacy; by witholding the piano from Boy Willie, Berniece deprives him of his access to American patriarchy.

Given all the piano symbolizes, the conflict over what to do with it resonates far beyond the personal relationship between the two siblings to the struggle of African Americans to rise up from racial oppression. As noted above, Wilson comes from a tradition of black thought and activism which emphasizes the vital importance of embracing both black cultural heritage and economic opportunity for racial survival and prosperity. Berniece and Boy Willie want to pursue these dual strategies but in rigidly divergent ways. Neither sibling will compromise, and both are willing to fight to the death for their respective visions for the piano. The divide is articulated not only in terms of how each sibling construes economic opportunity and cultural heritage but in terms of gender. Berniece's and Boy Willie's diverse visions are made all the more irreconcilable by their attachment to monolithic constructions of black femininity and masculinity. Gender stereotypes inform Wilson's rendering of family history, the immediate dramatic circumstances, and the indications for the siblings' respective futures.

In Wilson's rendering of the Charles family history, the piano bears the marks of generations of both racial oppression and sexist gender ideology. Sutter's grandfather, the white slavemaster, traded Berniece and Boy Willie's great-grandmother (also named Berniece) and Doaker's father, then a small boy, for the piano as an anniversary present for his wife. The act degraded the black woman as the white master's dispensable property and emasculated her black husband who was powerless to keep and protect her. In spite of her husband's generosity, the WASP domestic goddess of the plantation mourned the loss of her faithful, subservient mammy, whose black femininity made her mistress's white womanhood more ideal by contrast. Furthering the black slave husband's humiliation, the white master made him carve his wife's and other relations' images into the piano to assuage not his own but his mistress's loss.

In this family history, the racist and sexist dynamics of oppression established under slavery are perpetuated by both blacks and whites after emancipation. Bereniece and Boy Willie's father, to avenge the degradation and emasculation perpetrated on his ancestors, lost his life trying to prove his own manhood by stealing the piano back from the Sutter family. From these events, Boy Willie derives a patrilineal injunction to sell for a profit and "make something" of himself. Bereniece, by contrast, relates to the past through Mama Ola. She tells her brother: "You always talking about your daddy but you ain't never stopped to look at what his foolishness cost your mama. Seventeen years worth of cold nights and an empty bed" (52). Her identification with her mother bears directly on her conflict with Boy Willie, whom she blames for causing her own husband's death through a similar act of black macho foolishness. Hence, with the piano, she pursues a matrilineal legacy of struggle to preserve family unity and cultural continuity.

Along with his rendering of family history, Wilson reinscribes traditional constructions of black womanhood and manhood in the characters' immediate dramatic circumstances. Though her uncle, Doaker Charles, owns the home in which she and her daughter live, Berniece, in stereotypical matriarchal fashion, is the dominant figure. Working as a domestic for "a big shot down there at the steel mill" (58), she is the primary wage-earner. The paradigm of the black mammy tending to the white home while neglecting her own is reiterated in Wilson's stage directions: "The house is sparsely furnished, and although there is evidence of a woman's touch, there is a lack of warmth and vigor" ("The Setting"). By implication, her dominance has feminized Doaker, whom Wilson describes as "a tall, thin man of forty-seven, with severe features, who has for all intents and purposes retired from the world though he works full-time as a railroad cook" (1). Doaker cooks and cleans while Berniece manages and provides.

Berniece not only exerts paradimatic matriarchal dominance over the household, but presumes custody of the piano. Moreover, Wilson aligns her with forces of white oppression in witholding the piano from Boy Willie; everytime Boy Willie tries to move the piano, Sutter's ghost becomes agitated along with Berniece. In keeping with black nationalist gender ideology, black matriarchy is shown to be complicit with white supremacy in the economic and sexual emasculation of the black male.

These circumstances cast Boy Willie in the conventional masculine activist role of disrupting the stasis of the Doaker household in order to dislodge the piano. Like the archetypal Western hero, Boy Willie must slay the guardian dragon to release the treasure. However, the dynamics of racial oppression render his quest to achieve manhood even more urgent than that of traditional Anglo-European heroes, especially amid Depression hardships. Contrasting diametrically with Berniece's matriarchal posture of containment, Boy Willie personifies obstreperous ambition. He has ventured up from the South to hustle, in addition to the piano, a truckload of watermelons. After unloading a particularly large number of melons on gullible whites, he celebrates via attempted sexual conquest. He violates his sister's house rules by trying to seduce a black female love interest, Gracie, in the Doaker livingroom with degrading metaphors of auto maintenance (73). As with Dussie Mae in *Ma Rainey*, Wilson accords willing, opportunistic Gracie little more depth than a cheap, one-dimensional Jezebel. Her presence merely establishes Boy Willie's aspirations to phallocentric black masculinity.

The stereotypical dimensions of these characters are exacerbated in critical accounts of the Broadway production. Playing Boy Willie, Charles S. Dutton is described as "a force of nature on stage, a human cyclone" (Frank Rich), "a human tornado of rage" (Jack Kroll), "bristling with high spirits and irrepressible energy" (Howard Kissell), "energiz[ing] the entire production" (John Beaufort). By contrast, S. Epatha Merkerson as Berniece is characterized as "quiet and dignified holding her ground against him" (Frank Rich), playing the role "with exquisite levelheadedness" (Linda Winer) and "with imposing dignity . . . [and] great strength held in reserve" (Howard Kissell). Such adjectives further inscribe the characterizations in the ideologically loaded constructs of resolute matriarch and phallocentric hothead.

The plot resolution and implications for the main characters' futures remain consistent with these gender stereotypes. After Boy Willie loses his physical struggle with Sutter's ghost and Avery's biblical exorcism fails to rid the house of danger, Berniece marshalls her reserves of great strength to overthrow the supernatural forces of white patriarchy with which she had formerly been aligned. She breaks her seven-year moratorium on playing the piano, which she imposed on herself after her mother's death out of fear of waking the spirits. Wilson describes her effort:

> The song is found piece by piece. It is an old urge to song that is both a commandment and a plea. With each repetition it gains in strength. It is intended as an exorcism and a dressing for battle. A rustle of wind blowing across two continents. (106)

Berniece invokes the primal power of her Afrocentric matrilineal heritage extending from Old Berniece to Mama Ola. In the process, she also mentions the name of Papa Boy Charles as if to subsume Boy Willie's patrilineal injunction in her incantation. Greater than Boy Willie, greater even than Christianity, the force she summons marshalls the ghosts of the Yellow Dog who manifest in the sound of the rushing train and silence Sutter's ghost. When positioned against—instead of in complicity with—white patriarchy, black matriarchy becomes a formidable force in overcoming racial oppression.

However, linking this force inextricably to black women also shores up traditional race/gender stereotypes, like superstrong motherhood. After witnessing this ultimate manifestation of Berniece's matriarchal power, Boy Willie, heretofore a torrent of brash verbosity, exits quickly and without protest, consigning the piano to his sister. Phallocentric black masculinity is utterly defeated with no indication for a vital future of either an economic or a sexual sort. Nor are alternate constructions of masculinity presented as viable options, given Doaker's withdrawal from life, Wining Boy's drunkenness, and Avery's impotence. By contrast, there is significant indication of a vital future for triumphant black matriarchy. Berniece is passing the matrilineal legacy, now stronger than ever, to daughter Maretha, whom she is grooming to be a piano player and schoolteacher.[15] Black matriarchy has silenced Sutter's ghost and Boy Willie's argument and ensured its own future; the strongest combatant has won. The battle lines between the sexes, which are as great a threat to racial advancement as white oppression, remain as deep as ever, indelibly inscribed in the monolithic gender constructs Wilson's play perpetuates from generation to generation.

Fences

With *Fences*, Wilson brings his history of the African American experience into the late 1950s and early 1960s. The primary focus, once again, is on the male hero, Troy Maxson's, quest for manhood, with the major female character, his wife Rose, drawn primarily according to how she affirms or thwarts his endeavor. Though following a similar overarching pattern of gender relations as in the plays set in earlier decades, this work offers greater complexity in the characterization of the female lead who is accorded more consciousness than her predecessors of her own and her male cohort's motivations. Her consciousness foregrounds not only the dynamics of racism and sexism which oppress all African Americans, but those which divide them male from female. The most far-reaching and insurmountable "fences" in this play, like those in *Ma Rainey* and *Piano Lesson*, prove to be those of gender.

The masculine gender construct circumscribing Troy echoes that of Levee and Boy Willie, with the notable difference that, unlike those protagonists, ages thirty-two and thirty, respectively, Troy is middle-aged and a husband and father. While occupying these two central patriarchal roles, Troy, as a black male crushed economically and sexually under white racism, still must struggle to prove his manhood. His home and job situation stand in marked contrast to the post-war affluence of white, middle-class suburbia whose baby boom peaked in the play's beginning year of 1957. He owns his house in the impoverished inner city but not by the fruits of his own labor; only the paltry sum the government awarded his war-injured brother enabled him to buy it. But for his skin color, Troy believes he would have fulfilled the American Dream as a star professional baseball player. Otherwise unskilled and illiterate, he is consigned to the dregs of the labor force as a garbage collector. If he could not swing his bat in the major leagues, he tries to do so perpetually at the opposite sex, bragging to his buddy, Bono, "I eye all the women. I don't miss nothing. Don't never let nobody tell you Troy Maxson don't eye the women" (5). With such phallocentric aspirations, Troy is Levee and Boy Willie twenty years later, still, in the words of Frank Rich, "a volcano of rage." But his quest is even more desperate and at times more poignant than theirs because he has less time; his own death becomes a palpable presence and, eventually, a reality in the play.

Rose's responses to Troy's quest reveal her consciousness of her position as a black woman, the extremity of his obsession with black manhood, and the indelibly gendered nature of the widening divide between them. Wilson tells us: ". . . her devotion to [Troy] stems from her recognition of the possibilities of life without him: a succession of abusive men and their babies, a life of partying and running the streets, the church, or aloneness with its attendant pain and frustration" (7). Living with Troy, however, she is compelled to embrace other feminine stereotypes of wife/motherhood. She dutifully washes, cooks, and nurtures their extended family and manages Troy's meagre paycheck to ensure that the bills are paid. Because he gives her "a house to sing in," she carries the projection of his economic and sexual aspirations to transcend barriers of race and class. He tells her: "We go upstairs in that room at night . . . and I fall down on you and try to blast a hole into forever" (44). She comes to realize that he sees her not as an individual entitled to pursue her own needs but as a functionary who fulfills expected roles, including that of passageway for the realization and release of his frustrated dreams.

Two major struggles occur which highlight the gendered nature of the "fences" between husband and wife. The first transpires over the future of their son, Cory. Incarnating stereotypical motherhood, Rose selflessly nurtures her son and urges him to take the best opportunity available to him, an athletic scholarship to college. Troy, however, commands Cory to refuse the scholarship, claiming to be saving his son from the racism which kept him out of the majors. Rose tries to remind Troy that those racial barriers had already been crossed by stars like Jackie Robinson and that what excluded him was his age, then forty. But Troy will not concede to any explanation which impugns his prowess, and he blindly perpetuates the destructive cycle of abuse perpetrated on him by his own oppressed and frustrated father. In the process, he also construes Rose's defense of her son as overmothering, constellating black male fears of the castrating black matriarch. Pained by the resulting deterioration of internal relational bonds, Rose pressures Troy to build a fence around their yard in a vain attempt to keep the family together.

Ironically, Troy does not complete the fence until after his second major struggle with Rose, which proves even more divisive than the first. When Troy's mistress, Alberta, becomes pregnant, he is forced to tell Rose of the longtime affair and the impending birth of his illegitimate child. Because she has fulfilled the prescribed roles of self-sacrificing wife and mother, he expects her to understand and forgive not only that he had the affair but that he will not give up Alberta and what she does for him. He loves Rose but claims she stifles him with obligations and responsibility; with Alberta, he finds freedom and laughter. Rose defies rigid gender prescriptions to assert her own needs, demanding to know from Troy, "What about me? When's my time to enjoy life?" (80), but he has no answer. After the shocking news of Alberta's death in childbirth, Rose again tries to reach her husband to no avail. Retreating into his own rage and grief, he pushes her away, insisting "Just give me some room to breathe" (83).

All chances for reconciliation are shattered when Troy brings his baby girl home from the hospital and tells her loudly enough for Rose to hear: "A man's got to do what's right for him. I ain't sorry for nothing I done. It felt right in my heart" (86). This statement reflects his utter self-absorption in his desperate and futile quest for manhood and inability to take the hand that Rose tried to extend to him across the now gaping gender divide. Rose agrees to raise the baby but permanently withdraws from Troy into an impenetrable fortress of black matriarchy with the devastating line: "From right now . . . this child got a mother. But you a womanless man" (86). The fence Rose had Troy build to keep him in now shuts him out.

Though Rose and Troy never reconcile, their children come together in a highly symbolic encounter in the final scene which takes place the morning of Troy's funeral seven years later. Still in her nightgown, Raynell emerges from the house to greet the day and tend her newly planted garden. Cory, his manner transformed, returns from a six-year stint in the marines and announces his engagement to be married. He has become a man in highly conventional, dominant cultural terms, and he asserts his new manhood by refusing to attend his abusive father's funeral. His refusal catalyzes Rose's long self-reflective speech foregrounding the gender dynamics that divided her so irreconcilably from her husband. Near the end, she tells her son: "I didn't know that to keep up his strength I had to give up little pieces of mine. . . . But that's what life offered me in the way of being a woman and I took it" (105). Cory is evidently moved by his mother's reflections. Honoring his father's memory, he joins his sister in singing Troy's favorite song about his old dog Blue.

The play ends in an apparent family reconciliation, but it is only momentary; signs of dissolution abound. Lyons' marriage fell apart four years ago because of his abortive and often illegal attempts to prove himself a man; Bono remains a lonely widower; and Gabriel is largely confined to a hospital. Though Cory plans to get married, his military experience may destine him for the American debacle in Vietnam which would exploit and kill so many members of his race. The only sure and hopeful future, symbolized in Raynell and her garden, rests with the female characters. As Rose tells Cory, Raynell renewed her life after the gulf between her and Troy became irreparable "like she was all them babies I had wanted and never had" (105). The line reinscribes Rose in black matriarchy and black cultural continuity, once again, in the mother/daughter bond. The "fences" of gender in this play, finally, do not come down.

Two Trains Running

Traditional patterns of black gender construction evident to varying degrees throughout the Wilson canon are well represented in his last play to reach Broadway, and the most recent in his historical chronology, *Two Trains Running*. The play is set in the Hill District of Pittsburgh in 1969, and the two trains running metaphorically to and from this place, Wilson tells us, are life and death. Each of us rides them both, he claims. In doing so, his female characters remain locked in stereotypical bipolar constructions of black femininity: castrating matriarch/maternal savior and Jezebel/madonna. As in previous works, these constructions materialize in relation to male characters' quests for black manhood intensified throughout African American history by circumstances of racial oppression. Such circumstances loom large in the Hill District as the city threatens to tear down the block of mostly black-run businesses, including Memphis Lee's diner, where the play's visible action transpires. Though the cast of seven restaurant regulars includes only one woman, the waitress Risa, other paradigmatic constructions of femininity are invoked through various male characters' oral histories of their respective quests.

The restaurant owner Memphis and wealthy landlord West articulate views of women framed within the dialectic of castrating matriarch/maternal savior. The feeling of freedom Memphis says he experienced after his mother's death testifies to his perception of her as oppressive and emasculating (58). His attendant preoccupation with phallocentric masculinity is evident in his sexual identification with his mule, murdered and dismembered at the hands of white men: "One of them reached down, grabbed hold of his dick and cut that off" (60).

Castration anxiety continues to inform his view of the opposite sex. He proclaims that Risa "ain't natural" because she "don't want no man" and scarred her legs to deter men's sexual advances. If she cut herself, he fears she may cut him and so discounts her as a potential sex object (50). Seeing women as either actual or potential castrating matriarchs, he behaves tyrannically toward them and is utterly blind to their needs and responses. After he barks a few orders at Risa, it is easy to understand why, to his bafflement, his wife of twenty-two years left him abruptly one morning when he asked her to get up and bake him some bread.

West, who, like Memphis, is middle-aged, currently single, and the owner of his own business, provides a diametrically opposite view of femininity. His lucrative primary occupation as funeral director is an extended metaphor marking his deep state of mourning for the wife he adored. Unlike Memphis, West not only loved her, according to Holloway, he understood her; "After she died West had nothing to live for but money" (52). The narrative implies, however, that he understood her primarily in terms of what she did for him, not for who she may have been as a person. Incarnating archetypal aspects of maternal savior, she provided him with his entire life force and ability to feel, to the extent that he is now literally preoccupied with death and always wears gloves. Though constructed as positive in the play, the role in which West cast his wife was ultimately no less narrow and demanding of the woman's self-sacrifice than that in which Memphis cast his.

Wolf and Sterling offer views of women reflecting the Jezebel/Madonna dichotomy. Members of a younger generation than that of Memphis and West and less settled in life, these black males energetically pursue an ethos of phallocentric masculinity. Both try to prove their manhood by brash gambling and sexual conquest. As his name suggests, Wolf is particularly predatory. He claims to have two women in Atlanta, one of whom puts aside her five other men to accommodate him (62). His conquest mentality compensates for deep-seated fear underlying constructions of the trecherous Jezebel. He tells Sterling and Holloway: ". . . when you lay down with her, you trusting her with your life. You lay down you got to close your eyes. It wouldn't be nothing for somebody to walk up and slit your throat." (70) With danger evidently comes excitement; Wolf has been trying to add the *bona fide* razor artist Risa to his list of conquests, but she has rebuffed him.

Within the phallocentric value system, Wolf makes winning Risa the ultimate test of manhood for Sterling. Just out of prison and eager to build a new life, Sterling wants to make Risa more a Madonna than a Jezebel, an inspirational icon of personal and racial uplift. Presenting her with flowers he stole from a dead man, he says: "I asked God to send me an angel. He said he couldn't do that but he'd send me a teasing brown . . . I wanna find out if you her" (59). Though Sterling values her as a positive force in his life, she is no less an object than in Wolf's view. He asserts: "Get Risa to be my woman and I'll be alright. That's all a man need is a pocketful of money, a cadillac and a good woman" (67). He expects her to relinquish her home and job at the diner and follow him to Vegas, where he plans to make his fortune at the casinos.

The positive poles of both dialectics of black womanhood inscribed in the male characters' narratives converge on the construction of Aunt Ester. From Holloway we learn that she is 322 years old, old enough by Wilson's calculation to link the current (1969) generation of African Americans with that of their first ancestors to arrive on American soil in slave ships. As such, she is perhaps Wilson's most explicit example to date of black maternal figures functioning as forces of cultural cohesion and continuity. Her affirmative matriarchal power is so great that she transformed an ordinary minister into Prophet Samuel, founder of the wealthy, influential First African Congregational Kingdom. His transformation has accorded him the high-rolling status of spiritual guru and sexual impressario above the white man's law. Not surprisingly, Holloway persuades Sterling to pay Aunt Ester a visit; her benediction promises passage on the life/manhood train.

In addition to the narratives of the male characters, Wilson also conveys a powerful ideological message about gender through Risa, the play's only female character. Her most outstanding characteristic, one to which almost every personage in the play refers at least once, is the fact that she has cut herself. Advising Sterling to play the number 781, she divulges that she has 7 scars on one leg and 8 on the other, but she will not say where the 1 is (55). Her modesty suggests she has mutilated her genitals, a supposition consistent with Memphis's claim that her self-inflicted scars have rendered her "unnatural," that is, "unwomanly."

On one hand, this is a compelling gesture of self-assertion and defiance of stereotypes within which traditional perceptions of black women would confine her. Refusing to be seen chiefly as a degraded sex object, Holloway tells us, "she figure if she made her legs ugly that would force everybody to look at her and see what kind of personality she is" (50). Though male characters' continued phallocentric responses to her indicate the futility of her strategy, she persists in her defiance, challenging Memphis on his claim that he treated his wife "like she was the Queen of Sheba," and taking her time filling his imperious orders.[16] She has also pledged allegiance to Prophet Samuel and, by extension, to the matriarchal deity, Aunt Ester.

On the other hand, her self-mutilation also indicates her extreme internalization of the racist, sexist ideology of black female degradation. Her behavior reflects the phenomenon of black female self-hatred described by black feminists, an abhorrence of and desire to destroy the black body which disqualifies her from meeting standards of ideal femininity under white supremacist capitalist patriarchy (hooks 10; Collins 79–80). In addition to economic necessity, internalized degradation and self-hatred keep her working for the abusive male chauvinist tyrant, Memphis. These forces also compel her to compromise her defiant sense of selfhood by agreeing to go to Vegas with Sterling, a man who represents much of what she had eschewed in the opposite sex.

Significantly, in falling for Sterling, Risa accompanies him to festivities marking the birthday of Malcolm X. Historicizing the play with this plot device, Wilson inscribes both characters within black nationalist gender ideology. Sterling's phallocentric masculine ethos is elevated via worship of the civil rights leader lauded for giving African Americans their "manhood," while Risa is destined to become "man's field to produce his nation."[17] She betrays not only her independence but her matriarchal allegiance to Aunt Ester in honoring a martyred prophet whose faith was rooted in the vehemently patriarchal Islamic teachings of Elijah Muhammed. Through association with Malcolm X, the romantic relationship between Sterling and Risa, rather than healing the gender divisions endemic to Wilson's racial history, indicates victory of the phallocentric black male over the potentially castrating black female.

Aligning Sterling with Malcolm X, Wilson realizes the vision of potential black manhood heralded in 1911 with the vibrantly promising but amorphous "shining man" nurtured by Mattie Campbell. Sterling's physical and spiritual conquest of Risa in 1969 marks the black male's triumph over feminine forces of emasculation embodied in Ma Rainey, Berniece, and Rose which defeated Levee, Boy Willie, and Troy during the intervening decades. While acts of white supremacist capitalist patriarchal oppression inform the historical context of the action and occasionally intrude directly on the plot, the stage is filled far more with the hero's struggle against these matriarchal figures than with his battles with white oppressors. The terms and course of the conflict follow patterns of race/gender construction molded during slavery, institutionalized in the Moynihan Report, and "fired in the kiln of black nationalism": as a means of economic and sexual emasculation of black males, white supremacism has both fostered and degraded entrenched black matriarchy which the hero, having internalized the phallocentric ethos of the dominant culture, must overthrow to become a man and gain control over his own destiny.

The tyranny and eventual overthrow of black matriarchy charted through Wilson's history cycle reinforce dominant gender ideology and contribute to the author's canonization and commercial success. Through the poetics of oral history, the playwright commodifies phallocentric black masculinity and renders black matriarchs alternately castrating and nurturing of the hero's attempts to self-actualize. This representational strategy shifts the blame for African American racial ills from white capitalist patriarchy onto black women, an ideological message familiar and palatable to the white-male-dominated critical establishment and middle-class audiences. As the black matriarchy thesis countered the feminist challenge of the 1960s, so Wilson's ambitious history of black matriarchal overthrow diffuses mounting dominant cultural anxieties surrounding powerful women across racial lines during the 1980s and 90s.

NOTES

1. See, for example, Michele Barrett, "Ideology and the Cultural Production of Gender," in *Feminist Criticism and Social Change*, eds. Judith Newton and Deborah Rosenfelt (New York: Methuen, 1985), 65–85; and Teresa de Lauretis, "Desire in Narrative," *Alice Doesn't: Feminism, Semiotics, Cinema* (Bloomington: Indiana University Press, 1981), 103–57.

2. In 1988, August Wilson became the first African American dramatist to have two plays running simultaneously on Broadway, *Fences* and *Joe Turner's Come and Gone*. Jack Kroll, "August Wilson's Come to Stay," *Newsweek*, Vol. 111, No. 15, April 11, 1988, 82.

3. This was the fate, for example, of Michele Wallace's *Black Macho and the Myth of the Superwoman* (1979), which exposed sexism within the ranks of the civil rights movement. See hooks 98–101.

4. Dates in parentheses refer to the years in which each play opened on Broadway.

5. Daniel Patrick Moynihan, *The Negro Family: The Case for National Action* (Washington, D.C.: U.S. Government Printing Office, 1965).

6. Pauli Murray, "The Liberation of Black Women," in *Voices of the New Feminism*, ed. Mary Lou Thompson, 87–102 (Boston: Beacon, 1970), 89, qtd. in Collins, 86.

7. Haki Madhubuti, *Black Men: Obsolete, Single, Dangerous?: Afrikan American Families in Transition: Essays in Discovery, Solution and Hope* (Chicago: Third World Press, 1990), qtd. in hooks 109.

8. Barbara Christian, *Black Feminist Criticism, Perspectives on Black Women Writers* (New York: Pergamon, 1985), 234, qtd. in Collins, 116.

9. See also Jacqueline Dowd Hall, "The Mind that Burns in Each Body: Women, Rape, and Racial Violence," in *Powers of Desire: The Politics of Sexuality*, eds. Ann Snitow, Christine Stansell, and Sharon Thompson, 329–49 (New York: Monthly Review Press, 1983), especially 333.

10. Barbara Christian, "An Angle of Seeing: Motherhood in Buchi Emecheta's *Joys of Motherhood* and Alice Walker's *Meridian*," in *Black Feminist Criticism*, ed. Barbara Christian (New York: Pergamon, 1985), 214, qtd. in Collins 1987, 4.

11. Elijah Muhammed, *Message to the Black Man in America* (Chicago: Muhammed Mosque of Islam #2, 1965).

12. Imamu Amiri Baraka, *Mwanamke Mwananchi* (The Nationalist Woman) by Numininas of Committee for United New Ark, 1971, 7, qtd. in Sizemore, 7.

13. For alternate and more detailed readings of religion in this and other works by Wilson, see Sandra G. Shannon, "The Good Christian's Come and Gone: The Shifting Role of Christianity in August Wilson's Plays," *Melus*, Vol. 16, No. 3 (Fall 1989–1990): 127–144.

14. bell hooks notes in her analysis of black manhood: ". . . it must be emphasized that the black men who are most worried about castration and emasculation are those who have completely absorbed white patriarchal definitions of masculinity" (93).

15. For a fuller discussion of the mother/daughter bond as a source of African American cultural strength and continuity, see Collins 1987, 3–10.

16. According to reviews of the Broadway production, this aspect of Risa's character was emphasized by actor Cynthia Martells and director Lloyd Richards. Clive Barnes, for example, described Martells' movements as "slow to the point of stop" in "'Trains' Doesn't Run," *New York Post*, 14 April 1992.

17. The line about the black woman's proper destiny in the Nation of Islam is taken from Elijah Muhammad's *Message to the Black Man in America* (1965), qtd. in Sizemore 6.

WORKS CITED

Barnes, Clive. "Fiery 'Fences.'" *New York Post*, 27 March 1987.

New York Critics' Theatre Reviews [cited hereafter as *NYCTR*] (1987): 316.

———. "'Piano Lesson' Hits All the Right Keys." *New York Post*, 17 April 1990. *NYCTR* (1990): 325–26.

———. "'Trains' Doesn't Run." *New York Post*, 14 April 1992. *NYCTR* (1992): 138.

Beaufort, John. "Plight of 1920s Blacks Superbly Portrayed in New Wilson Drama." *Christian Science Monitor*, 16 October 1984. *NYCTR* (1984): 198.

———. "'Fences' Probes Life of Blacks in '50s." *Christian Science Monitor,* 27 March 1987. *NYCTR* (1987): 318–19.

Collins, Patricia Hill. *Black Feminist Thought: Knowledge, Consciousness, and the Politics of Empowerment.* London, New York: Routledge, 1991.

———. "The Meaning of Motherhood in Black Culture and Black Mother/Daughter Relationships." *Sage,* Vol. 4, No. 2 (Fall 1987): 3–10.

Dance, Daryl C. "Black Eve or Madonna?: A Study of the Antithetical Views of the Mother in Black American Literature." In *Sturdy Black Bridges: Visions of Black Women in Literature,* eds. Roseann P. Bell, Bettye J. Parker, and Beverly Guy-Sheftall. Garden City, NY: Doubleday, 1979, 123–32.

Davis, Angela. *Women, Race, and Class.* New York: Random House, 1981.

Dill, Bonnie Thornton. "The Dialectics of Black Womanhood." *Signs: Journal of Women in Culture and Society* Vol. 4, No. 3 (1979): 543–55.

Freedman, Samuel G. "A Voice from the Streets." *New York Times Magazine,* 10 June 1987, 36, 40, 49, 70.

Gilkes, Cheryl Townsend. "From Slavery to Social Welfare: Racism and the Control of Black Women." In *Class, Race, and Sex: The Dynamics of Social Control,* eds. Amy Swerdlow and Hanna Lessinger. Boston: G.K. Hall, 1983, 288–300.

Henry, William A. III. "Righteous in His Own Backyard." *Time,* 6 April 1987. NYCTR (1987): 320.

hooks, bell. *Black Looks: Race and Representation.* Boston: South End, 1992.

Hornby, Richard. Review of *Joe Turner's Come and Gone. Hudson Review* (Autumn 1988) 45: 518.

———. Review of *Fences. Hudson Review* (Autumn 1987) 40: 470–72.

King, Mae C. "The Politics of Sexual Stereotypes." *The Black Scholar* (March-April 1973): 12–23.

Kissell, Howard. "'Ma Rainey's Black Bottom.'" *Women's Wear Daily.* 12 October 1984. *NYCTR* (1984): 200.

———. "One Man's Failure Is Another Man's Smash." *New York Daily News,* 27 March 1987. *NYCTR* (1987): 315.

———. "A Bitter 'Lesson.'" *New York Daily News,* 17 April 1990. *NYCTR* (1990): 324–25.

Kroll, Jack. "So Black and Blue." *Newsweek,* 22 October 1984. *NYCTR* (1984): 199.

————. "Nine Innings Against the Devil." *Newsweek*, 6 April 1987. *NYCTR* (1987): 320.

Lorde, Audre. *Sister Outsider*. Trumansberg, NY: The Crossing Press, 1984.

O'Neale, Sondra. "Inhibiting Midwives, Usurping Creators: The Struggling Emergence of Black Women in American Fiction." In *Feminist Studies/Critical Studies*, ed. Teresa de Lauretis. Bloomington: Indiana University Press, 1986, 139–156.

Rich, Frank. "Stage: Wilson's *Ma Rainey's* Opens." *New York Times*, 12 October 1984. *NYCTR* (1984): 196–97.

————. "Theater: Family Ties in Wilson's 'Fences.'" *New York Times*, 27 March 1987. *NYCTR* (1987): 314–15.

————. "The Clash of Cultures." *New York Times*, 27 March 1988. *NYCTR* (1988): 251–52.

————. "A Family Confronts Its History in August Wilson's 'Piano Lesson.'" *New York Times*, 17 April 1990. *NYCTR* (1990): 322–23.

————. "The Long Wait: August Wilson's *Ma Rainey's Black Bottom*." *Black American Literature Forum*, Vol. 25, No. 1 (Spring 1991): 135–46.

————. "August Wilson Reaches the '60s with Witnesses from a Distance." *New York Times*, 14 April 1992. *NYCTR* (1992): 139–40.

Shannon, Sandra. G. "The Good Christian's Come and Gone: The Shifting Role of Christianity in August Wilson's Plays." *Melus*, Vol. 16, No. 3 (Fall 1989–1990): 127–42.

Simon, John. "'Two Trains Running.'" *New York Magazine*, 27 April 1992. *NYCTR* (1992): 135.

Sizemore, Barbara A. "Sexism and the Black Male." *The Black Scholar* (March-April 1973): 2–11.

Wallach, Allan. "Fenced In by a Lifetime of Resentments." New York Newsday, 27 March 1987. NYCTR (1987): 319.

Wallace, Michelle. *Black Macho and the Myth of the Superwoman*. New York: Dial Press, 1978.

————. *Invisibility Blues*. London and New York: Verso, 1990.

Watt, Douglas. "'Ma Rainey's': Mostly, It Swings." *New York Daily News*, 12 October 1984. *NYCTR* (1984): 197.

————. "'Fences Is All Over the Lot." *New York Daily News*, 3 April 1987. *NYCTR* (1987): 316–17.

———. "Star Key to 'Piano Lesson.'" *New York Daily News*, 20 April 1990. *NYCTR* (1990): 324.

Weales, Gerald. Review of *Ma Rainey's Black Bottom*. *Georgia Review* (Fall 1985) 39: 622–23.

Wilson, August. *Fences*. Introd. Lloyd Richards. New York and Scarborough, Ontario: NAL, 1986.

———. *Joe Turner's Come and Gone*. New York and Scarborough, Ontario: NAL, 1988.

———. *Ma Rainey's Black Bottom*. In *Black Thunder: An Anthology of Contemporary African American Drama*. Ed. and Introd. William B. Branch. New York: Penguin, 1992.

———. *The Piano Lesson*. New York: Plume, 1990.

———. *Two Trains Running*. *Theater*, Vol. 22, No. I (Fall/Winter 1990–1991): 40–72.

Wilson, Edwin. "Theater: Wilson's 'Fences' on Broadway . . ." *Wall Street Journal*, 31 March 1987. *NYCTR* (1987): 317–18.

———. "Theater: A Lesson in Life." *Wall Street Journal*, 18 December 1987. *NYCTR* (1987): 328.

Winer, Linda. "August Wilson's Haunting 'Piano Lesson.'" *New York Newsday*, 17 April 1990. *NYCTR* (1990): 323–24.

———. "Grappling with their Stations in Life." *New York Newsday*, 14 April 1992. *NYCTR* (1992): 136.

Developing His Song
August Wilson's Fences

Joan Fishman

It is fascinating to explore one writer's process of playwriting, and the work of August Wilson is prime material for the study of the movement of a play from its first to final draft. Wilson's play *Fences* stands as an exemplary product of the developmental process functioning in contemporary American theater. Wilson developed *Fences* over more than five years and through more than five drafts. This play has had readings and productions at institutions which are pillars of contemporary American playwrighting. It had its first reading in 1982 at New Dramatists in New York. In July of 1983, *Fences* was developed at the Eugene O'Neill Theater Center in Waterford, Connecticut. In April of 1985, *Fences* opened at the Yale Repertory Theater in New Haven, Connecticut, and, later that year, it moved to the Goodman Theater in Chicago for further modification. *Fences* then played in Seattle and San Francisco, and it opened at the 46th Street Theater on Broadway in March of 1987.

The text for *Fences* did not change in isolation and—although it would be difficult to assign a specific change to a specific individual—directors, actors, designers, lay people and professional critics have all influenced the work. Constraints of the commercial theater also impacted on its development. *Fences* ran 3.5 hours when it played at the O'Neill Center. Wilson cut significantly before rehearsals at the Yale Repertory Theater, but another 30 minutes had to go to bring the play to the 2 hours and 15 minute playing time which was considered more appropriate.

Over months and years, Wilson's plays were drafted and
redrafted, expanded and cut through hours of rehearsals and
performances.

The development of *Fences* is a study in refining the level
of responsibility in each of the characters, responsibility both to
themselves and to those around them. As Wilson clarifies the
themes of his play, he explores the balance and conflict between
the characters' pursuits of their personal goals and their
commitment to family.

Examining the changes in the individual characters in
successive drafts of *Fences* reveals Wilson's continued redefining
of the issues for himself and his efforts to balance these issues
through the actions of the characters. To follow these changes is
to examine both the progressive deepening exploration of a
theme by a playwright and a progressive refining of the theme's
presentation.

August Wilson began writing *Fences* in 1982, immediately
following his work at the O'Neill Center for the development of
his play *Ma Rainey's Black Bottom*. Wilson, poet recently turned
playwright, was eager for interaction with theater professionals
and had submitted four plays to the O'Neill Center before *Ma
Rainey* was accepted. Wilson's experience with *Ma Rainey* was
very positive; it was scheduled for production at the Yale
Repertory Theater and there was talk of Broadway. But Wilson
became worried about being a "one-play playwright." He
remembers thinking "What do I do now?" (Freedman 80). And
so, on the bus heading home from the O'Neill Center, Wilson
wrote the first scene of *Fences*.

Fences focuses on the family of Troy Maxson. Born in
poverty in the South, Troy has fought hard throughout his life.
He fought to use his talent for baseball to earn his living and was
pushed back by the white establishment. He fought the
pressures of the street but, nonetheless, landed in prison. Now,
in his middle years, Troy is fighting to uphold the lessons of
responsibility he has learned and striving for balance with his
wife, Rose, his brother, Gabe, and his sons, Cory and Lyons. But
the more he struggles to stand upright, the more he stumbles as
his dreams for his family clash with his own personal desires
and the desires of those around him. In his pursuit of a more

stable life for his son, Troy denies Cory the one thing he desires most: the opportunity to play college football. And in pursuit of responsibility to himself and the drive to feel more alive, Troy has an affair and brings home the other woman's child to Rose, following Alberta's death in childbirth.

Wilson's inspiration to write *Fences* was partially the result of commercial pressures. While Wilson's previous play, *Ma Rainey's Black Bottom*, achieved much critical and box office success, the play was criticized by conventional critics for the non-narrative aspects of its structure and for its bifurcated focus on two equally prominent characters. Wilson reacted to the criticism as a direct challenge, and he responded: "*Fences* was me sitting down and saying, okay here is a play with a large central character" (Devries 25).

But the play has strong personal ties as Troy, this central character, seems drawn from people in Wilson's life. Wilson was abandoned by his natural father but found strong guidance from his stepfather, David Bedford. Bedford's personal history is akin to Troy's story. Following a disappointment in sports, a serious brush with crime brought lessons of responsibility and a more conventional post-prison life. Bedford had been a football star in high school and had hopes that a football scholarship would lead to a career in medicine. No scholarship was offered. So he robbed a store to get money to go to school, killed a man, and spent 23 years in prison. When he came out, Bedford met Wilson's mother and began working in the city sewer department. Bedford died in 1969 when Wilson was 24.

However, *Fences* is not autobiographical. Wilson writes, "There are no incidents in the play that are specific to my life. [Rather] the cultural context of the play is my life" (Tallmer 28). And in this cultural context, Wilson explores themes close to his heart. "We have been told so many times how irresponsible we are as black males that I try and present positive images of responsibility. I had to write a character who is responsible and likes the idea of family" (Devries 25). "White America looks at black America in this glancing manner. They pass right by the Troy Maxsons of the world and never stop to look at them. They talk about niggers as lazy and shiftless. Well, here's a man with responsibilities as prime to his life" (Watlington 109).

Wilson started *Fences* with the image of a man standing in his yard with a baby in his arms, perhaps an homage to the great American painter Romare Bearden's *Continuities,* which features this same image. What followed the expansion of a single image and early writings on a bus ride were draft after draft of the play. These drafts continually honed the actions and attitudes of the characters as Wilson explored issues of responsibility to destiny versus family. It is Wilson's approach to the issues of responsibility which ultimately makes the play universal and allows him to examine issues which cross cultural lines.

Wilson considers Romare Bearden his artistic mentor, and he was heavily influenced by Bearden's goal of exploring "in terms of the life [he] knew best those things which are common to all culture" (Moyers 55). Although *Fences* is specific to black America, focusing on a black family molded and shaped by the forces of racism, Wilson offers universal husband-wife conflict and father-son conflict. But even more cross-cultural are the play's internal conflicts. As his characters wrestle with their individual decisions, Wilson explores the internal pressuring forces which influence decisions of responsibility and the frequent inability of another person, even a family member, to understand the choice of a spouse or a parent.

In the first drafts of the play, Wilson presents Troy as his standard of responsibility; he sets up the character of Lyons, Troy's son by his first marriage, as a dramatic counterpoint to Troy. Lyons is trying to make a life as a musician, but he cannot make ends meet. He often arrives on Troy's payday to borrow a few dollars, and it is during the exchange which surrounds this ritual, the only opportunity for interaction between these characters, that the Lyons role is continually redefined by Wilson.

Early in the first draft of the play, Troy defines Lyons for us as lazy and shiftless; although Troy's opinion may not be objective, it is our only reference for Lyons. Wilson sets up the comparison between the two men by showing Troy—having just arrived home from work, tired and burdened—handing over money to the free-spirited Lyons.

But for Wilson, the issue of responsibility had been made too obvious here; the scale weighing the two men is tipped too heavily in Troy's favor. Thus, as Wilson moved from his first to second draft of the play, he began to make Lyons more responsible. Wilson deleted Troy's "lazy and shiftless" description along with an additional line about Lyons being on welfare. He also dropped Troy's comment that if Lyons doesn't know by now how to get by in life "what hope is there for [him]?" (I:16). Wilson continued this tack as he proceeded through his rewrites. In a later version, Troy's derogatory comments are cut back further. Deleted is Troy's question "What about them rogues you be running in the street with . . . them dopeheads?" (I:15) Wilson also changed Lyons' age from 37 to 34, allowing him a little more time yet to grow fully into manhood.

Lyons' pursuit of a career in music is one of the first arenas for Wilson's examination of responsibility to personal destiny versus family. Early in his work, Wilson seems to be less supportive of the choice to pursue destiny at the cost of family. In his initial vision, Wilson made Lyons more cavalier in his decision to be a musician, and Lyons' success was modest. But as the drafts of the play progress, Wilson lent weight to the validity of the pursuit of Lyons' dream by making Lyons more successful at his music. In an early version, Lyons speaks vaguely of playing somewhere; in later versions, Lyons mentions specifically that he is playing at an established club, "The Grill." In the final draft, acknowledgment of Lyons' success comes from outside as Troy's friend Bono, who has seen in the papers that Lyons is playing at "The Grill," comments that you have to be good to play there. Although ultimately Lyons' pursuits will not provide a stable career, at this point Lyons' choice is more validated.

Thus Wilson has established the pursuit of personal destiny as not without merit. However, Wilson continues to factor in the issue of financial responsibility. Music does not support Lyons. He continues to borrow from Troy. But again Wilson moved to a position of greater support for Lyons as the drafts progress.

In all the versions of the script, Lyons comes to Troy to borrow money on Troy's payday. In the first draft of the play, Lyons returns the second payday to borrow again. But as Wilson moved into later drafts, Lyons returns on the second Friday to return the money he previously borrowed. Although he will borrow the same money again in the future, the return is a very important gesture and a significant change in the character in that Lyons not only has the money but chooses to return it.

Connected with his financial responsibility is Lyons' familial responsibility. In his exploration of this aspect of the character, through the relationship of Lyons with his wife, Bonnie (whom we never see), Wilson again moved away from his original, more negative image of Lyons to one more overtly upright, and then to one of compromise. In the first draft, when Rose invites Lyons to stay for dinner, he responds that he has to get home to Bonnie. Here Troy comments "Listen to that nigger. He got ten dollars in his pocket . . . time Bonnie see him it be two o'clock in the morning. Talking about he got to get home" (I:50).

In order to eliminate this denigrating impression, Wilson dropped any reference here to Bonnie in the next draft; Lyons cannot stay for dinner because he must pick up "his horn" and get down to the club. But Wilson had now avoided the conflict by trading Bonnie's place for that of the music; thus responsibility to destiny and family are not in conflict. So Wilson returned to Bonnie. In the version developed at the O'Neill Center, Wilson reintroduced Bonnie at this juncture but makes Lyons more responsible than in the first draft: Lyons leaves to pick up his wife and head down to the club.

Perhaps at this point Wilson felt he had not been true to his original vision and that to some degree the thematic tension had been lost in that Lyons' internal conflict had been mollified. Thus in the final version, Rose tells Lyons that Bonnie called to say he should pick her up. Later, Rose reminds Lyons of his responsibility; she, like the audience, is unsure that Lyons will remember. The ambiguity successfully addresses Wilson's desire to create only a potentially more responsible Lyons.

Through the relationship of Troy to his sons, Wilson explores the influence of a father on a child despite the child's efforts to thwart this influence. Lyons' effort to separate himself from Troy became clearer as the play progresses. In the first versions, Troy generally criticizes Lyons' choice not to work, and Lyons responds that music helps him to get up in the morning and find his place in the world. The argument is too general to point to Lyons' fundamental effort to be different from his father. In the Yale Repertory Theater version, the argument becomes more pointed as Lyons denies his father's lifestyle:

> Troy: Why ain't you working?
>
> Lyons: Aw Pop, You know I can't find no decent job . . .
>
> Troy: . . . Get you on the rubbish if you want to work . . .
>
> Lyons: Naw, Pop . . . thanks. That ain't for me. I don't wanna be carrying nobody's rubbish. I don't wanna be punching nobody's time clock.
>
> Troy: What's the matter—you too good to carry rubbish? You too lazy to work and you wanna know why you ain't got what I got. (IV:44)

With both his sons, Troy tries to promote reponsibility to family over responsibility to personal pursuits. And when faced with the young men's instincts to make the opposite choice, Troy denies his influence. He tells Rose that she's been "mothering" Cory too much, and he tells Lyons that he was "raised wrong." Troy chooses here to abdicate his responsibility completely for his sons' behavior. But in the final version, Wilson affords Lyons the opportunity to make a statement on Troy's irresponsibility regarding Lyon's upbringing.

> Lyons: If you wanted to change me, you should have been there when I was growing up. I come by to see you . . . ask for ten dollars and you want to talk about how I was raised. You don't know nothing about how I was raised (V:19).

Troy does not respond. Ultimately it becomes clear through Troy's actions that his sons are following in his footsteps.

Wilson moved consistently from a more glaring contrast between Lyons and Troy to the revelation of greater, though unacknowledged, similarity between them. The two men believe through most of the play that they are quite different. But Lyons' life will follow much like Troy's life. As young men, both pursued what they believed to be their personal destiny at great cost to themselves and those around them; Lyons' inability to make a life in music and Troy's inability to make a life in baseball led to loss of a first marriage and to prison. Later in life, they settle down, a result of their own failures combined with a greater understanding of the need to make different choices in order to survive. In the final version of the play, Lyons echoes one of his father's mottos and he tells his half brother "You got to take the crooked with the straights" (V:94). Although he has come to appreciate that one must address all that life demands, he, like his father, will still never deny the feeding of their life force—music for Lyons and a sexual rejuvenation for Troy.

Troy's relationship with and responsibility to his second son, Cory, whom he has raised, is a vital part of the play. A high school senior, Cory has been recruited to play football. But Troy will not sign the papers to permit this. Although it would be Cory's choice to pursue his future in sports, Troy, as the father of a minor, is in a position to make the choice for him. Wilson sees Troy as "trying to prepare his son to rassle with the world the father knows is out there; he doesn't want his son to follow in his footsteps" (Christianson 12).

Although Wilson presents Cory's position sympathetically, he supports Troy's decision: "When blacks went to universities on athletic scholarships, they were in fact exploited. Very few got an education. Troy is correct when he tells the kid that the white man ain't gon' let you get nowhere with that football. As a man born in 1904 and illiterate he's telling his son to get a job so he won't have to carry garbage" (Palmer 47).

Despite Wilson's ultimate support for Troy's decision, he fully understands its negative impact on Cory. This was an important element for exploration when Wilson set out to write the play: "My generation knew very little about their parents. Your parents didn't tell you everything; many times they didn't mention their past, and this led to misunderstandings. Children didn't realize why their parents seemed so cruel at times" (Christianson 13).

Cory does not understand Troy's actions, and his response is to cut off communication. Wilson makes a very strong choice in the play by having Cory lie to his father. Cory tells Troy that he continues to hold his job at the A&P grocery, but the demands of high school football have made him quit. Cory's irresponsible behavior is partially the result of imitative behavior—an inherited tendency to pursue responsibility to personal goals over responsibility to family needs—and partially a response to Troy's denial of Cory's opportunity in sports. Having established this serious act of irresponsibility, however, Wilson was undecided about Cory's other actions as he took into account the tendency of the audience to balance Troy's decision against Cory's behavior.

In the first draft, Cory does his chores reluctantly, and he skips school. But it seemed to Wilson that Cory's right to pursue his dreams needed to be supported by behavior more deserving of reward. So from here, Wilson moved him to the other end of the spectrum as the helpful Cory fulfills all of his mother's demands. But this detail tipped the scale too far in his favor and undercut the strength of his rebellion in response to Troy's action. In later drafts, Cory again neglects his chores. In the final version, he also resumes skipping school.

Cory's responsibility to his father and Troy's responsibility to his son are central to the play. As Wilson worked on *Fences,* he labored over the extent of this relationship. In the first version of the play, there is an extended scene between Cory and Troy in which they discuss the purchase of a new television set. Cory doesn't understand why they can't buy one, and Troy tries to explain the financial running of a household. The scene concludes with Troy offering to pay for half of the television set if Cory comes up with the other half. Here we have an opportunity to see father and son interact in a nonconfrontational manner, a rarity in the play, and also to see Troy exercising fatherly responsibility beyond feeding and clothing his son.

During work at the O'Neill Center, this section of the play was effectively moved from the second to the first half of the play where it serves as groundwork to inform the later conflicts between Troy and Cory. At the Yale Repertory Theater, the entire section was dropped from the play in an effort to shorten the work.

But the omission of the exchange between Troy and Cory left too big a gap in the portrayal of Troy's exercising of familial responsibility. At the conclusion of the play in all the drafts, Cory complains of a lack of understanding and emotional support from Troy, and he provokes Troy by asking what his father ever gave to him. Troy responds: "Them feet and bones. That pumping heart. I give you more than anybody else is ever gonna give you" (V:86).

In providing life itself and then the basic necessities to maintain that life, Troy has, in his eyes, fulfilled his obligation to his son, and he is angry with Cory's implication that he has somehow failed. Without the long scene between Cory and Troy in which we witness a productive exchange, we see only that Troy has provided the bare bones and can less eagerly support Troy's vision of familial responsibility. With the reinclusion of the television scene in the final version, and its accompanying advice by Troy, it is clear that Troy has made some effort to offer intangible sustenance to his son, despite the limitations of his personality. In the final version, Wilson also uses this scene for Troy to explain his decision regarding recruitment more extensively. In earlier drafts, Troy had challenged Cory in anger to give up football: "You go on and get your book learning where you can learn to do something besides carry people's garbage" (I:28). In the final version, Troy's attitude is more quiet and his speech intended to be more inspirational:

> You go on and get your book learning so you can work yourself up in that A&P or learn how to fix cars or build houses or something, get you a trade. That way you have something can't nobody take away from you. You go on and learn how to put your hands to some good use. Besides hauling people's garbage. (V:35)

Troy moved from the expression of bitterness over his own life to the expression of a positive dream for his son.

It is important to see that Troy has good intentions, as the play reveals his failings. As a younger man, Troy pursued his personal destiny in baseball at the cost of his family. Now, later in life, he professes to have made responsibility to others his priority. But Troy's efforts are neither wholehearted nor entirely successful, and Wilson uses Cory to help make this point. As the play was refined, Wilson gave Cory a greater understanding of the workings and failings of his own family, particularly his father. In early drafts, Cory was angry at his father and revealed his emotions in more naive, sophomoric outbursts: "I hate your blood in me" (I:86). As the drafts progressed, Cory challenges

Troy on substantive issues. At the play's close in the final draft, Cory points up to Troy his mistreatment of Rose, "I don't know how [Rose] stand you . . . after what you did to her" (V:87). He also challenges Troy regarding an action relating to Troy's brother Gabe: "It ain't your yard. You took Uncle Gabe's money he got from the army to buy this house and then you put him out" (V:87), Although Cory's understanding of these issues is incomplete, it pierces the core of Troy's view of himself as a responsible man by forcing him to address two issues which pit responsibility to self against responsibility to another.

The structure of the play leads its dramatic conclusion to be the physical and emotional conflict between Troy and Cory. Recognizing the flaws in his father and needing to make his own choices, Cory has become a man. There isn't room in the house for two men, and a simple argument about Troy moving over on the steps so that Cory can pass into the house blows up into the final exchange the two will share.

In earlier drafts, the final scene was potentially more violent. In the first drafts, at the height of the confrontataion, when Cory picks up Troy's baseball bat, Troy brings out a gun, points it at his son, and the stage direction reads that he cocks the trigger. Wilson dropped this detail before the Yale Repertory Theater production when he read that Marvin Gaye had been shot by his father. Thus in the later drafts, the only weapon in the scene is the baseball bat, symbolically more powerful in its meaning to Troy, and physically more threatening in that its use requires a physical closeness between the two men.

But the conflict also continued to change in other ways. In the production at the Yale Repertory Theater, Cory swings the bat once and then retreats into the alley as Troy continues to approach. The conflict is interrupted by the arrival of Rose. Cory leaves the yard.

Wilson realized that the interruption left the conflict unresolved. Thus, in the final version of the play, Rose does not enter, and the climax of the play is more complete as Wilson provided himself with the opportunity to explore the complex relationship between father and son more fully. Cory swings the bat once and misses—then he swings again and misses. Troy offers him the chance to swing a third time, having positioned himself as a target impossible to miss. Now, Cory cannot swing. The two men struggle for the bat, and Troy takes it away. Troy prepares to swing, but he stops himself. Defeated, Cory leaves the yard and does not return until after Troy's death.

Perhaps the issue of responsibility of one family member to another is best exemplified here. Of all the versions, this final one is the one where Cory and Troy are least in emotional control, where the anger is the most visceral and intimate. And yet it is in this version where we clearly see that neither one can intentionally injure the other.

The play concludes after a passage of eight years and the death of Troy. The final issue of Cory's responsibility is explored through his indecision regarding attendance at Troy's funeral. In the first draft, Cory tells Lyons he won't go to his father's funeral; Cory says he's given his father seventeen years of his life and he'll give no more. Lyons responds with outrage, challenging Cory's ethical sense: "How you gonna go home to your wife after you betray your mama?" (I:95)

Wilson was bothered by what seemed to him the unnatural exchange between the half brothers combined with Lyons' sermonizing. For this reason, and the sake of running time, for the first performance at the O'Neill Center, Wilson cut the long discussion Cory had with Lyons explaining his reasons for leaving, and Cory merely wanders away during discussion among the other characters. The audience response was quite negative, and for the second O'Neill performance, the entire discussion with Lyons and Cory's subsequent departure were dropped.

Both of these choices were unsatisfying for Wilson. In the Yale Repertory Theater version, Cory tells Rose that he is not going to the funeral and Wilson assigned to her the part previously assigned to Lyons. Rose, having survived the most damaging irresponsibility in Troy, is a more powerful spokesperson for the maintenance of responsibility in the face of its injuries.

Rose reminds Cory about that which Troy did offer to them and how his offerings could be reconciled with their expectations. Cory decides to stay for the funeral. In the final version, Wilson rearranged the material in the scene to strengthen the exchange. Where Cory was the first to arrive for the funeral, now he is last. By having Lyons already at the house before Cory's arrival, and by adding interaction between Cory and his half sister Raynell, all preceding Rose's speech to Cory, Cory and the audience are presented with a much more powerful and harder-to-deny family presence. Cory knows he must go to the funeral, and in this final draft, Wilson provides Cory's only verbal acknowledgement of his decision. Cory says to Raynell, "You go on in the house and change them shoes like Mama told you so we can to Papa's funeral" (V:100).

As Rose speaks late in the play about Troy's goodness, her character is the result of significant change through the drafts. Rose is the victim of Troy's greatest familial irresponsibility—his affair with Alberta. But through the successive drafts of the script, Rose moves toward greater forgiveness and understanding, making Troy's infidelity all the more dramatic and ugly.

The most significant change in Rose is in her day-to-day relationship with Troy and how this, in turn, affects his relationship with Alberta. In the early version of the play, Rose is a much more nagging wife. She bothers Troy constantly about his drinking (which is considerably greater in the early drafts). She reprimands Troy for his neglect of Cory, and when she is tired of Troy's shouting, she tells him to go shout somewhere else.

Although certainly none of these faults independently promotes Troy's wandering, they perhaps provide an excuse for Troy. As the versions progress, this side of Rose almost completely disappears, and Troy's affair is an even greater violation of his marital responsibility. In the later versions of the play, Wilson also makes Rose more suspicious that Troy is having an affair. In the first versions, his pronouncement that he will be a father comes as a complete surprise to Rose. But in later versions, Rose catches inconsistencies in Troy's explanations of his whereabouts, and the audience senses her awareness.

Additionally, Wilson spells out for the audience the extent of Rose's suffering by reinserting an original scene which had been cut during the development process. In an exchange six months after Rose learns of Troy's infidelity, she confronts him on his continuing attention to Alberta. The scene had been cut to shorten the script, but Wilson rightly missed the opportunity to impress on the audience Rose's oppression by the continuation of the affair. So Wilson put the scene back in the script. But he makes an important change from the original. In the first version, Rose threatens Troy; "I ain't gonna stand for this much longer. You living on borrowed time with me" (I:75). When Wilson reinstated the scene, he dropped the line, and Rose promotes Troy's independent decision to end the affair. The exchange becomes more philosophical without losing its emotional charge as Rose points out the fallacy in Troy's theory that his physical presence in bed at the end of every night fulfills his obligation to his household regardless of where he has been up to that point.

As Wilson makes Rose smarter and her suffering greater, our empathy for her is stronger. And Rose's decision to accept Troy's bastard child but sexually give up its father—the action in all drafts of the play—makes more sense as the action of a woman who has withstood her burden longer and has recognized the impossibility of change in her husband.

Rose stands in the center of the play as a model of responsibility but also as an example of the cost of responsibility to others at the expense of self. In response to Troy's explanation of his affair, Rose responds that she also has needs and wants not satisfied at home, but ultimately she sees no options for herself simply because, as she explains to Troy, "You my husband" (V:71).

In her relationship with Cory, Rose becomes progressively stricter with her son. But she does it for Cory's sake, seeing how Cory's greater responsibility at home might help win Troy to his side. Again, Rose is not rewarded. This effort by Rose is counterpointed by an increased disregard for her authority by Cory. Where he heeded her instructions in the early drafts, by the final version Cory outwardly ignores her demands.

Rose's selflessness moves toward an ultimate commitment outside of herself—that is, to the church. In successive versions of the play, Rose becomes more involved with the church, participates more in its events, sings more of its hymns, and ends the final version of the play completely engrossed in it.

Troy remains independent, somehow able to reconcile his juxtaposed impulses and actions. The complicated balance within this character was carefully defined by Wilson. Troy changes considerably through the different drafts of the play, sometimes by the mere deletion of an individual line or through a significant change in a speech or scene. Again, most of the changes contribute to the ramification of the issues of responsibility.

In the early drafts, Troy was a more active crusader. But as the play progressed, his references to those on the street, those who had been dealt a bad lot, his comments on how blacks should treat blacks, all disappear. The result is that his remaining concerns regarding equality are those more personally focused— his right to drive the garbage truck previously driven only by whites or his desire to have Rose shop at the more expensive Bella's market where Troy has been extended credit. These changes all contribute to a more selfish Troy.

There are other small behavioral changes in Troy. His drinking, for example, is greatly reduced with each draft. In an early version Troy refers to drinking as a way "to get a break from being responsible," and so it was a natural choice for Wilson to change this detail and deny Troy this crutch (II:69).

A significant change in Troy's character which again impacts heavily on the issue of responsibility is his relationship to religion. In early drafts, Troy reflects his Christian upbringing, wrestling with his due to the heavens and the heavens' due to him. In the first draft, following Alberta's death in childbirth, Troy rails at Jesus, asking for salvation in the face of his trials. This speech, combined with other similar references, presents a Troy who feels less in control of his destiny in the face of greater power. It offers the potential for abdication of responsibility, and so Wilson moved Troy away from this position.

At the O'Neill Center, the salvation speech and accompanying references were dropped. Through the next few drafts, Wilson provided Troy numerous mentions of the devil and his general tone, though humorous, is much more sacreligious, perhaps as a form of denial. This is, interestingly, juxtaposed with Rose's progressive involvement with the church and religion—perhaps as a reflection of her desire to hand over responsibility. During development at the Yale Repertory Theater, Wilson added a speech for Troy. After Alberta's death, Troy believes he can defeat death, and he challenges "Mr. Death" to try to come for some one close to him or Troy himself: "You come up and knock on the front door. Anytime you want. I'll be ready for you" (IV:59). Thus, Troy's perception of his ability to be responsible for his own fate has changed markedly.

Often a seemingly small change in the text can have a significant impact on the development of a character. Such is the case in a scene centered on Troy's relationship with his brother Gabe, who has been partially incapacitated as a result of a war injury. Troy used much of Gabe's veteran's compensation for the injury to buy his house, and Gabe lived with Troy for many years. Just before the play opens, Gabe has moved to his own apartment, taking his monthly compensation with him. Although Troy continues to profess his support for Gabe's independence, near the end of the play, Troy signs the papers which send Gabe to the hospital and split his income between the hospital and Troy. Although this action is included in all of the drafts, as the play progressed the scene was extended very modestly; the impact is considerable. In early drafts, Rose challenges Troy on his action, and Troy denies signing the papers. In later drafts, Wilson added a line as Rose reminds Troy, "You went back on yourself, Troy. You gonna have to answer for that" (V:75). This single remark combined with Rose's lengthened attack allow for Troy's change from controlled anger in early drafts to extreme confusion in the later one. Troy denies having taken the action, then denies the outcome of the action as Rose undertands it, and, finally, in an added detail, denies understanding the ramifications of his action by claiming, "Hell, I can't read, I don't know what they had on that paper" (V:75). Here Troy is plagued by the inconsistencies of his definition of responsibility.

Structurally, Wilson made another small, but significant, change in this section of the play. In the first few drafts, this scene opens with the discussion of Gabe's incarceration and then moves onto the issue of Troy's continued attention to Alberta. In later drafts, Wilson reversed the action. Rose first addresses Troy's infidelity and then moves on to Gabe. By having Rose move from Troy's responsibility to her into Troy's responsibility to Gabe, Wilson extended the issue outward from the more personal to the less personal and the ramifications are greater. Early in the scene, Troy can manipulate the point of view to defend his position. But the building of one incident on another, combined with Rose's increasing selflessness, undercuts Troy's strength, and the line-up of his distorted priorities becomes too great a foe.

Other small changes in Troy's dialogue also impact on the examination of his responsibility. In an early draft, Troy's comments on Cory's disobedience: "You wanna be grown . . . wanna do what you wanna do . . . alright. But when the time comes to pay the consequences . . . you got to pay them . . . that go for me too" (II:42). Although this statement is prophetic for Troy regarding his own actions, it is a truth Troy ultimately does not apply to himself, and so Wilson dropped this in later drafts.

In each successive draft, Wilson gave more prominence to Troy's affair with Alberta. It was a logical choice for Wilson, as Troy's reconciling of his relationship with Alberta reveals the greatest juxtaposition of responsibility to self and to others. Troy's friend Bono increasingly mentions Troy's attentions and challenges Troy on his actions, providing the affair more and more space in the text. Bono's reaction to the situation remains constant. In all the drafts, Bono tells Troy, "You responsible for what you do." But Troy's different response in different versions dramatically changes his position on the action. In the early drafts, Troy says he accepts responsibility for his action, that he knows what he's doing and is doing it because he wants to. In later drafts, this part of the speech is cut, and the remainder reads differently: "I ain't ducking the responsibility of it. As long as it sets right in my heart. . .then I'm okay. Cause that's all I listen to. It'll tell me right from wrong every time" (V:63). Lost is the indication that Troy sees greater harm in his action and is willing to suffer the consequences. Now, it sits alright with him.

Despite that which Troy preaches to all the other characters in the play, ultimately his responsibility to himself far outweighs his responsibility to them. Indeed, none of the characters finds a successful balance. Lyons, following his father's example, pursues "his dream" straight into jail. Rose, fearing her husband's example, denies her dreams in a selfless devotion to her church. And Cory, having had his dream denied him, has joined the army. For Wilson, society's institutions loom as forces which often engulf and guide the lives of those who ultimately cannot take responsibility.

The five available drafts of *Fences* reveal the changes which survived pads and paper napkins. They also reflect a developmental process in which many participated and which Wilson strongly supports. Wilson feels that an author needs an extended period of time to discover a play. Workshops and rehearsals offer a valuable opportunity: they provide "a chance to see what works and doesn't work. Some things you simply can't tell unless you see it staged. On paper you could read it a hundred times and not tell" (Stern 18A).

Working on his play around the country afforded Wilson the opportunity to listen to the opinions of many theater artists and laymen about his work. All of these were carefully taken into consideration by Wilson who used his instinct as the barometer for the validity of the input; "I go inside myself and find out what's there. If it's not there, nobody will put it there" (Stern 19A). Some ideas were incorporated and some rejected. At the encouragement of another playwright, Wilson made Troy's relationship with Alberta more overt. Yet Wilson rejected a producer's idea to have Troy's brother, who believes himself to be the saint whose blowing of the horn opens the gates of heaven, play the saxophone as opposed to the trumpet.

For Wilson, the process of refining his play was closely associated with Lloyd Richards, who was, when *Fences* was developed, Artistic Director of both the Eugene O'Neill Theater Center and the Yale Repertory Theater, as well as the stage director for the three major productions of *Fences*. Wilson feels artistically comfortable with Richards: "We're coming from the same place. It's Lloyd's understanding of the characters that lets me trust him. At times, he knows the characters better than I do. We have a sort of comradeship. Neither of us has to battle to impose his vision, because our visions are the same" (Freedman 80).

Richards, the veteran theatre director, enjoyed working with Wilson, the poet turned playwright: ". . . the wonderful thing about working with a writer who hasn't been experienced ... he hasn't been hemmed in by the rules ... We don't need the well made play. We need the fullness of expression" (Freedman 80).

Still, from the play's inception and continuing through its development, Wilson pursued his goal to make *Fences* a more traditional play than that which he had previously written. Wilson has strong feelings about the effort.

> I should have written *Joe Turner* after *Ma Rainey* and then *Piano Lesson. Fences* was the odd man out, in the sense that it was not the kind of play I wanted to write. But all these people who are used to theater kept trying to tell me my work should be something different. ... After telling people that I knew how to write that kind of play, I asked myself, do I really know how to write that kind of play? So I wrote *Fences* in answer to the challenge that I'd given myself. (Watlington 109)

Fences was more conventional and ultimately more commercial than any of Wilson's plays which preceded or followed it. Runs at regional theaters throughout the country sold out, and the Broadway production grossed eleven million dollars in one year. Because of its more conventional structure and because of the streamlined nature of its character development, *Fences* is prime material for the study of the development of a playwright's vision for a single play. The play has a simplicity in the direct relationship between Troy and each of the other characters and in the direct impact of each of these relationships on the presentation of the play's main themes.

The audience's ability to understand the complexity of the conflicts within the characters is central to the effectiveness of the play. Many of the characters in *Fences*, like those in our lives, make what seem to be irresponsible choices. Wilson's goal was to examine such choices by revealing the pressures which influence a decision and, thus, to understand the individual. To look at the intent of a life is to uncover nobility and dignity and, ultimately, to see the contribution of an individual.

The changes in the drafts of *Fences* reveal Wilson's continuing effort to explore the internal life of the characters and, thus, to clarify his theme. Each character's progression in *Fences* can be placed readily in the perspective of the developing vision for the play as a whole. Thus the ramifications of a change, from the modification of a single line to the loss of an entire scene, can be examined and measured in the light of the overall movement toward clearer expression of Wilson's message.

The draft of *Fences* read for the first time publicly in the spring of 1982 at New Dramatists was powerful and moving. Many plays begin and end their theatrical lives with no more consideration than this play had received up to this point. But Wilson continued to work on his play, revising, re-revising, experimenting, redefining. The result, a dramatic text very close to the original vision in the strength of its energy and the depth of its message, and yet very far in its cohesion and clarity, speaks powerfully to the validity of American play development especially as practiced by an open and extremely clear-minded playwright.

WORKS CITED

Christianson, Richard. "August Wilson: A Powerful Playwright Probes the Meaning of Black Life." *Chicago Tribune* (February 5, 1988) Section 13: 12–13.

Devries, Hillary. "A Song in Search of Itself." *American Theatre* (January 1987): 22–26.

Freedman, Samuel. "Wilson's New Fences Nurtures a Partnership." *New York Times* (May 5, 1985): 80.

Moyers, Bill. "America: A Conversation with Bill Moyers." *American Theatre* (June 1989): 13–17, 54–56.

Palmer, Don. "He Gives a Voice to the Nameless Masses." *New York Newsday* (April 20, 1987): 47.

Stern, Gary. "Playwrights Agree that the Workshops Process is a Major Aid in Rewriting." *Backstage* (June 8, 1984): 18A-19A.

Tallmer, Jerry. "Fences: Anguish of Wasted Talent." *New York Post* (March 26, 1987): 28.

Watlington, Dennis. "Hurdling Fences." *Vanity Fair* (April, 1989): 102–110.

Wilson, August. *Fences*. (unpublished property of New Dramatists, 1982). Version I.

———. *Fences*. (unpublished property of August Wilson, June 1983). Version II.

———. *Fences*. (unpublished property of The Eugene O'Neill Theater Center, August 1983). Version III.

———. *Fences*. *Theater* (Summer/Fall, 1985). Version IV.

———. *Fences*. (New York: Plume Books, 1987). Version V.

Subtle Imposition
The Lloyd Richards–August Wilson Formula

Sandra G. Shannon

When August Wilson got off the train in New Haven, Connecticut, en route to the first Yale Repertory Theater rehearsal of *Ma Rainey's Black Bottom*, his demeanor in no way foreshadowed that this was a man who would later win two Pulitzer Prizes in drama and make a serious impact upon the course of American theater. Frankly, his biggest concern at this point in his career was steadying himself to meet the cast and the director of this fledgling work-in-progress. He had just undergone an extensive and rigorous ten-week crash course in playwrighting at the prestigious Eugene O'Neill Center. He had already attracted the attention of prominent producers, and now his play about black jazz musicians of the 1920s was to be staged at one of the nation's top drama schools by noted director Lloyd Richards—then Dean of the Yale School of Drama and Artistic Director of the Yale Repertory Theater. Even though Wilson had received the equivalent of a Ph.D. degree in playwrighting, he apparently still felt vulnerable and, to some extent, overwhelmed by all that success in the theater business entails.

But once inside the rehearsal session, Wilson's insecurities began to dissipate as Lloyd Richards demonstrated not just his much touted skills at directing, but his profound sensitivity to and understanding of Wilson's commentary on the blues, black musicians, 1920s Chicago, and the white-controlled recording industry. Wilson recalls,

I didn't know Lloyd as a director, and I didn't know how
these things were going to turn out. And he went into
rehearsal, and we read through the script, and the actors
started asking questions. I'm all prepared to answer all
these questions, and they ask a question about Toledo, and
Lloyd spoke up, and Lloyd answered the question. Not
only was it correct, but it gave me some insight. I said "I
didn't know that about Toledo." This went on, but from
that moment I visibly relaxed. I said "Everything's going
to be alright." (Personal interview)

Wilson's initial *Ma Rainey* rehearsal session with Lloyd Richards
exorcised from him a powerful "demon" (one that has since been
the cause of his on-going feud with Paramount Pictures over
Fences)—his fear that his work, grounded in the cultural roots of
black America, would lose its texture in the hands of those alien
to the culture.[1] Also, in this one session, Wilson saw in Richards
a man whom he could trust implicitly in conveying the essence
of his work to the stage.

Certainly the pairing of noted directors and little-known
playwrights is not uncommon, but what is it that, from the
outset, cemented the relationship between these two men in an
unprecedented five-play collaboration on works depicting the
black experience? Since *Ma Rainey's Black Bottom*, August Wilson
and Lloyd Richards have perfected a formula which has
maneuvered *Fences, Joe Turner's Come and Gone, The Piano Lesson,*
and now *Two Trains Running* on a steady course from
brainstorming sessions to Broadway. What seems to be a key
ingredient in the Wilson-Richards formula is the tremendous
amount of respect that each man has for the other. As a result,
egos are held in check, one listens to the other, and differences of
opinion are handled ever so diplomatically. So compatible is
their working relationship that baffled reporters and
interviewers frequently ask "Do you ever argue?" And they just
as frequently respond with a grin or an emphatic "No."

But as with any serious, long-term working relationship,
first impressions of good manners and politeness lay the
groundwork for mutual and frank professional decisions that
must be made later—what Lloyd Richards refers to as "subtle
imposition." As he sees it, his job is

to extend August's thinking ... which means to understand it and even to provoke it. Sometimes people think they know things that they don't consciously articulate. And so my job becomes to get all of that out of him, out of my perceptions of what might be there, and to shape that in a theatrical way ... I coax him to discover what I want him to discover and reveal it in a manner in which I would like it revealed. You can call it subtle imposition (Backalenick 18).

For example, Richards used subtle imposition to convince Wilson to make both major and minor changes in his first version of *Ma Rainey's Black Bottom*. Even when Richards first read the script of the play at the O'Neill Center, he observed that the play's most glaring problem was that it was actually two plays under the guise of a single title. He also noted that Wilson had written a play requiring five major musicians in five major roles. After he had outlined the play's flaws, in his typical Socratic fashion, he queried Wilson until he got the solutions that he wanted: Should the two plays (one about Ma Rainey and the other about her band) be separated or blended together? Should we search for five actors who are musicians or five musicians who are actors? Should we even worrry about live music, or should we simply pre-record the scores? One of Richards's subtly imposed solutions was to relegate Ma Rainey more to the background and focus instead upon her band.

Out of all of Richards's suggestions for improving *Ma Rainey*, perhaps the easiest for Wilson to accept was de-emphasizing the role of the central female character. This change was an agreeable one for Wilson, for, as his subsequent plays demonstrate, his writing is grounded in a decidedly male ethos. He explains in an interview,

> "You've got to understand the sociology of it. The transition from slavery to freedom was a cultural shock for blacks. All of a sudden black men had to ask themselves things like, 'What is money?' 'What is marriage?' Black women, for all their own struggles, were relatively stable. Economically, they had control of the house. But what were black men supposed to do to make a living?" (Rocha 38).

Despite Wilson's preoccupation with black men, *Ma Rainey's Black Bottom*, as its title implies, is informed by the blues—an undeniably female dominated genre. The blues aesthetic, which informs each of Wilson's plays, evolved historically from the psyches of female blues greats, such as Ma Rainey and Bessie Smith. It is they who essentially gave life to this art form and carried it to the masses. Men, who were frequently alluded to as cheaters, loafers, and deserters both in their lives and in their lyrics, are marginal. As Samuel Freedman notes, "They were proud and tragic, indomitable and exploited and they cast a jaundiced eye at men" ("What Black Writers Owe" 8). Thus, the paradox that Wilson and Richards create in their decision to sideline Ma Rainey is that the play remains "willingly inscribed within the female language of the blues" (Rocha 39). Paradox notwithstanding, however, Ma Rainey, who represents "the sine qua non of Wilson's universe" (Rocha 39), yields the spotlight in the definitive version of the play to her all-male band. Although Wilson and Richards amicably agreed to de-emphasize Ma, this early evidence of competition and ambivalence between Wilson's male and female characters begins a pattern of plays dominated by the stories of black men and, to a noticeably lesser degree, lacking a forum for black women.

Another dilemma that Richards had to address in the original version of *Ma Rainey* was whether to "use a blend of live and recorded music which enabled the actors to learn what they could in a short time" (Nelson 12). On April 6, 1984, *Ma Rainey's Black Bottom* opened at the Yale Repertory Theater starring five actors who had learned to sing and play the blues during rehearsal. Gertrude "Ma" Rainey faded from the spotlight she occupied in the original script, and the through line of the play focused upon the black men in her band. Although several critics still grumbled about the lack of emphasis upon the play's namesake, others, such as Malcolm Johnson of the *Hartford Courant*, considered the edited script "astonishingly polished," "terrifically powerful," "deeply wrought," and "most eloquent" (1).

No doubt Lloyd Richards is aware of August Wilson's reputation among both producers and directors as an uncompromising artist. From the long-standing controversy surrounding his demands for a black director for Paramount's proposed screen version of *Fences* to his early refusal to allow producers to cast *Ma Rainey's Black Bottom* as a musical,[2] Wilson has stood his ground. This unwavering defense of his work's artistic integrity was sorely tested during a 1987 production of *Fences* in San Francisco and later in New York. As actress Mary Alice (who starred as Rose in the play's Broadway production) recalls, critics in New Haven, Chicago, and San Francisco had great difficulty with the play's ending. Specifically, they complained that the final scene during which Gabriel attempts to blow his horn to open the Pearly Gates for Troy was, in the words of one critic, "so silly that it was ridiculous!" (Alice, personal interview). With *Fences*'s Broadway debut imminent, producer Carol Shorenstein, who had invested some $850,000 in the play, feared that it would be doomed in New York if it continued with its unconventional ending. With this in mind, she staged a series of meetings with key figures involved in the play and decided—without Wilson's input or approval—to change the ending of *Fences*.[3] Several alternate endings were proposed and tested on stage, yet none proved satisfactory.

During the tempestuous run of *Fences* in San Francisco and subsequently in New York, Wilson and Richards simmered. The subtle imposition that had so aptly characterized their working relationship had turned to outright rebellion—not against each other, however. Instead, their mutual anger cemented an already solid alliance against mounting pressure to alter the play. As the play's director, Richards, had no intentions of altering Wilson's work, despite heavy criticism from Shorenstein. Panicking over his noncompliance, Shorenstein took drastic measures to fire Richards and replace him with a director who would acquiesce to her suggested changes. At this point, Wilson could no longer contain his anger: "It is your right to fire the director," he told her. "But you cannot hire another director without my approval" (Alice, personal interview). Shorenstein apparently withdrew her campaign.

Ironically, none of the suggested changes for *Fences*'s ending turned out to be an improvement over Wilson's original finale. From her perspective as a character, Mary Alice believed all along that the play's original ending was appropriate, given the depressing turn of events that the audience witnesses. She notes, "The audience was already dealing with the fact that this man that they had experienced for close to two hours was dead, and there's a whole scene that deals with the fact that he's dead. And so what they needed was something that would give them this release, and the original ending provided that" (personal interview). According to Mary Alice, Gabriel's frustrated attempts to sound his horn, his "slow, strange dance" (Wilson 101), his howling/singing, and his last words, "That's the way that go" (101) drew laughter from the audience and raised their spirits just before the curtain fell.

Unable to find a suitable alternative for the play's ending and acknowledging Wilson's anger, Shorenstein reluctantly took *Fences* to New York, still harboring grave doubts about its potential to succeed and about keeping Richards as its director. Ironically the play opened on Broadway on March 26, 1987, to rave reviews—its original ending intact. Wilson and Richards savored their victory and grew even more confident that the two of them could withstand the sometimes overwhelming pressures of the theater industry.

While *Fences*'s obscure ending posed the greatest consternation among theater critics, *Joe Turner's Come and Gone* initially puzzled pre-Broadway audiences who strained to discern a resolution to the protagonist's conflict. Thus, Wilson's unrefined genius posed yet another challenge for Lloyd Richards, who ultimately succeeded in fine-tuning the play from Yale Repertory Theater to Broadway. While the play was in rehearsal, Wilson, Richards, and several other observers noted that the original script ended with a lingering question as to whether Herald Loomis, a vagrant and ex-member of Joe Turner's kidnapped workforce "finds his song." What audiences needed, according to Richards, was a more emotionally rewarding catharsis, since they had learned of this man's lengthy incarceration and had witnessed his frustrated search for his wife (i.e., his "starting place") for much of the play. But it was not until Wilson had sat through several intensive rehearsals of the play that he discovered a solution to Loomis's incomplete portrayal: "I came up with the idea of ending the first act with him on the floor unable to stand up. When he stands at the end, you can read that as him finding his song" (Savran 297).

While the definitive version of *Joe Turner's Come and Gone*—considered by many to be Wilson's best play—leaves both readers and audiences with fewer questions, it still is significantly open-ended. Admittedly oblivious to Shakespeare's tragedies as well as Aristotle's *Poetics*, Wilson pays little attention to the tragic convention calling for a reversal of fortune for the protagonist. In the final turbulent scene of *Joe Turner*, Loomis and his ex-wife Martha engage in a verbal confrontation which reaches its climax when Loomis, in a graphic attempt to denunciate her God, slashes his chest, smears blood over his face and exclaims, "I'm standing! I'm standing. My legs stood up! I'm standing now!" (93). Apparently Wilson sees this self-sacrificial mockery as a major epiphany for a man who, for so long, has been defined by forces other than his own. Unfortunately Wilson's attempts to demonstrate this realization seem clearer in the accompanying stage notes than in Loomis's startling actions. Wilson translates the spectacle eloquently:

> (Having found his song, the song of self-sufficiency, fully resurrected, cleansed and given breath, free from any encumbrance other than the workings of his own heart and the bonds of the flesh, having accepted the responsibility for his own presence in the world, he is free to soar above the environs that weighed and pushed his spirit into terrifying contractions.) (94)

Buoyed by Wilson's poetic interpretation, Loomis ends the scene with a simple "Goodbye, Martha" (94).

As has become Wilson's trademark, *Joe Turner*, like his other four published works, steers away from the moral or neatly resolute ending. Instead, the playwright is, as usual, an instructor who carries his students to the threshold of awareness but leaves them there to ponder. This artistic strategy continues to be the source of much debate between Wilson and Richards. While Wilson is adamant about maintaining the original integrity of his work, Richards is faced with the job of translating it to suit the needs of audiences on one hand and financial backers on the other. Subtle imposition, compromise, and obstinacy have served them well in these endeavors.

When Wilson and Richards turned their attention to staging *The Piano Lesson*—the fourth play in the playwright's proposed series of ten—it was clear that Wilson was not yet convinced that his pattern of obscure endings was cause for change, and, once again, Richards had to resort to subtle imposition to convince him to rewrite the play's final scene. The original script of *The Piano Lesson* provided no clear resolution to the play's central conflict—who determines the fate of a two-hundred-year old piano bearing carved emblems of the Charles family's slave ancestors.

In an early draft, Wilson's ending features two significant actions, yet, alone, neither settles the dilemma that rages throughout much of the play: Will Boy Willie succeed in taking the piano from Berniece's house to be sold for land or will Berniece continue to keep the untouched instrument in her living room as simply a memento of her past? After failing to chase away Sutter's spirit, which attaches itself to the piano, Boy Willie engages it in a wrestling match. Also, while the two are entangled, Berniece comes to a sudden realization that she must play the piano. As she begins to play, she discovers a simple chant that turns into "her song": "I want you to help me" (107).

For Wilson—who maneuvers events in *The Piano Lesson* to address the theme of what one should do with his heritage—Berniece's decision to play the piano was the only resolution worth divulging. While she protects the piano from becoming a pawn in Boy Willie's quest for land and knows the stories behind each of its carvings, she does not fully come to terms with what the instrument means to her until she plays it. For Berniece, then, playing the piano is equivalent to finding her song or, as Herald Loomis explains in *Joe Turner's Come and Gone*, finding her "starting place." What should one do with his heritage? According to Wilson's emphasis in an early draft of *The Piano Lesson*, one must not simply acknowledge it but also draw strength from it.

Despite Wilson's preference for a spiritual resolution to the dilemma in *The Piano Lesson*, Richards tried to convince him that audiences simply wanted to know who gets the piano. Thus, before the play reached Broadway and acquired its present published form, Wilson had to be subjected to more of

Richards's subtle imposition disguised as Socratic questioning: "There are a lot of wonderful stories here. But which one do we want to tell?" How do Berniece and Boy Willie's stories fit together? What role does the piano play? Why did Berniece stop playing the piano? What happens to the piano after the play ends?" (Freedman, "Leaving His Imprint"). Richards did not expect immediate answers to these questions; they were merely an invitation to his colleague to share his visions for improvement. Convinced by Richards's prodding, Wilson rewrote the final scene extending the action beyond the wrestling match to reveal that Boy Willie rescinds his claim on the piano. Thus the new ending reveals that this powerful icon is to remain in his sister Berniece's home as a testament to their slave ancestors:

> Boy Willie: Wining Boy, you ready to go back down home? Hey, Doaker, what time the train leave?
>
> Doaker: You still got time to make it.
>
> (Maretha crosses and embraces Boy Willie.)
>
> Boy Willie: Hey, Berniece . . . if you and Maretha don't keep playing on that piano . . . ain't no telling . . . me and Sutter both liable to be back.
>
> Berniece: Thank you. (The lights go down to black.) (108)

While Wilson liked the idea of an open-ended final scene with curtains falling on Boy Willie wrestling with the pesty ghost of the piano's former owner, Richards's concerns went beyond the immediacy of the play to the audience: "The fact is you have to have a resolution to the evening for the people who are sitting there. So we looked and tried things—various things to find a resolution to the play. Until then, I devised a finish that we never considered an ending. But it was a finish for the evening while we were still working on the end" (Shannon 129). Richards later noted that with the average theater ticket priced at approximately $25 or higher, anyone who had to hire a babysitter, get all dressed up, pay for parking, etc., at least deserves a play with an ending. By the time the two men had reached an agreement on how to fine tune *The Piano Lesson*, Richards had become what one writer calls "an implant specialist." According to Richards, "the play was missing a lot in terms of its thinking and filling out, and it hadn't found its conclusion yet. We've really had to build it up" (Migler 139).

Although Richards and Wilson were satisfied with the altered ending, the play still came under harsh attack from one of their shrewdest critics. Former Dean of the Yale School of Drama and *New Republic* critic Robert Brustein notes in an overall condemnation of the play that, even though the revised ending is a definite improvement over a previous version, it still "tacks a supernatural resolution onto an essentially naturalistic anecdote" (29). Despite Brustein's complaints, *The Piano Lesson* went on to earn Wilson a Pulitzer Prize, and, like *Fences*, the play rose above enormous skepticism over its unconventional ending and promoted an even closer alliance between the director and the playwright.

The Wilson-Richards formula also nurtured his fifth published play *Two Trains Running*, from the Yale Repertory Theater to Broadway. The play, which was set in a cafe in Pittsburgh's Hill District, appeared on Broadway in 1992 to respectable reviews and was eventually nominated for that year's Pulitzer Prize in drama. When questioned about his biggest challenge in directing the fifth of Wilson's chronicles of the black experience, Richards noted, "We're still working on the through-line of the play—the basic action that moves the play" (Shannon 133).

One factor which is often underplayed when describing this successful duo is the common ground they share as black men in a traditionally white-controlled industry. Certainly their ten-year relationship has been prolific yet not without an occasional brush with green-eyed demons of professional envy or sheer racism. At such times, Richards, in his characteristic wisdom and candor, extends the jurisdiction of his subtle imposition to counsel Wilson on the politics of surviving as a black man in a predominantly white business. For example, previous dean of the Yale School of Drama Robert Brustein (who is white), in a transparent effort to discredit both Richards and Wilson's work at the Yale Repertory Theater, charged that Richards, his immediate successor, was violating Yale Rep's mission by promoting the work of August Wilson. In a seething article disguised as a review of *The Piano Lesson* (Brustein is drama critic for *The New Republic*), Brustein rebukes August Wilson for "[limiting] himself to the black experience in a relatively literalistic style," labels *The Piano Lesson* as "an overwritten exercise in a conventional style . . . the most poorly composed of Wilson's four produced works," and believes that the playwright's projected ten-play cycle of plays is "monotonous, limited, locked in a perception of victimization" (28).

Brustein was equally perturbed by Richards's decision to use Yale Rep's facilities to promote a black playwright writing exclusively of the black experience. He calls Wilson's plays that have passed through the Rep on their way to regional theaters and ultimately to Broadway "McTheater," which he defines as "the use of sequential non-profit institutions as launching pads and tryout franchises for the development of Broadway products and the enrichment of artistic personnel" (28). It is not difficult to see past these charges to detect the professional envy and racism that seep into this review. As Hilary DeVries of the *Boston Globe* sees it, the former dean's idea of Wilson and Richards's work at Yale was "the cultural equivalent of affirmative action" (46).

Of course, both Richards and Wilson were aware of Brustein's motives, but Richards, who most assuredly had discussed the matter with his colleague, decided to ignore the provocative charges. No sign of bitterness could be detected as he told one reporter, "The question is, are you interested that the work of the artist be seen? Are you interested that the work of Yale Rep be shared in all areas, including New York? I don't see it as a conflict between commerce and art" (Cole F5). Richards, a veteran of the theater, successfully sidestepped this quagmire Brustein had created, and his work with Wilson goes uninterrupted even after his June 1991 retirement from his twelve-year position at Yale.

Perhaps most heartening about Richards's relationship with Wilson is that it has become more than simply a director-playwright phenomenon. To Wilson, "Lloyd," as he calls him, is a father, a boxing coach, a business advisor, and, most importantly, a sensitive black man who shares his artistic vision. Wilson readily admits,

Because we share a commonality of experience, I think we
share a commonality of vision. I wouldn't have to be at
rehearsal and Lloyd, knowing me and knowing the overall
arc of my work, would know how I would want a scene to
play or what the values of that scene would be (Barbour
14).

Richards knows first-hand the people about whom Wilson
writes. Having grown up fatherless (Albert Richards died of
diphtheria when Lloyd was nine) in Detroit during the
Depression years, Richards, like Wilson, saw, through a young
boy's eyes, the deferred dreams of his people turn into poverty
and squalor.

Like Wilson, Richards was forced to mature early to
assume the role of caretaker and breadwinner for his family.
Unfortunately the already fatherless Richards also had to
contend with a mother who eventually lost her eyesight due to a
progressively worsening case of glaucoma. Still, the young
Richards persevered: "With his brother Allan, Lloyd supported
the family, shining shoes, running elevators, selling newspapers,
sweeping up in barbershops" (Freedman, "Leaving His
Imprint"). This unwelcomed responsibility thrust upon Richards
prepared him well for the responsibilities that he now faces in
the theatrical limelight. The same shrewd business sense and
quiet strength that he exhibited as a young black boy of the 1930s
turned breadwinner still accurately depicts his demeanor as one
of the most respected black men in theater today.

August Wilson, no doubt, draws much of his present
stamina from similar domestic hardships. His German-born
biological father did not meet an early death; however, he
essentially abandoned Daisy Wilson and her five children,
leaving them to survive on Welfare assistance and wages from
her job as janitor. As the eldest son, Wilson quit school in the
ninth grade and accepted odd jobs in the downtown Pittsburgh
"Hill District" area. His quest for work led him to the area's
tobacco shops, bars, and coffee houses. Years later the people
whom he met in these settings were to provide a steady supply
of characters for his cycle of plays.

Even though Richards boasts of his proven director's
strategy, which he calls "subtle imposition," its success is also

predicated upon the chemistry of Wilson's personality. Wilson the man is polite and unpretentious. He is not altered by ceremonies or awards, preferring the quiet of his hotel room to gala affairs, photo ops, or autograph seekers. He is a good listener and is not easily offended by harsh criticism of his work. In fact, he is one of a few playwrights who actually enjoys reading critical reviews of his plays—good and bad. Moreover, he thrives on revision and welcomes opportunities to sit in on play rehearsals and editing sessions with Richards to discover ways to improve his work. He is extremely self-motivated, preferring to always have a work in progress even as one of his titles appears on a Broadway marquee or another headlines at one of the country's numerous regional theaters. In addition, Wilson can be just as adamant as Richards, especially concerning who handles his work and how it is converted to the stage or screen. In fact, his uncompromising artistic belief is currently a thorn in the side of Paramount Pictures, whom he has challenged to hire a black director for a proposed film version of *Fences*.

From Wilson's perspective, his relationship with Richards has come full circle, evolving from a professionally distant director-playwright collaboration to a warm and trusting father-son team. Although his initial meeting with Richards was fraught with apprehension and anxiety, now he seems quite comfortable in going so far as to regard Richards as his surrogate father. In a recent unpublished interview, he admitted "I have certainly grown up without a father, and he [Richards] is about twenty-five years older than me. So, yeah, I defer to him in that regard" (Personal interview). In another interview he confesses, "I write something and run to him for his approval, like a kid" (Charles 64). Perhaps the best indication of the trust and, I daresay, love that exist between these two men may be seen in Wilson's determination to continue his work with Lloyd Richards ad infinitum. He told one reporter, "Because of him, I found a home . . . I will follow Lloyd wherever he goes" (DeVries 20).

In the early 1980s a little known poet-turned-playwright and a celebrated director came together because of a play with promise. Yet the relationship of these two men has endured for approximately ten years now—past the grueling initiation at the

O'Neill Center and past the helpful stage workshops conducted at the Yale Repertory Theater. Together, August Wilson and Lloyd Richards have tapped into The Great White Way and are enduring admirably the rigors associated with their success. Their common bond as black men producing plays of the black experience in a white-dominated industry has made them necessarily interdependent and, to some extent, protective of each other, closing ranks and sidestepping controversy when they feel threatened by the press or other intruders. In his attempt to interview Wilson while at Yale University, novelist and critic Ishmael Reed noted, "Getting to see Wilson was like arranging to view a gem on loan from a private collection. Access is granted (and barred) by Lloyd Richards" (93).

Although he has two grown sons of his own, the now seventy-year-old Lloyd Richards finds great comfort in passing along his business savvy and his artistic vision to his forty-seven-year-old protege. This satisfaction is mutual, however, for Wilson readily acknowledges this man's role in determining his present status as one of America's premiere playwrights. Richards's manipulation of Wilson's plays and expert advice concerning the playwright's business maneuvers may have indeed been carried out in a subtle manner. However, the two Pulitzer Prizes and long list of other prestigious awards that have brought Wilson both national and international prominence in no way suggest that Lloyd Richards's brilliant insight has been an imposition.

NOTES

1. For details concerning Wilson's demand for a black director for Paramount Pictures's proposed film version of *Fences*, see Wilson's "I Want a Black Director" in *Spin* October 1990 or the *New York Times* (26 Sept. 1990). See also David Dufresne's "In Hollywood Dreams Don't Pan Out." *The Day* (1 April 1990): F1, F4.

2. In an unpublished personal interview, Wilson explained that before he began working with Lloyd Richards, he came close to selling the rights to *Ma Rainey's Black Bottom* to producers who wanted to convert the play into a musical. His decision to allow Richards to stage the play at the Yale Repertory Theater was all the more difficult because "These producers wanted to do the show on Broadway, and the Dramatist Guild's minimum for an option is $2,500 for a play. But *they* were offering me $25,000!" (Wilson, Unpublished Interview, 9 Nov. 1991).

3. For details concerning the controversy over changing *Fences*'s ending, see Richard Christiansen's "Artist of the Year: August Wilson's Plays Reveal What It Means to be Black in This Century." *Chicago Tribune* (27 Dec. 1987): 13:F9–F10.

WORKS CITED

Alice, Mary. Personal interview. 15 April 1993.

Backalenick, Irene. "A Lesson from Lloyd Richards." *Theater Week* (16 April 1990): 16–19.

Barbour, David. "August Wilson's Here to Stay." *Theater Week* (18–25 April 1988): 8–14.

Brustein, Robert. "The Lesson of 'The Piano Lesson.'" *New Republic* 202 (21 May 1990): 28–30.

Charles, Nick. "August Wilson: Stages of Black America." *Emerge* (April 1990): 62–65.

Cole, Gloria. "Theater-Maker at Yale." *Fairpress* (21 June 1990): F1–F6.

DeVries, Hilary. "Drama Lesson." *Boston Globe Magazine* (24 June 1990): 20+.

Freedman, Samuel. "Leaving His Imprint on Broadway." *New York Times* (22 Nov. 1987).

———. "What Black Writers Owe to Music." *New York Times* (14 Oct. 1984): 2:1–17.

Johnson, Malcolm. "Ma Rainey's Visceral Attack on American Racism." *Hartford Courant* (7 April 1984): 1.

Migler, Raphael. "An Elegant Duet." *Gentleman's Quarterly* (April 1990): 114.

Nelson, Don. "Splendid Shake-Up." *Playbill* (Dec. 1984): 6–12.

Reed, Ishmael. "In Search of August Wilson." *Connoisseur* 217 (March 1987): 92–97.

Rocha, Mark. "A Conversation with August Wilson." *Diversity: A Journal of Multicultural Issues* 1 (Fall 1992): 24–42.

Savran, David. *In Their Own Words: Contemporary American Playwrights.* New York: Theater Communications Group, 1988.

Shannon, Sandra. "From Lorraine Hansberry to August Wilson: An Interview with Lloyd Richards." *Callaloo* 14 (Winter 1991): 124–135.

Wilson, August. *Fences.* New York: New American Library, 1986.

———. *Joe Turner's Come and Gone.* New York: New American Library, 1988.

———. Personal interview, 9 November 1991.

———. *The Piano Lesson.* New York: Plume, 1990.

Alternatives . . .
Opposites . . . Convergences
An Interview with Lloyd Richards

Richard Pettengill

Lloyd Richards has completed his tenure as Dean of the Yale School of Drama and Artistic Director of the Yale Repertory Theatre, positions which he held from 1979 to 1991. Since 1968, he has been Artistic Director of the National Playwrights Conference at the Eugene O'Neill Theatre Center in Waterford, Connecticut. He directed the original Broadway production of Lorraine Hansberry's *A Raisin in the Sun* in 1959, and has directed all of August Wilson's major plays, including *Ma Rainey's Black Bottom*, *Fences*, *Joe Turner's Come and Gone*, *The Piano Lesson*, and *Two Trains Running*. I spoke to Mr. Richards prior to the start of rehearsals of the Goodman production of *Two Trains Running*, which ran from Jan. 15 to Feb. 28, 1993, and then ran at the Regal Theatre, on Chicago's south side, from March 4 to March 14, 1993.

Richard Pettengill: You've worked with August Wilson for over a decade now. What are some of the ways in which you work together?

Lloyd Richards: There is one basic principle that I've established and that is that I am not the playwright. And I will not be the playwright. My responsibility is to stimulate, provoke, and to get him to function at the top of his ability. August has realized that. We were doing a play, and I said to him one day, "There's one scene too many." I gave him back the script, and I went about doing what I was doing. And he waited and waited for me to tell him which scene was the one that should be cut; I never told him which one was too many. So he went and he looked at the script, and he looked at the script, and he studied it and he discovered what was for him one scene too many. And he gave me back the script, and he does not know to this day whether it was the same scene I had in mind. And I will never tell him, because he discovered what he had to discover about that play.

RP: What are some of the problems in August's plays that you and he have worked to resolve?

LR: With all the plays we've worked on different problems. *Ma Rainey* was two short plays. Do we put them together? Do we keep them apart? We made the same decision; we had the same commitment, and the same feeling about it. His second play, *Fences*, was a very different problem: instead of two short plays, he ended up writing a play that was four hours and fifteen minutes long. So, our problem was to shape the play, to find the spine in all of the material and pull the spine through. There's one speech in that play that really was key in the discovery of its spine. It's in the second act when Troy speaks to Death; he challenges Death and he says "This is between you and me." That speech originally had been a speech to God. One day I said August, this man doesn't speak to God, never has; in the first act he spoke to Death. He has lived death, he lives with death on a daily basis. August said absolutely right; he rewrote that, and it affected everything else throughout the play. August is wonderful. Here is a playwright who didn't know what it was to be a playwright, so he made all kinds of wonderful mistakes. In *Fences* he didn't know that you don't end a scene with a character on stage with the last line, who has to start the next scene—six months later—in a different costume! You don't do that. But I don't tell him things like that. I don't want to teach him playwrighting. I want those so-called mistakes, because those so-called mistakes are part of the impulse of the writer. They are my problem. I have to find a way to deal with whatever comes out of that impulse, but I don't want to stop it from coming out. So I say as little as possible in the beginning about structure, because I don't want him to write my play, I want him to write his play. And then I deal with what I get and try to shape it so that it really is his ideas.

RP: *Joe Turner's Come and Gone?*

LR: Joe Turner . . . I'm fascinated by it. The questions with *Joe Turner* were really the evolution of the plot and the development of a character, Bynum. My work was to help develop the line of that character through the play. He became a very moving character who made things happen. The boarding house is a way station, one of the way stations of life which could have been in the desert, it could have been anywhere. In August's world, way stations are where people stop for a moment and refresh themselves. They engage in talk and action, they are encountered, and they proceed.

RP: And *The Piano Lesson*, which you brought here on its way to Broadway?

LR: *The Piano Lesson*, a wonderful play that has no end. We went into rehearsal, and I knew there wasn't an end to the play. The third week of rehearsal I said to August, okay, we haven't been able to develop an end for this play. What I will do is devise a finish to the play, but we will have to go on working. We worked for a year and a half trying to find the end of that play. We took it all around the country devising finishes for it. August would say to me that the play doesn't end, it just goes on, and the fight between Boy Willie and the devil goes on. Well okay, all right, I gave up and tried to do things onstage with that. But it wasn't until a year and a half later (when we were in Los Angeles on our way to New York) that I said August, people are waiting for the resolution between Boy Willie and Berniece about the piano. I said, do you know what we're doing? We're not dealing with the other rights to the piano. The Sutters have a right to the piano too. That ghost is here, his rights are being disregarded.

He agreed that we weren't dealing with that sufficiently. We had to develop that right. So we worked back all the way through the play, texturing in that right, the right of the Sutters to the piano. The speech came in about Miss Ophelia and when, how, and why the piano was carved, and when and how the piano was taken. In the end, Sutter was the one who lost the piano. Boy Willie was able to give it up to his sister, and we were able to resolve the question of the play. Not the conflict, because it would go on forever. It will re-emerge in other ways. We were able to resolve that part of it for this time. It took us a year and a half to do it. In the meantime, it was still a wonderful evening of entertainment.

RP: And on to *Two Trains Running*.

LR: We came to *Two Trains Running*, and he said, I got you this time, this time we got no middle. We got to work out the middle. We have the beginning, we have the end, we didn't have the middle. That doesn't mean there weren't wonderful speeches and exchanges, but in terms of the structure, we did not have that play we were looking for; it took time to develop it. This had to do with how each character grew in terms of his own challenge; it was sharpening the challenges of the characters, in particular Sterling—and to a great extent—Memphis. Each play presented a different problem and each one we approached differently. August and I, in some way or another, think very much alike. Our value systems seem to be very similar to one another. I don't have to say a lot, he doesn't have to say a lot; I know what he's getting at, he knows what I'm getting at. With that kind of basis of understanding, you don't need to do a lot of talking.

RP: Can you comment on *Two Trains Running* in light of August's other plays?

LR: August has done here what he has done in all the plays he has written. His plays have centered themselves in a decade and have illuminated the life of an oppressed people during that time. He has not approached the plays as historical chronologies of the events of a time, or even as dialogues on the problems of a time. He has approached everything through characters, characters who any of us may have encountered or avoided encountering on the street. He has put them in a position where we can get to know them through their attempts to deal with the issues of their time as they affect their everyday lives. And in their struggle to live, to survive, to thrive, to respect themselves, one begins to perceive these people in their time; you see the history flowing to the time and flowing from it as it affects the lives and the decisions of those characters.

Two Trains is centered in Pittsburgh—which isn't just a place where August's life is centered, it's also where the rivers converge, where the boats of the various rivers come and go, one behind the other. They pick up baggage, baggage and people, baggage of ideas, and it all flows into and out of this cistern. So, we're back in Pittsburgh, where we're examining how the issues of the sixties affect the lives of the people who are living then. It is to be remembered that Kennedy has been shot, that King has been shot, that Malcolm is no longer there. The greatest leaders in many decades in this country are suddenly gone, and the problems that were unsolved are still there and are unsolved. The place is Pittsburgh, the convergence and the byway or bywater. In *Joe Turner's Come and Gone,* again, that boarding house too was a byway. Lee's restaurant is also a byway. The significant action takes place elsewhere. The consequences are confronted here.

RP: How has your own view of Pittsburgh evolved?

LR: Pittsburgh has become fascinating to me through dealing with August's plays. When I was young and living in Detroit, if you were on your way to New York the trains passed through Pittsburgh, and you were conscious of a couple of things about Pittsburgh: the heavy pall of smoke as you approached, the burning coke that made the steel, the fire. You were also conscious of the fact that somebody's under it. There's somebody under that fire. Who's under that fire? It made me think and wonder. As we were getting ready to do *Fences,* and we began to research it, we found that Pittsburgh was one of the first cities in terms of cleaning up the environment, and by the time of the play they had cleared away a lot of that smoke. And so I couldn't use smoke in the production. I had to find out about Pittsburgh; it's a place that has continually intrigued me. I couldn't take it for granted.

By setting his plays in Pittsburgh, August is sharing his adventure in the crossroads of life.

RP: *Two Trains* is not a plot-laden play, but rather a character-driven one. Can we go through the characters to get your thoughts on some of them?

LR: The names of the characters are always very interesting. I think the characters come first with August, and then the name goes on the character, and they go on because of what the characters suggest about themselves.

Wolf is just that, he is a loper, he is a survivor. Wolves are very intelligent animals, and they are lopers and they are survivors. A wolf finds his way to survive in a hostile enviroment. The streets are a hostile environment, and when a wolf goes out into that hostile world, his expectation always is that it will be a hostile world. He's a wolf, he's a loner, he's a survivor. He survives because he's on the alert always to what might happen. That doesn't mean he's the world's brightest man, but he is wary, so he survives.

Memphis. His salvation is in the fact that he will follow through. His life is askew until he can go back and finish the thing he should have finished a long time ago, which was the salvation of his own dignity. Until he can go back and pick up that challenge, he is a dignified man without dignity.

Risa is a woman of principle. She is a very strong-willed, determined, competent human being. She runs the restaurant. She is living in a man's world, and she does it at her own pace. She believes what she believes, and acts in terms of that. I have tremendous respect for that character. I've seen men in the theatre who become so exasperated with Risa because they can't control her. She is moving at the rate she knows will permit her to last the entire day and will take care of everything that emerges in that day. Her scarring of ʌer legs might be seen as a manifestation of a loss of control, as an act of derangement, but it is a highly controlled act. Wonderful character. There were times when we thought about giving her more lines, she doesn't need more lines.

West is a survivor. West knows how to operate in the world of work. West has found his way to live in a white man's world by adopting the practices of the white man into the black world. He has learned the economics of the society, but he is wise enough to know that he can't necessarily survive in a white man's world. He could if he was white, but he knows enough to know that he isn't. He is not without sensitivity or appreciation. He is not just a survivor, he is a thriver.

Sterling learns to employ principles, values, and the value of taking action for what one perceives as right. He learns to do that in the course of the play, to define right and to act. He learns the difference between taking a gun and going into a bank and taking some of what you think you should get, and taking a stone and smashing a window and taking a ham for a man's coffin. Those are both described as crimes, but there is a significant difference between those crimes.

Hambone takes a stand: Give me my due, give ɾ ʔ what's promised me. He is perceived to be mad because of his commitment to that principled position. How strange that he would be thus perceived. There are resonances in the line: "he don't even know his right name" which is said about Hambone, but can be said about every black person that exists in this country, because they have all been separated from their names. How can one reconstruct oneself without even a name to go back to? Or a place? Africa is a big continent. And so this man, Hambone, who has been struggling for his dignity, does not have a home or a name.

RP: How about Aunt Ester, an important character who is only spoken of in the play?

LR: Anybody who comes back from Aunt Ester doesn't have
     a prescription, or an answer, but they all come back with
     faith and their ability to act. Aunt Ester's is a place of
     personal, spiritual revival of oneself, which is what any
     good watering hole should be. She is the idea, the person,
     the spirit that holds the mirror up to you and says "This is
     what you can be." She is that.

RP: The title, *Two Trains Running*, is derived from the blues,
     but what does it suggest beyond that?

LR: Two trains suggests alternatives. Alternatives suggest
     opposites. Opposites, or what seem like opposites, can
     also be convergences, all of which are possible in terms of
     understanding *Two Trains*. The important fact is that the
     alternative exists, in terms of which one questions the
     validity of a choice.

The Historical Perspective
An Interview with August Wilson

Richard Pettengill

August Wilson visited Chicago for the opening of the Goodman Theatre's production of *Two Trains Running* on Jan. 25, 1993. He came by the theatre for this conversation, which took place on the lunch counter of the *Two Trains* set.

Richard Pettengill: In *Two Trains Running* you chose to keep the major historical events of the period offstage.

August Wilson: The play does not speak to the so-called red lettered events of the sixties, because at the time all of that was going on—the assassination of Martin Luther King and Bobby Kennedy and all the anti-war administrations, etc.—people were still living their lives. You still had to go to work every day, you still had to pay your rent, you still had to put food on the table. And those events, while they may have in some way affected the character of society as a whole, didn't reach the average person who was concerned with just simply living. And so in *Two Trains* I was more concerned with those people and what they were doing and how they were dealing with it, than I was with writing a "sixties" play.

RP: Did the title come first?

AW: The title came first. The title came from a blues song called *Two Trains Running,* and actually that phrase is in several blues songs. It's most commonly followed by the line "two trains running, neither one going my way. One running by night, one run by day." There were two ideas in the play, or at least two ideas that have confronted black America since the Emancipation, the ideas of cultural assimilation and cultural separatism. These were, in my mind, the two trains. I wanted to write a play about a character for whom neither of these trains were working. He had to build a new railroad in order to get to where he's going, because the trains are not going his way. That was the idea when I started out exploring.

RP: And how did you view the two trains when you had finished?

AW: In this play there are actually three ways you can change your life, but one of those ways, Prophet Samuel, is dead, so that one is gone. So there's Malcolm X, symbolized by the rally, although he never became as important a part of the play as I originally thought he might. The other way is Aunt Ester, who became more important than I thought she was originally going to be. So from my original idea— that there was a character for whom neither train worked—I ended up saying that you need both Malcolm X and Aunt Ester in order to change your life.

RP: How did the characters evolve as you wrote?

AW: The characters, as I write them, they grow, they change. West, the undertaker, was originally a much larger role than he is now, somehow a more important part of the play. I was fascinated with the idea of the personification of Death, and moved him in from some of my earlier work. In *Fences*, for example, Troy wrestles with Death. Here I wanted to actually bring Death on stage; here he is in person, this undertaker with these gloves on. But when I began to write the play and work with the characters, a lot of that became unimportant to the story. What happened was that it became largely about Memphis at one point, and then it was more about Sterling at another point. And gradually it became really about Hambone, because he is the one character that affects everyone else in the play. He's the one character who, when he dies, changes things. There are some big changes. Sterling pretty much stays the same: he comes in, he knows what he wants, he knows what he's about. But I did not know that Hambone was going to affect all the rest of the characters in quite the way he did.

RP: Where did Hambone come from?

AW: I just this moment remembered that Hambone was a character from a short story I wrote many years ago, a man who refused to accept less than what he felt he was due. That turned into the character of Hambone, and it was a matter of placing him somewhere in the play.

RP: And Holloway?

AW: Holloway became the character that knows everything. If you say, "How long Ruffin been dead?," he'd say "Oh she been dead twenty-three years. Died right after the war." He'd say "Where you going? I'm going to get some cigarettes. What kind you smoke? I smoke Kools." He'd say "You can't go down over there, you got to go down over there. He charge two cents more than . . ." Whatever the situation is, any question anybody has, he's the character who knows the answer. Consequently, in order for him to know the answer, Holloway's got to ask a lot of questions: "When she die? How long they been married?" I discovered in the process of writing the play that whenever you get stuck and you don't know where you're going, you just ask that character a question. You trust him and he'll tell you the answer. So a lot of the things that came about, a lot of the exposition, a lot of the things I found out about the characters, I got from Holloway by simply asking him. Once I had that character in the play, it became easier to write the other parts.

RP: Is Aunt Ester related to Bynum in *Joe Turner*, in that she helps people to find their song?

AW: It's all basically the same theme. Aunt Ester says it most clearly: you've got to return to your past. If you drop the ball, you have to go back and pick it up. There's no need to continue to run to the end zone, because it's not going to be a touchdown. You got to have the ball. It's a matter of reclaiming the past, as opposed to discovering who you are. I think we know who we are, but it's a matter of reclaiming and saying—irrespective of recent political history—that we come from a long line of honorable people.

RP: Memphis is certainly focused on reclaiming the past.

AW: Absolutely. That's why we can crystallize more on that character. He became the one who was the least complete without doing that. Having played by the rules, so to speak, and in the end up still losing the game, he said "Let me make up some rules, I'm tired of all of you making up the rules all the time. I got some rules of my own."

RP: Memphis's name links him to the South. Was that conscious on your part?

AW: It was, yeah. Memphis, again, is a character from a short story I was writing a long time ago. There's Memphis and another character from the story, a woman character, name of Selma. These are both cities. Then, of course, I've got Toledo in *Ma Rainey's Black Bottom*. That's not a bad idea, naming characters after cities. Troy too. So Memphis for me is a special name. I always say that if I had a male child, I would name him Memphis. It's also an Egyptian God. I like the name a lot, I might even rename myself that. (Laughs).

RP: Memphis owns the restaurant, but who runs it?

AW: Risa, without question. At some point I realized that nobody in that whole restaurant can do anything without Risa. (Laughs). They can't exist. It's Risa this, Risa that. There's a point in the play where Sterling talks about "if you get fired" and she says, "I ain't worried about getting fired." Memphis wouldn't know what to do without her, so there's no question of that. One of the early questions I had was: why did Memphis's wife leave him? Then I thought, well, if you just hang around here for a minute and watch how he deals with Risa, then it will come to you why his wife left him. At some point I knew why she left.

RP: I'm interested in the question of Risa's scars. Some Africans scar themselves to make themselves more beautiful.

AW: (Laughs). That came from the same place as Hambone wants his ham. It's just something that popped in my head. Starting out I knew that Memphis's wife had left him, but I didn't know why, so I decided that his wife was not going to be a character in the play and that the only female character in the play was Risa. So I thought, Risa has to carry the wife's story. She has to carry the story for all of the women mentioned in this play.

One of the large ideas that men and women wrestle with is the question of self-definition: women define themselves in terms other than the terms men define them in. Men see Risa as someone to sleep with, in terms of sex, in terms of her body. The scars on her legs became a rejection of that definition. I don't think I pushed it as far as I could have. The reason is very simple: I didn't understand it as well as I would have liked to. I think I was just on the edge of it. So I resolved that I would explore fully, or at least more fully, in my next play, the whole idea of male/female relationships.

RP: There's clearly more to her self-scarring than the explanation she offers.

AW: The only thing I knew was that I did not want a moment in the play where you say O.K., now she's going to tell you why she did this. I don't know exactly why she did it, so I couldn't have written the moment if I had wanted it. I had a couple of things earlier on that defined her more, but for some reason I took them out. This may seem odd, but I liked her flat, or flatter, than the men in the play. I thought it might make her stand out more, or call attention to her. It might make you wonder who she is and how she functions in that world with all of those men. I didn't have the space and time within the play to fully develop her character. And as I looked at her, she became more interesting being not quite fully developed.

RP: Wolf is another significant character name.

AW: Wolf is very interesting. It's real subtle in the play, but I think that the one thing Wolf is lacking is a male/female relationship; he cannot trust anyone. Wolf likes his women in the daytime, because he doesn't want to close his eyes. And I thought, how sad. He becomes one of the most defined characters because of that aspect. All through the play, he makes constant reference to that. And in his whole relationship with Risa, he's so intensely jealous of Sterling. In a sense, he's incapable of things which Sterling can do. He's incapable of trusting or even of loving, and he knows this. So as opposed to being a womanizer, he's almost the opposite of what his name would imply.

RP: He depends on the notion that if he dies, all the women in Pittsburgh are going to cry.

AW: It's all a sham, though. The idea is no one will want to show up at his funeral, no one's going to cry. That's his tragedy, there's no woman that's going to cry when Wolf dies. Maybe Sterling, maybe Memphis might pause and say "You know, Wolf was alright with me." But there isn't any woman anywhere so far in his life that is going to cry. So he goes, "when I die, every woman in Pittsburgh gonna cry." That's just bragadoccio stuff, whistling in the dark. He defines his character in a simple stroke with a line like that. It's very poignant for me; it's just like, man, he doesn't have anybody. And then he watches Sterling come in and get someone.

RP: How did Aunt Ester evolve as you worked on the play?

AW: As I was writing her, somehow she became 322 years old. I asked myself: Can I do that, can I write a character that is 322 years old? I said, yeah, I can. If only one person in this play believes that this woman is 322 years old, then that's how old she is. Now, any thinking person will stop and think it's impossible for us to live to be 322 years old. So, let's say that Aunt Ester is a very old woman who claims to be 322 years old, claims to be ageless, timeless. In actuality, she's probably only 97. But she's old, and she's still alive; it seems like she's been here forever. Beyond that, of course, she represents the entire 349 years that blacks have been in America. She represents our tradition, our philosophy, our folk wisdom, our hobbies, our culture, whatever you care to call it. All of that is alive, and you can tap into it if you know where to go, what to say.

I find it interesting that Bynum, in *Joe Turner's Come and Gone*, has to pass a couple of tests. When he meets the shiny man on the road, the man asks him does he have anything to eat because he was hungry. Bynum didn't say "go get your own food, I just got an orange for myself." He gave the man an orange, and the man said to come and go along the road a little ways with him. You have to do all these things in order to be shown the wisdom. Sterling knows he's got to go back to see Aunt Ester. He goes back, she's asleep, and so he goes back again. If he doesn't go back the third time, he's missed it; he never has the experience of going to see Aunt Ester, and he never gets whatever it is she has to give him. You have to work to earn that, it's not just there for you. All that is what I was trying to do there.

RP: West doesn't earn the experience.

AW: Oh no, West, of course not, he values money over everything. I don't know why it's that way, but somehow the more money you have, the wealthier you are, the more important money becomes for you. The man in the play who is most capable of throwing twenty dollars in the river doesn't want to do it. The man who has two dollars, Sterling, says if he had twenty dollars, he'd throw it. He didn't even have twenty dollars to throw, but if he had it, he would. And when he got it, he did.

RP: What do you think drives Memphis, as opposed to Holloway?

AW: Memphis is a little different than Holloway. Memphis's got something to say about everything and he generally finds something wrong in everything. "People ain't doing this right, they ain't doing that right, this one ain't doing the other thing right. That boy ain't got good sense. Risa ain't cooking things right. This ain't going right." All the way through. "West cheating the people here, telling the people this." You name it, anything that comes up, he jumps right on it: Black Power, Vietnam. "I don't want that Malcolm X."

RP: There's a kind of rivalry between him and Holloway, which we see when they each tell the story of Hambone and Lutz.

AW: Holloway's telling the wrong story. Memphis always tries to straighten the person up if they don't know the full story: "That ain't how it went." Also, it's so easy for us to say, "Here's the white man mistreating black folks again." But it's much more interesting, I think, if you can see how that happened. Memphis says, "Lutz told him if he painted his fence he'd give him a chicken. Told him if he do a good job he'd give him a ham. He think he did a good job and Lutz didn't." So then Hambone goes, "How you doing boss? Yeah, good job ain't it? Where's my ham?" And Lutz says, "Nahh, I don't think it's a good job, take a chicken." That becomes more plausible than someone just trying to cheat someone out of a ham. I mean, who would do that? So the differences in the story become important in that regard; then you can understand that it's really just a misunderstanding and they're both stubborn men. It's just, "I want my ham. Take a chicken." Which one of them is going to break down? And of course the longer that went, I'm sure, the firmer Lutz's resolve got. Memphis says, "Lutz ain't gonna give him no ham . . . cause he don't feel he owe him. I wouldn't give him one either." Memphis would do the same thing. If he does not owe you fifty cents, he's not going to give you fifty cents. If he owed you he would give you. He pays his bills, he pays Risa her due. There's not even a dispute about the three dollars, he takes her word. "I told you I put the three dollars back . . . Well here . . . take this . . ." But if he don't owe you, you not gonna get it. And that's the way Lutz is. Lutz don't owe him a ham. He ain't gonna pay what he feel he don't owe.

RP: Once Hambone dies, there's a sense of lost opportunity.

AW: Oh yeah, without question. Holloway's the one who lays out why Hambone might have more sense than you or me, but even though Hambone's having a hard time with people in life, most everybody lets down a little after his death. Once he's dead, he can't get his ham. Lutz can no longer suddenly break down and give him his ham. It's impossible, because he's no longer there. Suddenly they feel the loss, what his death means. Everyday he goes by without his ham, and the possibility always exists that he might one day get it. But when you remove that possibility, it becomes evident to everybody that he never got his ham. I think that's the sense they feel.

RP: Would you want to encourage audiences to keep open the idea of two trains when thinking about the play . . . different possibilities for interpreting that title?

AW: Oh yeah, sure, and they have to be aware of the choices that we as black Americans need to make. We've been debating an idea for maybe sixty or seventy years now, and I think it's time we have really intensive debates and make a decision to go down one of those roads or the other. What I have discovered is that the people ultimately will decide. You cannot force a solution. The people as a group will decide that this is the thing to do, just like most of us ended up in the North. We all originated in the Southern plantations, but somehow we live all over the United States . . . as far as Seattle, of all places, which is where I live. Somehow that was the right thing to do, to leave. So I think people ultimately will decide. It may be this generation who decides and moves collectively in one direction or another.

RP: You've said before that African Americans have made some incorrect choices, referring to their leaving the South. What should they do now?

AW: Well, I think we need to make an honest assessment, an analysis, of where exactly we as a people are. I think if we do that, we'll find out that we're in a worse position in American society in 1993 than we were in 1940. If you look at the Black American communities in 1940, when we were operating under the idea of separate-but-equal, we had communities that were economically viable. You couldn't play on the white baseball league, so you started your own, you had a Negro baseball league. This Negro league had Black owners as well as Black players. And on Sunday, the people in the communities got together and went to the ball park. They paid their two dollars and they watched the ball game and they cheered. Mr. Smith sold his peanuts, and Mr. Johnson sold his chicken sandwiches. But then once you say, "OK, you guys can play in the white major leagues," you no longer have a Negro baseball league and you no longer have a Negro community. It's the same thing with businesses. When Black women could not go into the department stores downtown and try on dresses, then they had a store in their own neighborhood that was black-owned. Once you say, "OK, you can go downtown now," then you no longer have a store in your neighborhood.

If we begin to make an honest assessment here, we will find out that we are in a pretty bad position. What we should do is to return to our ancestral homeland in the Southern United States. If five million people were to move to, let's say, Alabama or Georgia, that's five million people that suddenly have to be fed. That means someone's going to have to own some supermarkets. That's five million people that need to be housed. Who owns the lumberyards? Just in the process of providing food, clothing and shelter, you create jobs for yourself. Then you begin an economic base. You build houses for five million people, then you take all that money and open you up a bank. Suddenly, we're talking about hundreds of millions of dollars here, just in lumber.

We do not have a relationship with banking capital, which is primarily the reason we are in the conditions that we are in. I walked down here today, in downtown Chicago. I thought I was in a city that was approximately 50 percent black, and yet everything I see is owned by whites. Every single thing. All these buildings are owned by whites. The post office is owned by whites. Every single thing, every business that you walk by, every

building, every house. They own the river. There's
nothing that you own. Truly you are an outsider. And it
should not be that way. Maybe we could own a couple of
things. Saks Fifth Avenue, that's ours. Lord and Taylor,
that's ours too. You can't own them all, but in fact white
people do. Suppose these five million people move down
to Georgia. Then we could build a Saks Fifth Avenue or a
Joe's Fifth Avenue or a Joe's Fourth Avenue which is
Black. Nike shoes? Why don't we own basketball shoes,
why don't we own the basketball team, the basketballs? If
five million people moved down South and you began to
own at least something, the houses you live in, the
supermarkets, food, shelter, and clothing, then you move
from there, you begin to vote. You register to vote the first
day you get there. You could get a couple of black
senators. Then the Senate will, in turn, represent you.
Let's say you elect a governor of the state of Georgia. If
the state of Georgia is 70 percent Black, then the resources
of the state go to whoever lives in the state, be they white,
black, or Chinese. The resources of that state are used to
further the life of those people. So this 70 percent, we tax
ourselves. Hey, we're raising taxes today. Sales tax 9
percent. Somehow you don't mind paying sales tax if you
see that it's coming back to you in some form or fashion.
You can cuss the governor out if you want to, but you'll
pay your 9 percent. You'll see it show up; they don't just
clean the streets in the white communities now. Now we
can have street sweepers every week, matter of fact we
can get together and vote on twice a week. If that was the
situation here, the city of Chicago would be entirely
different. All these buildings and all these things generate
money and jobs, and none of it ever goes to the Black folk
that make up approximately 50 percent of the people that
live here. Just imagine if 50 percent of that went to the
Negro . . . overnight he would be in an entirely different
position. The proof of this is if you look at the Saudi
Arabians or the Arabs 50, 60, 70, 80 years ago before the
discovery of oil, and all of a sudden they were doing OK.

They discovered the oil, you see. It's the same kind of situation.

I think we should all go back. We should all move tomorrow, while we still can before the government says we can't. We should move down there and register to vote, elect ourselves as representatives within the framework of the Constitution of the United States of America, and begin to provide do-for-self food, clothing, and shelter. I think if we did that, fifty years later we'd be in a much stronger position in society than we are today. If we continue to stay up here in the cities and go along the path that we're going along now, I'm not sure we're going to be here fifty years from now.

RP: Do you feel that there's an actual chance of this movement coming about?

AW: I think the people will discover that themselves. The people will say, "Why don't we go on back." It may already be happening as we sit here. Maybe we just need to spur them on a little bit. The fact is that we came up North around 1915 through 1940. It wasn't overnight. If we did it then we can go back now. Why not? This time the people going back are much different people. We're more educated people. We're more politically sophisticated people. I think if we go back, we'll have a lot of things to offer. When the Soviet Jews were migrating into Israel, they were welcomed with open arms by the Israelis because they were bringing skills, knowledge, and services to them. It strengthened their country. We have human resource and potential, and we waste it; we should begin to utilize it for ourselves. As Africans in America, we are the most educated Africans on the planet Earth. We have doctors, lawyers, hydraulic engineers . . . you name it, there are Black people in the United States of America who do it, and the only difference is they work for white people as opposed to working for themselves. If you put all these skills together, then you're going to have doctors and people who know how to build houses and who know how to

build machinery and construct factories and things of that
sort.

RP: Do you see a movement in a place like Atlanta toward
black empowerment?

AW: I think so. I think you will find that more in Atlanta than
in some of the other places. If you could duplicate Atlanta
in D.C.—or Chicago for that matter—it would be very
interesting; Atlanta remains a kind of beacon of light in
that regard. But if you triple the black population of
Atlanta, then you have that much more potential; it
doesn't have to be in Atlanta, it could be somewhere else.
Let's have a bunch of Atlantas all over—why not! We're
35 million people.

RP: To return to your writing, what have you been working
on since *Two Trains*?

AW: I'm writing a play called *Seven Guitars* which is set in the
40s. It's a murder mystery of sorts about a guy named
Floyd Barton. He used to be Floyd Banister until someone
told me there was a baseball player named Floyd
Banister, so I changed it to Floyd Barton. I hope there's
not a football player named Floyd Barton. It's a murder
mystery in the sense that by trying to find out who it is
that killed Floyd Barton, we have to look at Floyd
Barton's life, the social content of his life in Pittsburgh in
1948. The idea came, again, from a short story I wrote
about a guy who was killed. By going through all the
boxes of papers in his room, you discover who he was
simply by looking at the contents of his life. So that's
what I'm doing, and the play is a flashback within a
flashback within a flashback. It's like a Chinese box where
you suddenly discover it's a flashback, and when you
discover where you are, that turns out to be a flashback
too. So eventually we arrive at a different place. Beyond
that, all the male characters in the play are blues
musicians. It's about their relationship to society, to white
society and to black society. Whereas in Black society they
are carriers of the culture, a very important part of
everyday life, in white society they are vagrants,
drunkards, they are constantly harassed by the police,

they've no visible means of support, they're in and out of jail, etc. So there are two different values at work here. The play is about blues musicians, one of whom is Floyd Barton, who has been murdered. But it's really unimportant as to who killed him. It's more important to find out what's beyond that, about male/female relationships. We see Floyd Barton and his relationships with various women in these flashbacks.

RP: Two years ago you spoke of this play as a series of short vignettes. Did you abandon that idea?

AW: I abandoned that idea, but I haven't abandoned that idea. That now belongs to another play. This one, as I worked on it, began to change. I've always said that if it doesn't change, you're not writing deep enough. So it changes and becomes something else. The idea of those little five-minute set pieces, I think I'm going to return to them.

RP: You'd also mentioned working on a play called *Moon Going Down*.

AW: That's become less of a project, primarily because I don't know anything about turpentine camps. I don't know why I got the idea of doing that. I always thought it would be fun to do an all-male play at a turpentine camp. I may do it one day. But it would have to be after I found out what a turpentine camp was and exactly how turpentine was made.

RP: We have learned a great deal from you over the past decade, through the plays. I'm curious to know how you feel your own perspective has grown over this period. And how do you view your earlier work from this vantage point?

AW: My views change every day in the sense that there are a lot of things that influence you every day just in the process of living. You hopefully become wiser, you gain more insights. As you get older there are some things that you can see more clearly than you could five years ago and certainly more clearly than you could twenty years ago. I'm the kind of person who likes to look back—I benefit from the historical perspective.

I can see myself as a young man, when we were trying to alter the relationship of Black Americans to the society in which we lived. One of the ways of doing that, of course, was to get some power, and also to alter our shared expectations of ourselves. But one of the things I realized as I was writing *Two Trains Running* was that we had isolated ourselves from the Sterlings of the world. We isolated ourselves from that energy. Somehow by trying to speak for the people we got way out in front of the people and left the people behind; we forgot to follow them where they were going. It was a romanticized vision; it was part of being young, part of youth. We were all 23, 25, all young men engaged in a society. What I would hope is that young men today are still involved in trying to alter their relationship to the society which now, more than ever, needs to be altered.

This is all to say that I enjoy the historical perspective. So therefore, after having written *Two Trains Running* and now working on *Seven Guitars*, I can look back and what becomes clear to me is how odd *Fences* is. It's the odd man out, so to speak. If you pull *Fences* out, a more natural progression of my work would have been from *Ma Rainey* to *Joe Turner* to *The Piano Lesson*. And yet *Fences* can also be the fulcrum, the centerpiece, the thing upon which everything turns. In other words, if you're fashioning a chain or something, I'm not sure that *Fences* should necessarily be the odd man out. Maybe we need another similar kind of play that would balance it or complement it.

RP: What was the particular challenge in your mind as you attempted *Fences*?

AW: Well, when I first went to the O'Neill with *Ma Rainey*, some of the playwrights and other people at the conference thought I was trying to write an autobiographical kind of *Ma Rainey*; they felt Ma Rainey should have been more involved in the play, but I said, no, no, I didn't want to do that. I wasn't trying to write a play where you had one big central character which all the things revolved around. I know how to do that, I said, and that isn't what I wanted to do. So I went home afterwards and I said to myself: now that you were telling all these people you know how to do that, do you really know how? And I said, yeah, I think I do and I sat down and wrote *Fences*. The challenge was to write a play that had a central character which was in virtually every scene, and the whole play spun around him. You could almost call it *The Life of Troy Maxson* or just *Troy Maxson*, but that would have been a bit pretentious; it just didn't work for me. My challenge now would be to write another one, to find a character that is as representative of Black America in the 1980s as Troy was in the 50s. I don't know who that character would be, but having found that character, then I think the more you know about him, you just put him in every scene. Have the events of the play surround and involve him and put in all the stuff you're supposed to do, like his growth and changing fortune or whatever. I'm not sure of all the rules, but you just intuitively find your way through to the ending.

RP: It seems to me that there is less attention in *Fences* than in the other plays to questions of Africa, identity, heritage.

AW: Yes, I'd agree. But these Friday night after-work rituals that Troy engages in have a particularly African American bent to them, though it was less so than the bones rising out of the ocean in *Joe Turner*, or the ghost in *Piano Lesson*, or Aunt Ester.

RP: Looking back on *Ma Rainey*, what comes to mind?

AW: I think *Ma Rainey*, the more I think about it, is probably my boldest play, structure-wise. *Joe Turner* is my favorite, but *Ma Rainey* starts to nudge out some of the others, coming in second place. Maybe it was all fresh to me then.

RP: Lloyd Richards has said that when you started out with *Ma Rainey*, it was two plays.

AW: Well, I started the play in '76, but at that time I didn't know how to write the male characters. Then by '81 I felt I could, so I started working with them and my tendency was to leave Ma out. I told my friend Claude Purdy that I'm planning on dropping Ma and having the play be about the four guys in the band. But he said no, don't do that, keep Ma in there. So the challenge from that point became how to blend the earlier parts of the play that I wrote in `76 with the parts with the four guys in the band room. There was this one moment, which for me was a crystallized moment (the audience probably didn't notice it) when Ma goes into the band room. She entered that space, and for me that was the moment that wedded those two plays together. Up until that point, as long as she stays in the recording studio, it was two different plays. But when she walks in that band room it was just like inserting the key in the lock, and the play was joined from that point on.

RP: Why is *Joe Turner* your favorite?

AW: I think because it is a large play in terms of the issues and things it deals with: large issues like the question of identity and spiritual isolation and spiritual discovery and redemption. The bones rising out of that ocean— when I wrote that I thought, okay that's it, if I die tomorrow I'll be satisfied and fulfilled as an artist that I wrote that scene. I think you can go a lifetime and not arrive at that scene which for me crystallized everything, because it was a symbolic resurrection of those Africans who were lost, tossed overboard during the Middle Passage, and whose bones right now still rest at the bottom of the Atlantic Ocean. It was like resurrecting them and marching them up on the ground and walking them around in Chicago right now. I'm not sure that anything I've written since then has crystallized as clearly what I wanted to say. With Loomis in that one scene, the defining moment, I found a way to crystallize that by having him slashing his chest. He was willing to bleed to redeem himself, because redemption does not come outside yourself. "You want blood? Blood make you clean? You clean with blood?" That one moment in which he becomes luminous, there's certainly not a moment like it in any of the other plays. So I think for all those reasons it's my favorite.

RP: The movement toward finding an ending to *Piano Lesson* was a long one, wasn't it?

AW: That's because I was stubborn, I think, and hopefully I learned something there. I didn't want to say what happened to the piano, because I didn't think it was important. But the audience, as I discovered, wanted to know, and they felt it was very unfair to sit there for three hours and not find out what happened to the piano. I always knew what happened: it was just a question of keeping the lights on for another two minutes at the end. Then we could see Boy Willie come down and say that he was leaving because Berniece had found the one perfect use for the piano: to exorcise Sutter's ghost. Then there was no way Boy Willie could take that piano. Up until that moment it was his piano, he had every right to take it until Berniece found a use for it. I always knew that, but I just didn't tell the audience. I'm wondering about that now as I'm getting into *Seven Guitars*, with the question of who killed Floyd Barton. I said earlier that it's really unimportant who killed Floyd, but I don't think I can set up this play and then tell the audience well, you know, you really don't want to know who killed him. I may have to figure out who did it and tell the audience.

So that was the problem with the ending of *Piano Lesson*, and also there was another problem: you have an ending that is supernatural in that here's a man wrestling with a ghost. In film you might be able to show that a little better. At one point we had pictures lining up in the backdrop which were the ghosts of the yellow dog. I think we should have stuck with that idea, but with like 2000 pictures, so that it becomes every man. When Bereniece is calling out the names of her ancestors, Papaboy Charles and Mama Ola, I always wanted people in the audience to toss out their grandmother's names, somebody *they* were calling on. I could just see this thing building, with more and more people shouting out things. Berniece's playing the piano, Boy Willie's wrestling with the ghost, she's calling, "Mama Ola, Papaboy Charles," and somebody in the audience is saying "I love Betty

Smith." I thought if you could actually do something like that it would be great. Anyway, I was being stubborn and resisting the idea of saying what happened.

RP: Looking back at *Piano Lesson*, having finished it, what do you feel you achieved in that play?

AW: I don't know if we achieved anything beyond raising questions: What should we do with our legacy? What would you do if this was your piano? What is our future? Why do we stay up here and let Boy Willie go back down and get some land, something under his feet?

Boy Willie empowers himself. He has a very good clear plan, the best plan of anyone I know that was presented in 1936 about his future. He understood that if you had a piece of land, everything else fall right up into place. You can stand up right next to the white man and talk about the weather, the price of cotton, anything else you want to talk about, economics, politics, whatever it is. Then you can stand and look around. Land is the basis of independence. People all over the world fight about what? They fight about land. Here's a man who says, "Just give me a little piece of land and I'll be satisfied, I'll build me a future with it. I can always get me another piano. With that cash in my pocket I'll get me six pianos; if that piano can help me get some land, let me get my land." It's just a question. Maybe he was right, maybe he was wrong, but I think the play stated the question clearly.

RP: Back to *Two Trains*, Lloyd has mentioned that finding the end was not the problem, it was finding the middle.

AW: I had the ending before I had anything else. After having wrestled with *The Piano Lesson* ending, I thought, well, I've got an ending here; Sterling taking a ham and bringing it to West. Then it was a matter of working backwards. I knew how it was going to begin, with Sterling coming in. What I wanted to do was set up this situation, this environment, and show you what that was like, and then have this new force come into that environment—something new to which everything in that environment had to adjust. So I had that and I had the ending, but how you got from there to there I wasn't quite sure. I didn't know what was going to happen with Sterling and Risa. I didn't know what his and Memphis's relationship was going to be. I didn't know if they were going to end up killing one another or what. I just knew this man was coming—he'd just gotten out of the penitentiary—into this environment, and he was going to cause everyone to respond to him. And the upshot of it is he's going to end up taking this ham and giving it to the undertaker. What his relationship with the undertaker was, I didn't know, I just knew it was the undertaker. I'm not even sure I knew how Sterling related to the play. So I think that's what Lloyd means—the middle was a question of finding all of that. In the first draft it was not clear, and I had to go clarify some of the steps to be taken to get to him bringing the ham. But I always knew that Hambone would die, and that Sterling would get the ham. Those are the things I knew. And even after we started rehearsal, it was a matter of how do we clarify this, and how do we get there? What happens after he hits the numbers? Does he get paid? Does he go up and confront them? How is this reported? Those kinds of things were on the page, but they still had to be clarified. The parts that obscured things just had to be cut, and it became cleaner and clearer. So that was the thing about finding the middle. But listen, I'd love to find the middle any day as opposed to trying to find the end. Give me a beginning and an end, and I'll find the middle; it's a much more enjoyable process.

Contributors

Eileen Crawford is an Assistant Professor of African and African American Literature at the University of the District of Columbia. Dr. Crawford's forthcoming book is entitled *Fragile Markings: A Study of the Development of National Literatures in Ghana, Nigeria, and South Africa.*

Marilyn Elkins is Assistant Professor of English at California State University, Los Angeles. The editor of *The Heart of a Man* (1991), she is the author of *Metamorphosizing the Novel: Kay Boyle's Narrative Innovations* (1993) and several journal articles on ethnic literature.

Joan Fishman is completing her doctoral dissertation, *Defining His Song: The Development of August Wilson's "Ma Rainey's Black Bottom", "Fences," and "Joe Turner's Come and Gone,"* in the Theatre Arts Department at the University of California, Los Angeles. Her essay, "Romare Bearden and August Wilson in the Tradition of African Performance" is included in *May All Your Fences Have Gates: Essays on the Drama of August Wilson,* (ed. Alan Nadel, 1993).

Patricia M. Gantt is an independent scholar of Southern literature, history, and folklore and has published numerous articles in these areas. Dr. Gantt is currently working on a book on the Federal Writers' Project.

Joanne Gordon is Associate Professor of Theatre Arts at California State University, Long Beach. The author of *Art Isn't Easy: The Achievement of Stephen Sondheim* (1990), she is also an accomplished professional director and the recipient of the *Los Angeles Times* Critics' Choice Award and *Dramalogue*'s Critics' Award for Outstanding Achievement in Directing.

Trudier Harris is the Augustus B. Longstreet Professor of American Literature at Emory University. She is the author of numerous articles and books on African American literature; her most recent volume is *Fiction and Folklore: The Novels of Toni Morrison* (1991).

Gunilla Theander Kester, a Fulbright recipient, is an independent scholar of African American and comparative literature. Dr. Kester's forthcoming volume *Writing the Subject: Structure, Tropes, and Doubleness in Five African-American Novels* analyzes how the subject formation in African American narratives anticipates postmodern reformulation of the *Bildungsroman*.

Kim Marra is an Assistant Professor of Theatre at the University of Iowa. She has published articles on theatrical gender production in leading theatre and American Studies journals and currently serves as secretary of the American Theatre and Drama Society.

Pamela Jean Monaco is completing her dissertation, *The Tie That Binds: The Role of the Family in Contemporary American Drama*, in the English Department at Catholic University.

Richard Pettengill is Director of Arts in Education at the Goodman Theatre, where he also serves as dramaturg on productions. He teaches dramaturgy at the Theatre School of DePaul University, has published extensively on film and theatre, and is treasurer of Literary Managers and Dramaturgs of the Americas, Inc.

Mark William Rocha is Associate Professor of English at California State University, Northridge, where he specializes in contemporary drama. His forthcoming volume is entitled *August Wilson and the Quest for American History*.

Sandra G. Shannon is Associate Professor of English at Howard University and a frequently published Wilson scholar. She has just completed the forthcoming study *The Dramatic Vision of August Wilson* (1994), funded by a grant from the National Endowment for the Humanities.